Leadership in Health Care

Acknowledgements

Leadership in Health Care

Jill Barr and Lesley Dowding

SAGE Publications
Los Angeles • London • New Delhi • Singapore

SAGE Publications Ltd
1 Oliver's Yard
55 City Road
London EC1Y 1SP

SAGE Publications Inc.
2455 Teller Road
Thousand Oaks, California 91320

SAGE Publications India Pvt Ltd
B 1/I 1 Mohan Cooperative Industrial Area
Mathura Road
New Delhi 110 044

SAGE Publications Asia-Pacific Pte Ltd
33 Pekin Street #02-01
Far East Square
Singapore 048763

Library of Congress Control Number: 2007931049

British Library Cataloguing in Publication data

A catalogue record for this book is available from the British
Library

ISBN 978-1-4129-2067-4
ISBN 978-1-4129-2068-1 (pbk)

Typeset by CEPHA Imaging Pvt. Ltd., Bangalore, India
Printed in Great Britain by The Cromwell Press Ltd,
Trowbridge, Wiltshire
Printed on paper from sustainable resources

Contents

Foreword

The constant state of change in the National Health Service during the past decade has been unprecedented since it was established in 1948. The number of targets and new initiatives as a result of the mountain of Department of Health policies and strategic documents has reached, arguably, unachievable levels. The task for clinicians and managers alike is almost Herculean. The development of new clinical skills and roles in health care have contributed to the clinical objectives. However, more and more clinicians are being expected to deliver the management agenda in addition to their clinical role, with little or no preparation for this important responsibility.

The high priority placed on the management of change, developing leaders, good communications, team working, development of organisational cultures and the equality and diversity of workforces requires managers to have an extensive range of knowledge and tools in their management repertoire. Many managers fall short of the task, as they are unprepared for the challenges that face them everyday. This is in part due to the pace and complexity of transformational change, and most certainly in the way that they have been prepared for their new roles as leaders.

Organisations involved in the delivery of health care are without doubt exciting and exhilarating places to work. They are also stressful environments for new managers to survive in and often hostile environments for existing managers to grow and flourish in. The need for sound decision makers has never been more important or more necessary. With the responsibility of leadership comes the accountability for finance, governance, communication, discipline and team development; because of this, longevity is often not on the menu.

Jill Barr and Lesley Dowding have captured in this book a fully comprehensive set of tools that anyone currently working in a leadership role or anyone aspiring to walk that immensely slippery path should not be without. This publication will travel well and will become a textbook that managers will treasure and return to over and over again. This book will make a valuable contribution to the induction of new leaders and the ongoing development of existing leaders.

Philip A P Begg
Associate Dean for Primary Care,
University of Wolverhampton UK and
Visiting Professor of Physicians Assistants,
University of Kentucky USA

Preface

Why this Book?

Effective leadership underpins the efficient and safe running of any clinical practice. Indeed in everyday life it may be necessary to use leadership skills in our family life in getting children to school in time, managing the domestic chores and planning for future holidays. The way in which we do it, and the effects it has on others, is important. Leadership is a topic that concerns policy through to practice in health care. The 'modernisation' agenda highlights the importance of leadership in clinical practice. The NHS Leadership Centre exemplifies the importance of leadership through a range of initiatives. Being able to give skilled and evidence based care is important, but it is also about working in a performance-measured health service to meet the expectations of society.

Leadership is a vital part of today's health care practice. Therefore, it is useful to have an understanding of the variety of theories supporting actions and applied to leadership practice in the UK. One view may be that leadership comes from within and is something that is with you from birth. Contrary to this is the idea that leadership skills can be learned or even developed. It is our belief that an ability to lead people in delivering a quality health service relies on developing these skills.

To this end, this book explores the underpinning theories of leadership and applies them to the health care scenario wherever it is practised. It debates the nature of leadership by examining diversity, individual values, the idea of team as 'hero' and the variety of skills required to achieve effective and efficient health care delivery.

Who is it For?

This book supports the health care professional (HCP) in identifying the application of leadership theory to their own clinical practice. It is applicable to all professions allied to medicine including adult, mental health, children's nursing, midwifery, health visiting, operating department practitioners and paramedic sciences, to name but a few. Theories offer the 'bones' for exploring the nature of leadership: the difficulty comes in applying those theories to practice.

Recognising the theory/practice gap is important because each informs the other when searching and developing more effective ways of delivering health care to a demanding public. Pre and post registration courses usually include aspects of leadership theory but it has been noted that some students experience difficulty in application; as such this book is for them.

How Do I Use It?

The chapters are designed to direct you as a health care professional, through a structured approach, starting with leading as an individual, through to team working and on to the organisational perspective, reflecting both micro and macro levels of health care systems.

Each chapter commences with a list of Learning Outcomes; followed by an Introduction outlining the content of the chapter. Within each chapter there will be a variety of activities with questions related to the content, self-knowledge, literature application, review questions, 'stop and think' activities and preferred styles. Each chapter will conclude with a Summary of Key Points, highlighting the ways in which the learning outcomes have been met and some suggested further reading.

Chapter 12 gives a résumé of the content of each chapter and a selection of activities to allow you to consolidate what you have read.

We hope that you will find this book – used in conjunction with other texts – a useful tool to aid you in interpreting and using effective leadership skills in your professional and personal lives.

Jill Barr and Lesley Dowding

Part 1

The Individual

1 The Nature of Leadership

Learning Outcomes

By the end of this chapter you will have had the opportunity to:
- ▸ Discuss the notions of leadership and followership
- ▸ Define leadership
- ▸ Discuss the importance of the changing context related to health care
- ▸ Compare leadership and management
- ▸ Debate the art and science of leadership.

Introduction

So you want to find out about leadership, but what does this mean exactly? How do you know that you are not already a leader? You may be thinking that you have only just started your career in one of the many health care professions and that the leadership issue will not raise its head for some years, but you could assume some leadership roles early on. Similarly, you may have been a qualified practitioner for some time and are about to move into a position that has a formal, recognised leadership role. Whatever the reason, this chapter will allow you to start to think about leadership and its role in your life and career.

The concept and theories of leadership have evolved and are continuing to do so, but how can a book on leadership help you to be a better leader? Daft (2005: 29) reminds us that it is important to bear in mind that leadership is both an art and a science. Leadership is an art because many of the leadership skills and qualities required cannot be learned and a science because there is a growing body of knowledge that describes the leadership process. By keeping this in mind we can understand how a variety of leadership skills can be used to attain the best possible care for our patients.

When first thinking about leaders in health care, we may identify people like Florence Nightingale (1820–1910), famous for her work at Scutari Hospital in the Crimea collecting data (the beginnings of research in nursing), in order to improve practice. Mary Seacole (1805–1881), another nurse, was refused an interview to go to the Crimea. Such was her belief that there was a real need for her talents there, she paid for herself to go, and went on to be known as 'Mother Seacole'. She is now held up as one of the first black women leaders. Dr E L M Millar highlighted the need for effective training within the Ambulance Service of the 1960s, which ultimately has led to the current technician training and paramedic degree (Kilner, 2004). These people did much for caring, through their pursuit of improved standards and acting as role models in the health care work they did. In today's society you might think of Margaret Thatcher, Nelson Mandela, George Bush or Tony Blair as being renowned leaders. Whoever you think of as an influential leader, they must be enthusiastic and love their chosen profession in order to command such respect and to be able to infuse others with energy and enthusiasm. Leadership involves people being led, so there must be those who are happy to be followers. We must, therefore, remember that effective leaders and effective followers may sometimes be the same people playing different roles at different times. This book will try to engender this verve for effective leadership. In order to address the identified learning outcomes, this chapter will introduce the nature of leadership, comparing management and leadership, evolving theories of leadership and the art and science of leadership.

Relationships between Leadership and Followership

Owen (2005: xiv) postulates that one barrier in the definition of leadership is the belief that leadership is related to seniority. However, he goes on to state that leadership is not about your position but how you behave. Think about the following situation in relation to leadership:

> Sue Potter is a third year student on placement in the clinical area. During the course of the day, she notices that a second year student in the same placement area often comes to ask her for advice related to patient/client care for a given situation. Sue happily explains the procedure to the other student, highlighting the current research supporting the action. A qualified member of staff also approaches Sue for information related to the research, as it was an area of care he had not been involved with for some time. Sue was happy to tell the qualified person what she knew and then started to reflect on her own abilities in leading and teaching. She then started to examine why people felt that they could come to her for information and support.

Although Sue was not yet qualified, she was clearly seen as a leader within that situation. The skills Sue demonstrated – being approachable and teaching others willingly – are those of leadership. Sue's example of supporting and sharing her knowledge can be applied to any field of health care provision. It is important then to examine some of the variety of definitions of leadership available. Daft (2005: 4) states that:

> scholars and other writers have offered more than 350 definitions of the term leadership

and concludes that leadership

> .... is one of the most observed and least understood phenomena on earth.

Tappen et al. (2004b: 5) suggest that there are a number of primary tasks involved with being a leader:

1   Set direction: mission, goals, vision and purpose
2   Build commitment: motivation, spirit, teamwork
3   Confront challenges: innovation, change, and turbulence.

So leadership would appear to be a people activity and occurs within group life; it is not something done to people. Without followers there cannot be leaders and without leaders there cannot be followers (Lyons, 2002: 91–93), so being an effective follower is as important to the health care professional as being an effective leader.

Activity

Can you identify situations when you have been a leader and when you have been a follower?

You might have been a leader during your time at school, as a prefect, sports team captain; or outside school as a *'gang'* leader, girl guide, boy scout, youth club leader; or even a member of a parent–teacher association. Conversely, you might also have identified those same situations as being times when you were a follower. Similarly, there may be times in your clinical area when you were a follower due to being unsure of yourself; but other times when you were a leader like Sue. 'Followership' is not a passive, unthinking activity. On the contrary the most valuable follower is a skilled, self directed team member who participates actively in setting the team direction; invests his/her time and energy in the work of the team, thinks critically and advocates for new ideas (Grossman and Valiga, 2000). Tappen et al.

(2004b: 5–6) suggest that there are a number of things you can do, in order to become a better follower:

1   If you discover a problem clearly you would inform your team leader of the problem but you might also offer a suggestion as to how it might be rectified
2   Freely invest your interest and energy in your work
3   Be supportive of new ideas and new directions suggested by others
4   When you disagree with the ideas explain why
5   Listen carefully and reflect on what your leader or manager says
6   Continue to learn as much as you can about your speciality area
7   Share what you learn with others

If you are to be an effective leader, it is vital that you recognise the opportunities for leadership all around you and that in these situations you act like a leader, influencing others in order to bring about change for a better quality of care provision. Leaders have to face some hard decisions in their work, remembering at all times that managing scarce resources such as equipment, pharmaceuticals and transport may not be easy, and that managing people is much more complex.

Defining Leadership

Leadership can be defined in a number of ways but is still an elusive concept. Indeed, key authors cannot agree on the nature or essential characteristics of leadership but offer a variety of perspectives. This indicates that leadership is thought to be about relationships. Leadership is a discipline that is evolving. A single definition that depicts the 'here and now' could be the one offered by Rost and Barker (2000: 3–12):

Leadership is an influence relationship among leaders and followers who intend real changes and outcomes that reflect their shared purpose.

Lansdale (2002) suggested that:

... effective leaders enable people to move in the same direction, toward the same destination, at the same speed, but not because they have been forced to, but because they want to.

Rafferty (1993: 3–4) offers us: 'vision that is driven ... from an emotional front and some practical ability to achieve that vision'. And also commented that leaders:

... inspire you, and whom others will follow, but who will trust you. They will trust in your integrity. ... Leaders care for the people they are leading/serving. Leaders try to strengthen and promote these people. ... They facilitate and help and encourage and praise.

However, Bernhard and Walsh (1995) identify leadership as a process that is 'used to move a group towards goal setting and goal achievement … and can be learned.' Whereas Stewart (1996) and Rafferty (1993) indicate that it is a combination of the two. Stewart (1996: 3) recognises leadership as discovering the way ahead and encouraging and inspiring others to follow. She agreed with the idea that leadership involved '… the spirit, personality and vision.' Rafferty (1993: 3–4) thought of leaders as people who 'have that combination of conceptual ability …'

Activity

Can you find a definition that fits in with clinical leadership?

Working with common definitions can lead into concept analysis: a deeper process involving antecedents, attributes and consequences being unpacked (Walker and Avant, 1994). At a deeper level, leadership could be seen from various perspectives as being:

- A characteristic trait – based in trait theory
- A position – based in the functional approach
- A quality – based in trait theory
- A process – based in functional approaches
- A power relationship – style, or the effect on group behaviour.

These perspectives will be developed further in Chapter 4. How you view leadership will influence your clinical beliefs, values and behaviours. Leadership must be a part of caring. Patients and clients deserve care that is *well led* at all levels of the NHS organisation.

Health Care – A Changing Context

Due to the driving technological forces and rising expectations, our health service has expanded to entail much greater provision than that envisaged when the National Health Service (NHS) was set up in 1948. The NHS had its history in a socialist ideology of health being a right for all, regardless of ability to pay. Its current complexity and philosophy has put great emphasis on leadership at all levels. It could also be said that the health service of today is seen by the public as a religion or a system of belief. This may be due to the expectation that the health service can cure all ills. The view that health is a much wider sought after accessible commodity is stronger than it was in the past. Sofarelli and Brown (1998) conducted a literature review and then strongly argued for the need to move from the previous bureaucratic NHS management model to a model of a leadership-focused health service. This new model is useful in order to cope with the apparent dramatic change and uncertainty in the health service today. In support of this, MacDonald and Ling (2002) identified that nurses today need specific leadership skills and clinical development in order to help them deal with this rapidly changing situation in clinical care. Indeed, this can relate to all health care professionals as changes are occurring rapidly everywhere. Rippon (2001), however, argues that leadership training per se will not produce the quality of leaders required to bring through change. A more sustainable solution lies with the development of what he terms 'growth cultures' in order to develop leaders with emotional intelligence. It is emphasised that leaders need to focus on *inward* rather than *outward* bound experiences, enabling a spiritual growth based on relationships and awareness (Wright, 2000). *Inward* could mean greater self-awareness and need for learning whereas *outward* could relate to expected behaviours. Depending on the model, the notion of growth cultures and change will be discussed further in Chapters 9 and 11.

Comparing Leadership and Management

There appears to be some ambiguity between the notions of leadership and management. Currently the terms *leadership* and *management* may be used interchangeably because the differences between them may not always be straightforward. Most of us think we can recognise leadership but we may not find it easy to find it in ourselves.

Activity

Jot down your ideas of the differences between a manager and leader in health care.

Current thinking indicates that managers have formal authority to direct the work of a given set of employees; they are formally responsible for the quality of that work and what it costs to achieve it. Neither of these elements is necessary to be a leader. Leaders are an essential part of management but the reverse is not true: you do not have to be a manager to be a leader but you do need to be a good leader to be an effective manager. Table 1.1 reflects the differences between leadership and management.

Table 1.1 Differences between leadership and management

Leadership	Management
• Based on influence and sharing • An informal role • An achieved position • Part of every health care professionals responsibility • Initiative • Independent thinking	• Based on authority and influence • A formally designated role • An assigned position • Usually responsible for budgets, hiring and firing people • Improved by the use of effective leadership skills

The amount of time taken up in leadership activities might differ from person to person (Sadler, 2003). Cunningham (1986; in Sadler, 2003) noted that leadership is an *'integral part'* of the management role and as such may not be seen as a separate entity (Figure 1.1).

Figure 1.1 Leadership within management
Source: Sadler, 2003
Reproduced with permission

However, Bennis and Nanus (1985) indicate that there are two other models to be considered. They are where leadership is seen as half-and-half of the same concept (Figure 1.2).

Figure 1.2 Leadership alongside management
Source: Sadler, 2003
Reproduced with permission

and where there is partial overlap (Figure 1.3).

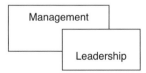

Figure 1.3 Leadership overlapping with management
Source: Sadler, 2003
Reproduced with permission

In each case the time taken for leadership functions will differ.

Overall, management is defined in relation to the achievement of organisational goals in an effective and efficient way. This means that planning, vision, staffing, direction and resources are the main concerns that need to be controlled. Managers often seem to have a bad press, due to the emphasis instead focusing on effective leadership. It should be remembered that

management and leadership should work together to achieve a common aim of effective quality patient care. Dowding and Barr (2002) discuss the potential effects of a wide variety of management approaches on practice. Examining these individually – or in some detail – is not the remit of this book. However, if you consider the history of management approaches, it

is evident that the way in which leaders and managers function within the health care system is greatly influenced by the overall management philosophy in place. Miner (1980) makes the point that '... the more we know about organisations and their methods of operation, the better the chances of dealing effectively with them'.

Therefore, it is necessary to view the different elements of an organisation in order to understand why it functions in a specific manner. It can also help to clarify how you might be expected to behave in a given situation in order to uphold the reputation of that organisation. Similarly, it may help us adopt management practices, which while 'old', might be the most appropriate for a given situation.

The Art and Science of Leadership

Donahue (1985) indicated that nursing has been called the oldest of the arts and the youngest of the professions. Stewart (1918) goes further to state that the science, spirit and skill of nursing was beginning to develop as it became apparent that love and caring alone could not ensure health or overcome disease. Nursing education, in the past, has concentrated on the science element or 'medical model', whereby nurses were told what to learn and when to learn it in relation to the disease and the disease process. More recently, it has been recognised that the patient is a person and not just a collection of symptoms. Nursing then became more 'art' focused concentrating on *holism* rather than medical/science focused, concentrating on the disease process. This is now changing to include a holistic approach, to not only deliver care in relation to a specific condition but also to include the family and regular carers.

Similarly, in other professions related to health care delivery, the initial purpose was to deliver care in relation to a specific condition, demonstrating little concern for the patient/client as a whole. Again, this is changing. In the same way, the notion of leadership and team working became the way forward for health care delivery.

The concept of leadership has evolved over the last century and continues to change. That isn't to say that the old ways of doing things are not good but that in today's business society there are different ways of getting things done; ways that enable 'management' and 'leadership' to work together. Leadership is both an art and a science. An art because of the many skills and qualities that cannot be learned via a textbook but a science because of the growing body of knowledge that describes the leadership process, leadership skills and the application of these elements within a given practice area. Knowing about leadership theories allows us to analyse situations from a variety of perspectives, understand the importance of leading an organisation to success and suggest well thought-out alternatives to enhance a quality practice. Studying leadership gives you skills that can be applied not only within the workplace but also in your everyday life. This book will lead you through a variety of situations as an individual and a member of a corporate body.

Summary of Key Points

This chapter has briefly looked at various aspects of leadership in order to meet the identified learning outcomes. These were:

- **Discuss the notions of leadership and followership** This was achieved by examining how you might already be a leader in some situations and a follower in others. Also, we examined what a variety of writers have said leadership is, so that you can select the definition that comes closest to your own perception of the role.
- **Define leadership** By selecting and understanding the multifaceted nature of leadership the benefits of effective leadership can be examined: as Daft said 'leadership is an emerging discipline that will evolve' (2005: 4–5). Don't expect to get it right every time but with knowledge of leadership approaches (see Chapter 4) you will get it right most of the time.
- **Discuss the importance of the changing context related to health care** The National Health Service (NHS) emerged due to a socialist ideology of health being a right for all, regardless of ability to pay. Leadership within the health service has always been seen as important because of the size of the NHS.
- **Compare leadership and management** This perennial argument related to the differences (or not) between leaders and managers. Much of the problem in understanding the concepts relates to the fact that the two philosophies are so closely linked and the words used are interchangeable, hence the possible lack of differentiation when we think and speak of leaders.

▸ **Debate the art and science of leadership** Stewart (1918) states that the science, spirit and skill of nursing was beginning to develop as it became apparent that love and caring alone could not ensure health or overcome disease.

Further Reading

Bower F (2000) *Nurses Taking the Lead: Personal Qualities of Leadership*. Philadelphia, PA: WB Saunders Company.

Cook M and Leathard H (2004) 'Learning for clinical leadership', *Journal of Nursing Management* 12 (6): 436–444.

Cook M J (2001) 'The attributes of effective clinical nurse leaders', *Nursing Standard* 15 (35): 33–36.

Mahoney J (2001) 'Leadership skills for the 21st century', *Journal of Nursing Management* 9: 269–271.

Sadler P (2003) *Leadership* (2nd edition). London: Kogan Page.

2 What Makes a Leader?

Learning Outcomes

By the end of this chapter you will have had the opportunity to:
- Recognise the importance of clinical leaders in health care
- Reflect on personal experiences of leaders in clinical practice
- Develop self-awareness
- Develop practice mastery through evidence-based practice.

Introduction

In the previous chapter, the concept of leadership was examined. It is now appropriate to scrutinise some of the experiences related to some of the leaders we have met in clinical practice. Highlighting the ideology related to clinical leaders in health care will lead us into the characteristics of a leader. Discussion related to leaders met in practice will lead on to a consideration of the possible reasons for their actions. In order to investigate one's own abilities there are a variety of tools that may be implemented; these tools will be administered and results discussed prior to conclusions being drawn. The notion of practice mastery and the need for evidence-based practice will be addressed as the chapter concludes.

Clinical Leaders in Health Care

Globally, health care has the same complex issues whether it is in a developed, developing or underdeveloped country. In Britain, the NHS was led by a succession of governments and their manifestos, which addressed their vision for improving the health service. Historically, health care was built on a system of vocational leaders such as doctors, nurses, midwives and ambulance technicians who used 'care and cure' methods to help people get better. Leadership has more recently been seen as important because of the size of the NHS. It is the largest European employer (NHS Careers, 2007) and the third largest world industry after the Red Army in China and the Indian Railway (Hibbs, 2005). Now clinical leadership, as well as educational and research leadership, will be required in the NHS to respond to the demands of society for the future.

Characteristics of a Leader

Maxwell (1999) maintains that there are 21 indispensable qualities of a leader. They are:

Table 2.1 Indispensable qualities of a leader (Maxwell, 1999)

Character	Charisma	Commitment
Communication	Competence	Courage
Discernment	Focus	Generosity
Initiative	Listening	Passion
Positive Attitude	Problem Solving	Relationships
Responsibility	Security	Self-discipline
Servanthood	Teachability	Vision

Activity

- Rank these qualities in the order you think most important.
- Justify why you believe in their importance.

Although it can be seen that the skills required are far reaching and require a great deal of thought and discussion from a personal perspective, the following have been highlighted:

Character: The disposition, quality or calibre of ability a person has is important. For instance, the way an individual handles a clinical emergency will either create respect or distrust for future events. Maxwell (1999:5) highlights a saying that states 'If you think you are leading and no one is following you, then you're only taking a walk.'

Charisma: This is about making others feel good about themselves by trying to see the best in others rather than concentrating on their faults. Napoleon Bonaparte called leaders 'dealers in hope' (Maxwell, 1999: 11). Whenever you meet someone new you try to make a good impression by doing things like remembering their name. Do it every day and it will increase your charisma, as people will recognise that you care about their feelings.

Communication: This element is vital, as good leaders must be able to share their knowledge and ideas with others in order to achieve organisational goals. Getting people to work together requires good communication, so without good communication you travel alone. Be clear in your writing and speaking but also be aware of the need for active listening. Giuliani (2002) (New York Mayor at the time of the 9/11 attacks) describes a successful leader as someone who is able to develop and communicate strong beliefs, accept responsibility, surround oneself with strong people but also to study, read and learn independently. It can be seen then that the position a member of staff holds in the organisational structure is associated with a particular pattern of expected behaviour and may be related to others' expectations of that role.

Passion: If, as Nightingale, Seacole and Millar demonstrated, you have a passion for your profession it is usually met with a positive response. The impossible might become possible. Passion is contagious; I recall hearing Beverly Malone, General Secretary of the Royal College of Nursing (2001–2006), speaking about the power to care in nursing at a theatre nurses conference, and how much power nurses hold even if they think they don't. The passion for nursing she imparted was terrific; I became excited about my profession again (as did most of the audience).

Servanthood: Maxwell (1999: 133) asserts that you have to love your people more than your position, thus being a servant leader. This is not a low skilled activity – it is about attitude. A true leader serves people by ensuring that their best interests are maintained. Maxwell (1999: 138) further stated that effective servanthood will be attained and the leader would:

Stop lording it over people and *start* listening to them;
Stop role-playing for advancement and *start* risking for others benefit;
Stop seeking your own way and *start* serving others.

It seems that today you cannot open a journal related to any industry without leadership in some context leaping out at you. This is because we are currently in a position of change, which is moving the business of organisations from the 'old style' management approach, emphasising stability and control, to a more rational approach which purports to encourage effective leadership that values change, empowerment and relationships. The management of change is another subject area to consider in order to understand how effective leadership can enhance the change process (Chapter 11 will address this further).

Experiences of Leaders in Clinical Practice

When we think about our own clinical experiences in the context of leaders, we may think about nursing role models and people we aspire to become. We remember three particular people in our professional experience and they were all quite different.

1 *Charge Nurse A* 'ran' the medical ward and linked to a CCU. It was my first nursing experience and I had nothing else to compare it with. He was a quiet but very efficient manager. I have to say I do not remember his presence very much, but there was a very happy team spirit, with each part of the hierarchy supporting and teaching others. There was a sense of belonging. From memory, the care on the ward was excellent and he set and monitored the standards. In those days it was task driven duties. There were constant emergencies but the team felt a sense of achievement at the end of the long shifts.
2 *Sister B* ran a surgical ward. Again the mode of working was that of task allocation but the ward was run with precision, in a military style. Everyone knew their allocated job, what was expected of them and the time frame in which they had to function. I recall being quite intimidated by Sister and would never dream of speaking to her unless she spoke to me first. Although this placement was very intimidating, at times, it was happy and the patients all felt that they were getting the best care possible in a very efficient and effective way; and the staff felt that they had done a 'good' job when they completed their shifts, however difficult it might have been.
3 *Sister C* by comparison was quite disorganised, nobody knew what was going on, what they were supposed to be doing and often there were panic situations where something had to be done all of a rush. Sister used to shout a lot when things were not done but, unless we were at 'panic stage', didn't tell us what we were supposed to be doing.

Each of these leaders, in their own way, demonstrated their style. Two were far more effective than the other but each reflected communication skills at differing levels. Indeed, Starns (2000) highlights the militarisation policy adopted in early British nursing history. Dame Katherine Jones, the first

Matron-in-Chief, wanted to link the registered nurse with the military 'officer classes'; she felt that the registered nurse status would be further secured by imposing the Army framework and style on civilian nursing. This might reflect the actions and leadership style of Sister B. Lewin et al. (1939) identified 3 main leadership styles

- Laissez-faire
- Directive/Autocratic,
- Participative/Democratic.

Activity

What style of leadership do you think Charge Nurse A and Sister C used?

Charge Nurse A appeared to be rather participative or democratic, while Sister C was of the laissez-faire style.

Lewin's categories have been used extensively since 1939. Wider categorisation of leadership styles are diverse and may include:

- *Coercive:* using many sanctions and few rewards; gives directives rather than directions; useful for simple, straightforward tasks.
- *Authoritative:* has clear vision and provides long-term direction; is prepared to justify and take responsibility for the direction; useful where there is a clear aim and people are buying into it.
- *Affiliative:* aims to avoid conflict and develop harmony; avoids confrontation; useful for getting to know people and how things are done around the school.
- *Democratic:* encourages participation and seeks consensus; aims to seek commitment through ownership; sometimes useful when the leader is not clear about the most appropriate direction.
- *Pacesetting:* focuses on task accomplishment to a high-level of excellence; tends to take the lead; useful in managing change.
- *Coaching:* encourages the development of others; identifies strengths and weaknesses; useful for long-term development of people and the organisation.

National Professional Qualification for Headship (NPQH), 2005

It is perceived that the most effective leadership style is that exhibited by democratic leaders. However, it should be remembered that one style will not be adopted for all occasions but that a mixture of styles will be required depending on the situation.

Leadership and Followership Styles

Having noted that there are a variety of clinical leadership styles, it would be useful to analyse one's own ability as a leader and a follower. Daft (2005) suggests that leaders who demonstrate a high level of self-awareness learn to trust their 'gut feelings' and realise that these feelings can provide useful information about difficult decisions. So in order to be successful, leaders must also look inwards to their hopes and dreams. Part of preparedness for leadership might be to test what sort of style you prefer as a leader by taking a Leadership and Followership Test of the type described by Frew (1977).

Table 2.2 Leadership and followership style test

Leadership and Followership Style Test

Section 1 – Leadership Profile

The following 20 statements relate to your ideal image of leadership. We ask that as you respond to them, you imagine yourself to be a leader and then answer the questions in a way that would reflect your particular style of leadership. It makes no difference what kind of leadership experience, if any, you have had or are currently involved in. The purpose here is to establish your preference for relating with subordinates.

The format includes a five-point scale rating ranging from *strongly agree* to *strongly disagree* for each statement. Please select one point on each scale and mark it as you read the 20 statements relating to leadership. You may omit answers to questions that are confusing or to questions that you feel you cannot answer.

	Strongly Agree	Agree	Mixed Feelings	Disagree	Strongly Disagree
1 When I tell a subordinate to do something, I expect her or him to do it with no questions asked. After all, I am responsible for what s/he does, not the subordinate.	1	2	3	4	5
2 Tight control by a leader usually does more harm than good. People generally do the best job when they are allowed to exercise self-control.	5	4	3	2	1
3 Although discipline is important in an organisation, the effective leader should intervene using disciplinary procedures and knowledge of the people and the situation.	1	2	3	4	5
4 A leader must make every effort to subdivide the tasks of the people to the greatest possible extent.	1	2	3	4	5
5 Shared leadership or truly democratic process in a group can only work when there is a recognised leader who helps the process.	1	2	3	4	5

Table 2.2 Leadership and followership style test (continued)

Section 1 – Leadership Profile (continued)

	Strongly Agree	Agree	Mixed Feelings	Disagree	Strongly Disagree
6 As a leader I am ultimately responsible for all of the actions of my group. If our activities result in benefits to the organisation, I should be rewarded accordingly.	1	2	3	4	5
7 Most people require only minimum direction on the part of the leader in order to do a good job.	5	4	3	2	1
8 One's subordinates usually require the control of a strict leader.	1	2	3	4	5
9 Leadership might be shared among participants of a group so that at any one time there may be two or more leaders.	5	4	3	2	1
10 Leadership should generally come from the top, but there are some logical exceptions to this rule.	5	4	3	2	1
11 The disciplinary function of the leader is simply to seek democratic opinions regarding problems as they arise.	5	4	3	2	1
12 The clinical problems, management time and worker frustration caused by the division of labour are hardly ever worth the savings. In most cases, workers do the best job of determining their own job content.	5	4	3	2	1
13 The leader ought to be the group member whom the other members elect to coordinate their activities and represent the group to the rest of the organisation.	5	4	3	2	1
14 A leader needs to exercise some control over his or her people.	1	2	3	4	5
15 There must be one – and only one – recognised leader in the group.	1	2	3	4	5
16 A good leader must establish and strictly enforce an impersonal system of discipline.	1	2	3	4	5
17 Discipline codes should be flexible and they should allow for individual decisions by the leader, given each particular situation.	5	4	3	2	1
18 Basically, people are responsible for themselves and no one else. Thus a leader cannot be blamed for or take credit for the work of subordinates.	5	4	3	2	1
19 The job of the leader is to relate to subordinates the task to be done, to ask them for ways in which it can be better accomplished, and then to help arrive at a consensus plan of attack.	5	4	3	2	1
20 A position of leadership implies the general superiority of its incumbent over his or her workers.	1	2	3	4	5

(Continued)

Table 2.2 Leadership and followership style test (continued)

Section 2 – Followership Profile

This section of the questionnaire includes statements about the type of boss you prefer. Imagine yourself to be in a subordinate position of some kind and use your responses to indicate your preference for the way in which a leader might relate to you. The format is identical to that within the previous section.

	Strongly Agree	Agree	Mixed Feelings	Disagree	Strongly Disagree
1 I expect my job to be very explicitly outlined for me.	1	2	3	4	5
2 When the boss says to do something, I do it. After all, he or she is the boss.	1	2	3	4	5
3 Rigid rules and regulations usually cause me to become frustrated and inefficient.	5	4	3	2	1
4 I am ultimately responsible for and capable of self-discipline based on my contacts with the people around me.	5	4	3	2	1
5 My jobs should be made as short in duration as possible, so that I can achieve efficiency through repetition.	1	2	3	4	5
6 Within reasonable limits I try to accommodate requests from persons who are not my boss, since these requests are typically in the best interest of the company anyhow.	5	4	3	2	1
7 When the boss tells me to do something that is the wrong thing to do, it is his or her fault, not mine, when I do it.	1	2	3	4	5
8 It is up to my leader to provide a set of rules by which I can measure my performance.	1	2	3	4	5
9 The boss is the boss. The fact of that promotion suggests that he or she is on the ball.	1	2	3	4	5
10 I only accept orders from my boss.	1	2	3	4	5
11 I would prefer for my boss to give me general objectives and guidelines and then allow me to do the job my way.	5	4	3	2	1
12 If I do something that is not right, it is my own fault, even if my supervisor told me to do it.	5	4	3	2	1
13 I prefer jobs that are not repetitious, the kind of task that is new and different each time.	5	4	3	2	1
14 My supervisor is in no way superior to me by virtue of position. He or she does a different kind of job, one which includes a lot of managing and coordinating.	5	4	3	2	1
15 I expect my leader to give me disciplinary guidelines.	1	2	3	4	5
16 I prefer to tell my supervisor what I can or at least should be doing. I am ultimately responsible for my own work.	5	4	3	2	1

Table 2.2 Leadership and followership style test (continued)

Scoring Interpretation

Now you have completed all the questions add together all the scores from Section 1 – Leadership Profile – and divide the total by 20. This will give you a score to match with the table below.

Following this, add together all the scores from Section 2 – Followership Profile – and divide the total by 16. Again, match your answer to the grid below.

Interpretations Score	Leadership Style	Followership Style
Less than 1.9	**Very Autocratic** Boss decides and announces decisions, rules and orientation.	Cannot function well without programmes and procedures, needs feedback.
2.0–2.4	**Moderately Autocratic** Announces decisions but asks for questions, makes exceptions to rules.	Needs solid structure and feedback but can also carry on independently.
2.5–3.4	**Mixed** Boss suggests ideas and consults groups, many exceptions to regulations.	Mixture of above and below.
3.5–4.0	**Moderately Participative** Group decides on basis of boss's suggestions, few rules, group proceeds as it sees fit.	Independent worker, doesn't need close supervision, just a bit of feedback.
4.1 and above	**Very Democratic** Group is in charge of decisions; boss is coordinator, group makes any rules.	Self-starter, likes to challenge new things by him or herself.

It should be noted that scores on this instrument vary depending on mood and circumstance. Your Leadership or Followership style is best described by the range of scores from several different test times.
Adapted from Frew (1977)

This test helps you understand how and why both you and your colleagues react within a particular situation. As a potential leader, this information can help you to develop and become effective. This test and the Myers-Briggs® tool will be addressed and explored further in Chapter 5 to demonstrate the benefits of 'knowing' oneself and others.

Assessing your Abilities/Skills

As well as using the Leadership and Followership Style Test, there are other ways of identifying your own abilities. One of these is SWOT analysis, which has long been thought of as an admirable way of identifying both individual and organisational Strengths, Weaknesses, Opportunities and Threats (SWOT). Tappen et al. (2004b) indicate that on an individual level, borrowing the SWOT tool from the corporate world can guide you through your own internal strengths and weaknesses, providing an analysis of external opportunities and threats that might help you in your job search or career planning.

Table 2.3 SWOT analysis

Strengths	Weaknesses
• Skills • Qualifications • Life experiences • Professional experiences • Punctual • Hardworking • 'Fit' with the job description	• Age • Gender • Skills; Experience • Time keeping • Planning/organisation • Narrow/broad focus
Opportunities	**Threats**

To be able to rectify:
• Insufficient appropriate
  skills
• Insufficient appropriate
  experience
• Insufficient appropriate
  knowledge
	• 'Fit' with the job description
	• Training
	• Career development
	• New courses
	• New experience

SWOT analysis is always a useful exercise to undertake and even keep within your portfolio. It can be used when applying for a new position or course as it clearly highlights your attributes and how they can be matched against the criteria for the position or course entry. It can also be a basis for the additional information requested when you have to indicate to appraisers during your annual Individual Performance Review (IPR). Together with identifying internal individual strengths and weaknesses an external situational analysis can identify how threats might be changed to opportunities in order to enhance individual and organisational performance.

Problem Solving Styles: The Myers-Briggs Type Indicator® (MBTI®)

Another point for consideration when leaders are being appointed relates to problem solving styles. For many the use of the Myers-Briggs Type Indicator® (1995) is one tool of identifying ways in which individuals differ in gathering and evaluating information for problem solving and making decisions. (Myers-Briggs Type Indicator®, Myer-Briggs®, MBTI® and the MBTI logo® are all trademarks or registered trademarks of the Myer-Briggs Type Indicator Trust in the United States and other countries.)

Four dimensions are considered within the tool, each has two polar aspects.

1 **Introvert (I) – Extrovert (E):** This dimension focuses on where people gain interpersonal strength and mental energy. Extroverts gain energy from

being around and interacting with others, whereas introverts gain energy by focusing on personal thoughts and feelings.

Table 2.4 Extrovert/introvert dimensions

	Positive Impact	Negative Impact
Extrovert	Spreads energy, enthusiasm	Loud mouth, does not include other people
Introvert	Thoughtful, gives space to others	Nothing worth saying? Uneasy networker

2   **Sensing (S) – Intuition (N):** This identifies how a person absorbs information. Those with a sensing preference gather and absorb information through the five senses, whereas intuitive people rely on less direct perceptions. Intuitivists, for example, focus more on patterns, relationships and hunches than on direct perception of facts and details.

Table 2.5 Sensing/intuition dimensions

	Positive Impact	Negative Impact
Sensing	Practical, concrete, detailed	Dull, unimaginative
Intuition	Creative, imaginative	Flighty, impractical, unrealistic

3   **Thinking (T) – Feeling (F):** This dimension relates to how much consideration a person gives to emotions in making a decision. Feeling types tend to rely more on their values and sense of what is right and wrong, and they consider how a specific decision will affect other's feelings. Thinking types tend to rely more on logic and are very objective in the decision making process.

Table 2.6 Thinking/feeling dimensions

	Positive Impact	Negative Impact
Thinking	Logical, rational, intellectual	Cold and heartless
Feeling	Empathetic, understanding	Soft-headed, fuzzy thinker, bleeding heart

4   **Judging (J) – Perceiving (P):** This dimension concerns an individual's attitudes toward ambiguity and how quickly a person can make a decision. People with a judging preference like certainty and closure. They enjoy having goals and deadlines and tend to make decisions quickly based on available data. Perceiving people, conversely, enjoy ambiguity, dislike deadlines, and may change their minds several times before making a final decision. Perceiving types like to gather a large amount of data information before making a decision.

Table 2.7 Judging/perceiving dimensions

	Positive Impact	Negative Impact
Judging	High work ethic, focused and reliable	Compulsive neat freak, uptight, rigid, rule bound
Perceiving	Work–life balance, enjoys work	Lazy, messy, aimless and unreliable

Clearly from these four dimensions 16 unique personality types can be identified. Owen (2005: 4) suggests that there is no 'leader type' but there are tentative suggestions that leaders are equally divided between extrovert and introvert. Leaders are, in the main, intuitive, feeling and judging (i.e., ENFJ or INFJ).

Activity

Try the following test to see what sort of personality you or your colleagues might exhibit.

Consider how this tells you what you are like and what the person you are dealing with is like.

Table 2.8 An example of a personality test

For each item below choose 'a' or 'b'. In some cases, both 'a' and 'b' may apply to you but you should decide which is *more* like you, even if it is only slightly more true.

1	I would rather:	a	Solve a new and complicated problem
		b	Work on something I have done before
2	I like to:	a	Work alone in a quiet place
		b	Be where 'the action' is
3	I want a boss who:	a	Establishes and applies criteria in decisions
		b	Considers individual needs and makes exceptions
4	When I work on a project, I:	a	Like to finish it and get some closure
		b	Often leave it open for possible change
5	When making a decision, the most important considerations are:	a	Rational thoughts, ideas and data
		b	People's feelings and values
6	On a project, I tend to:	a	Think it over and over before deciding how to proceed
		b	Start working on it right away, thinking about it as I go along
7	When working on a project, I prefer to:	a	Maintain as much control as possible
		b	Explore various options
8	In my work I prefer to:	a	Work on several projects at a time, and learn as much as possible about each one
		b	Have one project that is challenging and keeps me busy
9	I often:	a	Make lists and plans whenever I start something and may hate to seriously alter my plans
		b	Avoid plans and just let things progress as I work on them.
10	When discussing a problem with colleagues, it is easy for me:	a	To see the 'big picture'
		b	To grasp the specifics of the situation

Table 2.8 An example of a personality test (continued)

11	When the phone rings in my office or at home, I usually:	a	Consider it an interruption
		b	Don't mind answering it
12	The word that describes me best is:	a	Analytical
		b	Empathetic
13	When I'm working on an assignment, I tend to:	a	Work steadily and consistently
		b	Work in bursts of energy with 'down time' in between
14	When I listen to someone talk on a subject, I usually try to:	a	Relate it to my own experience and see if it fits
		b	Assess and analyse the message
15	When I come up with new ideas, I generally:	a	'Go for it'
		b	Like to contemplate the ideas some more
16	When working on a project, I prefer to:	a	Narrow the scope so it is clearly defined
		b	Broaden the scope to include related aspects
17	When I read something, I usually:	a	Confine my thoughts to what is written there
		b	Read between the lines and relate the words to other ideas
18	When I have to make a decision in a hurry, I often:	a	Feel uncomfortable and wish I had more information
		b	Am able to do so with available data
19	In a meeting, I tend to:	a	Continue formulating my ideas as I talk about them
		b	Only speak out after I have carefully thought the issue through
20	In work, I prefer spending a great deal of time on issues of:	a	Ideas
		b	People
21	In meetings, I am most often annoyed with people who:	a	Come up with many sketchy ideas
		b	Lengthen the meeting with many practical details
22	I tend to be:	a	A morning person
		b	A night owl
23	My style for preparing for a meeting is:	a	To be willing to go in and be responsive
		b	To be fully prepared and sketch out an outline of the meeting
24	In meetings, I would prefer for people to:	a	Display a fuller range of emotions
		b	Be more task oriented
25	I would rather work for an organisation where:	a	My job was intellectually stimulating
		b	I was committed to its goals and mission
26	On weekends, I tend to:	a	Plan what I will do
		b	Just see what happens and decide as I go along
27	I am more:	a	Outgoing
		b	Contemplative
28	I would rather work for a boss who is:	a	Full of new ideas
		b	Practical

In the following, choose the word in each pair that appeals to you more:

29		a	Social
		b	Theoretical
30		a	Ingenuity
		b	Practicality
31		a	Organised
		b	Adaptable
32		a	Activity
		b	Concentration

(Continued)

Table 2.8 An example of a personality test (continued)

Scoring

Count one point for each item, circled in the inventory, listed below

Score for I (Introversion)	Score for E (Extroversion)	Score for S (Sensing)	Score for N (Intuition)
2 a	2 b	1 b	1 a
6 a	6 b	10 b	10 a
11 a	11 b	13 a	13 b
15 b	15 a	16 a	16 b
19 b	19 a	17 a	17 b
22 a	22 b	21 a	21 b
27 b	27 a	28 b	28 a
32 b	32 a	30 b	30 a

Totals

Circle the one with more points:

I or E

(If tied on I/E, don't count No.11)

Circle the one with more points:

S or N

(If tied on S/N, don't count No.16)

Score for T (Thinking)	Score for F (Feeling)	Score for J (Judging)	Score for P (Perceiving)
3 a	3 b	4 a	4 b
5 a	5 b	7 a	7 b
12 a	12 b	8 b	8 a
14 b	14 a	9 a	9 b
20 a	20 b	18 b	18 a
24 b	24 a	23 b	23 a
25 a	25 b	26 a	26 b
29 b	29 a	31 a	31 b

Totals

Circle the one with more points:

T or F

(If tied on T/F, don't count No.24)

Circle the one with more points:

J or P

(If tied on J/P, don't count No.23)

Your Score is: I or E ....   S or N ....   T or F ....   J or P ....

Your personality result is: *(Example: INTJ; ESFP; etc.)*

Activity

Do you think your MBTI personality type is correct?

I remember thinking how accurate the assessment was, even though I hadn't given the questions much thought. Within clinical practice I found the knowledge of my type gave me a greater insight into how I interacted with both patients and colleagues. It made me more aware of how other people worked so that when they were asked to complete a job they went about it in their own way and not necessarily the way I would have done. However, they achieved the required outcome, so that was fine. In terms of writing this book, one of us is a linear thinker and the other thinks in circles, arrows and flamboyant diagrams; we complement each other's strengths and weaknesses. Effective teams need a variety of personality types otherwise conflict, complacency and apathy would occur.

Reflective Practitioner

Increasingly, we are asked to maintain a professional portfolio that demonstrates an ability to reflect and improve practice. In order to do this effectively we must utilise a model of reflection. There are many identified within the literature, however, the one selected must be understandable, useable, effective and fit for the intended purpose. Schön (1987) differentiated between reflection-in-action and reflection-on-action, in later literature he also talks of reflection-before-action. Each of these indicates when reflection should take place, i.e., or before, in and on action. It is thought that reflection-before-action is likely when the practitioner has met a specific situation before and draws on past memories and records in order to influence the way in which the current situation is handled. In-action, on the other hand, is normally limited as the need to act quickly in complex situations is paramount, by comparison on-action takes place once the incident has been dealt with and assists the practitioner to gain insights and make amendments as necessary. One of the models used most often is that described by Gibbs (1988) (Figure 2.1) wherein a series of questions are posed. By answering these questions in order, one can work through an experience, learn by it

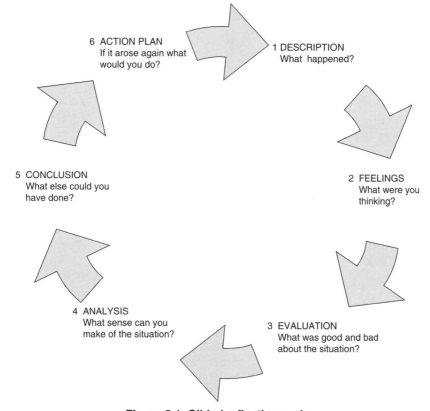

6 ACTION PLAN
If it arose again what
would you do?

1 DESCRIPTION
What happened?

5 CONCLUSION
What else could you
have done?

2 FEELINGS
What were you
thinking?

4 ANALYSIS
What sense can you
make of the situation?

3 EVALUATION
What was good and bad
about the situation?

Figure 2.1 Gibbs' reflective cycle

and review it later. Reflection is an excellent process by which to learn and this is most certainly the case for the newly emerging leader. In order to become effective it is useful to critically analyse any situation, taking care to discover the parts that can be improved upon. Taylor (2000), when talking of the value of reflection, states that there are three main kinds of reflection: technical (based on scientific method and rationale), practical (leads to interpretation, description and explanation of human interaction) and emancipatory (leads to transformative action), which are categorised according to the kind of knowledge they involve and the work interests they represent. Each type is important in developing the effective practitioner within the clinical area.

Activity

Think about what reflection means to you.
To what extent does your definition agree with that of the authors mentioned here or in other books you have read?
Keep a record of your thoughts to refer back to as you progress in your career.

I normally use Gibbs' model of reflection to consider the direction of my career, identifying what I want to change and what I am doing well. It is a way of moving forward. It does, however, feel a bit cumbersome at times but once you are used to using a model of reflection – and reflecting on action – it goes a long way to improving practice.

Practice Mastery – Evidence-based Practice

During the 1990s the trend was to speak of the need for evidence-based practice within nursing and midwifery (Pearson et al., 1997; Shorten and Wallace, 1997). This could be considered another way of saying that nursing and midwifery practice should be based on effective research rather than rituals, traditions and whims. It is this evidence-based movement that is testing the validity of long-standing procedures, seeking to replace them with newer, research-based ones.

Being able to master your own specific professional practice may come after many years in a clinical area. Sometimes time can be lost when you put yourself in the hands of others to direct your professional development. When people look back, they realise that they could have reached career fulfilment much earlier, if they had relied on their own determination. 'Self-mastery' is about empowering *yourself* to reach your own goals and dreams. Kanter (1991) notes its importance in today's world. It is about knowing and realising your full potential, rediscovering new ways and insights towards taking actions that will enable you to get where you want to go. Bennis et al. (1994) identified that we all have a large amount of untapped potential that can be used within the work situation to achieve personal growth and mastery. Self-mastery is about being driven by vision and also seen as being able to act as a focaliser, a facilitator, a synergiser as well as a co-creator, learner and shaper.

In terms of professional practice, mastery is about continuously focusing on trying to improve your own skills and knowledge. What do you want to learn today, what skills do you want to gain this week, this month, this year and what achievements have you planned for the next five years? Being a 'master' in your particular practice means there is no chance to stay still. Along with new skills, the ability to critically understand how these skills benefit patients and clients and how they can be improved is all part of searching and mastering the evidence base underpinning practice.

Summary of Key Points

This chapter has briefly looked at various aspects of leadership in order to meet the identified learning outcomes. These were:

- **Recognise the importance of clinical leaders in health care:** We all learn from observation of our role models.
- **Reflect on personal experiences of leaders in clinical practice:** We will learn things that we will not wish to repeat in our practice setting and at the same time there will be elements that we would wish to carry forward.
- **Develop self-awareness:** The development of self-awareness through the use of tools such as SWOT analysis and the leadership/followership tools can only serve to enhance the care you offer and career prospects.
- **Develop practice mastery through evidence-based practice:** In all professions it is important to ensure that the care offered is current and based on reliable evidence. It is only in this way that we can develop mastery of our individual professions.

Further Reading

Reynolds J and Rogers A (2002) 'Leadership styles and situations', *Nursing Management* 9 (10): 27–30.

Rocchiccioli J T and Tilbury M S (1998) *Clinical Leadership in Nursing.* Philadelphia, PA: WB Saunders Co Ltd.

Tappen R M (1995) *Nursing Leadership and Management* (3rd edition). Philadelphia: F A Davis.

Wedderburn Tate C (1999) *Leadership in Nursing.* London: Churchill Livingstone.

3 Diversity, Values and Professional Care

Learning Outcomes

By the end of this chapter you will have had the opportunity to:
- ▸ Examine the breadth of the concept of culture
- ▸ Discuss the importance of cultural diversity influencing health and health care
- ▸ Discuss leadership in the context of cultural diversity and explore theoretical models of transcultural care
- ▸ Examine the theoretical models of transcultural care
- ▸ Critically reflect on personal transcultural care and leading the culturally diverse

Introduction

It is essential that leaders recognise the importance of health care individuality; how it relates to the delivery of health care to patients and clients as well as to the uniqueness of staff team members. Health care professionals (and their leaders) bring a richness of individuality into the relationships they have with their patients. We will discuss the value of trait theory and the variety of personality characteristics that are valued in actual and potential leaders (Chapter 4 explores this further). In terms of your own self awareness, a number of self evaluation exercises, such as Myers-Briggs® (1995) can help to highlight differences. Whether we are more reflective or extrovert than others can help us recognise how these can be used as leadership strengths. The value of individuality, however, cannot be isolated from the roles and responsibilities required within an organisation such as the health service. Regardless of individual differences in staff, patients and clients will also want to understand what they can expect as a standard of care from the health care staff involved. This chapter will attempt to relate the notion of cultural diversity and values in the present climate of public accountability.

What is Culture?

Culture is an important aspect of diversity within the health service. What do we mean by culture, though? Sardar and Van Loon (1997: 4–5) noted several definitions of 'culture', such as one by anthropologist E.B. Tylor (1832–1917)

> Culture is that complex whole which includes knowledge, belief, art, morals, law, customs and other capabilities and habits acquired by man as a member of society. (1871: 1)

This is an all-encompassing definition that helps us to understand how individuals assemble into subgroups within society. What kind of different cultures can we see represented in health service staff? Cortis (2003) points to diversity differences in a broad classification of ability, age, ethnicity, gender, religion and sexuality. At a deeper level, culture can be seen as more than just group identity but as a way of determining deeper notions of:

- Values
- Attitudes
- Beliefs
- Ideas
- Behaviours

These are important for individual human development. The 'worldview' of different societal groups helps individuals in them to define themselves and form values related to their lives and the world they live in. This gives a sense of identity, belonging and self worth in order to be mutually supportive and to survive in society (Kagawa-Singer and Chung, 1994; Leininger, 1997). Kelly-Heidenthal (2004) identifies a model reflecting the ways people differ (see Table 3.1).

Table 3.1 Characteristics of culture (Kelly-Heidenthal, 2004)

Characteristics of culture
• Culture is both learned and taught
• Culture is shared
• Culture is social in nature
• Culture is dynamic and adaptive

The development of *biculturalism*, for instance black and ethnic minority people living in a predominantly white country, has also been seen as a recent feature in the UK. Many people describe a feeling of 'twoness', where they live in two worlds: one life at home and the other at work. They sometimes find themselves striving to adopt cultural behaviours and attitudes that will help them be successful in a white dominated country, while at the same time maintaining ties to their racial and ethnic community and culture. This leads to the development of sociocultural skills and attitudes as they integrate both the dominant culture and their own (Daft, 2005: 446).

Culture and health are linked as a functional aspect in society and relates to their influence on the values, beliefs and practices of promoting health and illness prevention. Culture gives reason for causation, detection and treatment/care of the ill and the well in order to determine social roles, expectations and relationships (Spector, 2000). *Cultural behaviour* can be recognised in our society through the various transparent dress codes, eating habits, music tastes or attendance at different social gatherings outside work, such as in the theatre, the mosque, the tennis or golf club, night club or even at the hen/stag weekend. On one hand, some of these exhibited behaviours can give an individual a sense of belonging, but on the other, may be seen as a superficial cultural identity that may lead to discrimination from outside groups.

Case 1

Paul is a 30-year-old man who is HIV positive. He lives with his partner at number 23 Lee Street. Paul is dying from an AIDS related illness. A community nurse has been asked to visit in order to provide support. Upon arrival at the flat, the nurse discovers Paul's partner is dressed up as a female, with lipstick and make-up. A group of gay friends are there, wearing gay pride T shirts, chanting songs, making speeches and playing music.

The nurse ordered them to be quiet while she carried out an assessment. She got cross when they didn't stop and asked them to have some respect for Paul while she tried to talk to him. Eventually she was able to proceed and finish her paperwork.

On her return to the health centre, she commented to her colleagues on what she described as 'the nonsense' going on at number 23 Lee Street, stating that 'these people have such weird behaviour'.

Case 2

Mrs Green is a 77-year-old lady who lives in her own three bedroom semi-detached house. All her relatives live outside the area and she only sees them when they come to visit on special occasions. Mrs Green's neighbour regularly visits to keep 'an eye' on her, doing her shopping and collecting her pension and helping her out generally.

Following a recent fall she was admitted to hospital. In planning for her discharge, the assessment team advise Mrs Green that she should really make arrangements to move into a residential home, where she would be safer. The patient responded by saying that she intended to stay at home as her neighbour was happy to look in and help her out. The Nurse advised Mrs Green that it was unfair to expect a neighbour to take on all that responsibility. Mrs Green then refused to discuss it further but the assessment team recorded that they recommended that the patient needed residential care.

Activity

- Identify and jot down issues that are unfair and hence discriminatory in these two case studies.
- Provide an alternative response that would help to promote anti-discriminatory practice in care delivery.
- You may wish to use these questions for discussion with colleagues.

You may have thought that in both cases scant regard was given to either Paul or Mrs Green's rights to live in the way they wished. Both of these people were regarded as different. While the nurse visiting Paul may have been quite correct in asking for, not ordering, some quiet it was wrong of her to pass comments about 'the nonsense' when she got back to the health centre. Of course, one could say that it is human nature to discuss the 'unusual' with one's colleagues. It is important to recognise, though, that the way Paul's friends dressed was irrelevant to the care offered. Similarly, while Mrs Green was made aware of the possible problems of her staying at home, and this could be documented, Mrs Green's personal views on her choices should also be aired, discussed and documented. It is easy to think that cultures are made up of people who are all the same and that they never change characteristics, however, it is important to see the diversity of deeper values even between people who have a common identity. The values and beliefs held by student nurses, the local Muslim community, members of an Elton John Fan Club, or a City Football Club members may be quite different.

Activity

Write down the obvious differences between individuals in your present working team.
If you found this difficult to remember, raise one of the following issues in your work group and then a social group and check out the various perspectives:

- Speed cameras
- Increasing the licensing hours
- Child Support Agency
- Changing the term 'Christmas lights' to 'festive lights'

Think back to when your team discussed an issue raised on the radio or in the paper and try and identify the various value statements that individuals made and how they differed from one another. Usually these are very emotive issues and can highlight people's values but also their difficulties with other groups in society. Generational, class and gender differences will underpin the diversity of values. Religious and ethnic group beliefs and values will all change over time. For instance, ideas concerning international issues, such as the ideologies in some of the global war zones or various new reproductive technologies such as cloning, can vary considerably even in one cultural section of society. Despite noting the differences in various cultures, Mulholland (1995) highlights the mistake in thinking that differences in minority groups are more important than similarities with other minority groups. It is therefore useful to actively engage in looking for similarities between different cultures.

Diversity of Values in Health Care

Recognising diversity creates a tolerance for the richness of values in our society as a whole but, on the negative side, can lead to the development of stereotypical ideas of people who don't belong to our specific subgroup. It is important to recognise the main cultural groups where adverse reactions occur in relationships at work and particularly in the health service. Those mainly suggested by social research are age, ethnicity and gender. Leaders and teams therefore need to always be aware of the diversity of values in working relationships and should seek to be sensitive and responsive to that diversity (Marquis and Huston, 2006).

Ethnic Diversity

Ethnicity has been defined in many ways but is often equated with race, colour or even confused with religion per se on a day-to-day basis. *Race* refers to the grouping of people based on biological similarities, such as genetic features (including skin colour), whereas *ethnicity* is seen as a generic term for how a group perceives its own identity (Kelly-Heidenthal, 2004). *Ethnocentrism* is the term for a belief that one's own culture is better than that of other groups, without considering the values of other groups, and is thus discriminatory. These issues raise concerns in our society as to how we can move cultural integration forward.

It is also important to identify the implications of culture for our health service. Harrison (2004) noted that around 13 per cent of NHS staff come from Black and Ethnic Minority groups. She highlights a Nursing Standard survey of diversity in the NHS. The response rate was similar to the racial breakdown in the NHS. Among the respondents were nurses from across the UK, working in a variety of settings and in all clinical grades. These were a few of the statements made by nurse respondents:

> 'Even I, as a senior nurse with a degree, am spoken to by my senior in a certain tone of voice.' *(Asian, Grade G)*
>
> 'I was left to take patients to the toilet and clean commodes all the time for 11 years because of my colour and ethnicity.'*(Asian, Grade F)*
>
> 'I hear racist comments on a daily basis from unqualified staff, such as health care assistants, boasting about joining or voting for the British National Party and ignorant comments are made on a frequent basis.' *(White, Grade E)*
>
> 'Each time you are on duty, for whatever reason, nobody else but you will remain on the ward until the end of the shift. Others are told to go early, which is unfair.' *(Black, Grade D)*
>
> 'One type of ethnic group of women will always make a fuss after surgery.' *(Reported to have heard this by a White, Grade D)*
>
> 'Twenty years ago, as a newly qualified RGN, I was the only white nurse on the ward and I used to get called names because of my pale skin. In the canteen a coloured lady refused to serve me when I asked for black tea.' *(White, Nursing Home Nurse)*

'I find it is the patients, especially older people, who are racist. They often make racist comments.' *(White, Grade E)*

'Most black nurses have to fight for everything, unlike white staff.' *(Black, Grade E)*

'I find staff from BME backgrounds seem to get preferential treatment. This is not equal.' *(White, Grade E)*

'It is extremely difficult for people from ethnic minorities to progress. They always have to have more qualifications and work harder.' *(Black, Grade F)*

'I work with Indians, Filipinos, Africans, Norwegians and many other nationalities. Where else would you get that? I love it. Differences in culture exist. We just have to recognise this and get on with the job.' *(White, Grade E)*

(Harrison, 2004: 12–13)

These views highlight that there is still racism in the NHS and the very real difficulty in changing institutional racism despite professional codes of conduct and education. This therefore raises important implications for primary, secondary and higher education in our society today. The *glass ceiling* is the invisible barrier, in ethnocentric organisations, that separates minority groups – such as women and black minority people – from progressing in their career, or if they do achieve better positions are paid unequally or are unequally valued. The NHS in its Modernisation Agenda (DoH, 2001a) has identified that all NHS staff should be given equal opportunities in the workplace, regardless of their gender, ethnicity or sexual orientation. The role of leadership should pay attention to this.

Age Diversity

Marquis and Huston (2006) note that different generations exhibit different value systems from each other, which influences health care (Martin, 2003; McNeese-Smith and Crook, 2003; Hill, 2004) (see Table 3.2).

There is an idea that the older generations of health workers, coined veteran or the silent generation, are seen as very respectful of authority, supportive of

Table 3.2 Different generation value systems

Year of Birth	Generation
1925–1942	Silent Generation or Veteran Generation
1943–1960	Baby Boomers
Early 1960–1980	Generation X
Late 1970–1986	Generation Y

hierarchy and disciplined. Baby boomers have similar traditional work values and ethics, but are seen as more materialistic and willing to work long hours. They have been taught to think more as creative individuals, and fit well with independent and flexible roles. Generation X, in contrast, defines success differently. They tend to lack an interest in one lifetime career in one place, and value flexible contracts and 12-hour shifts, which gives them more scope for other activities during the rest of the week. Generation Y is seen as the first group that is globally aware, seeking roles that will push their limits. They are seen as self-confident, optimistic and socially conscious.

Activity

- How do you think all these generations can work together in a clinical environment?
- Do you think it can cause conflict?

You may observe from your clinical practice that all these generations can work effectively together as long as they respect where others are *coming from* and what their individual expectations of team working are. Of course there may be conflict at times but this is all part of team working.

Gender Diversity

It has been identified that 78 per cent of the one million NHS staff are women, but that there are proportionally fewer women in senior management posts and NHS managerial culture is still controlled by a transactional leadership style (Markham, 2005). Differences in leadership style can be linked to gender as highlighted in research by Rosener (1990), which concluded that men were more likely to be transactional leaders whereas women had a preference for transformational styles. This has to be seen within the context of the late 1980s and may not necessarily reflect the truth today.

Gender has also been seen to influence communication. Grohar-Murray and DiCroce (2002) suggest that men and women communicate differently in groups. Women tend to be more passive in groups and, as new leaders or managers, are more hesitant in speaking to groups.

Activity

- How do you feel when having to speak to small groups of peers?
- How do you feel when having to speak to large groups of peers?
- How do you feel when having to speak in groups of people you do not know very well?

Initially I was quite worried about having to talk to group peers because I always felt that I had nothing of interest to say; they would all know far more than I did about any given subject. Once I got over my initial lack of confidence and found I could contribute to discussions, raise issues and make a reasonable attempt at getting my point of view or experiences over to others I felt more at ease with this activity. Like all things, it's getting over that initial barrier. It is, however, much easier to speak to a group of people you do not know as you have fewer preconceived ideas of their expectations of you or you of them.

Although men and women work alongside each other in the NHS, they are socialised quite differently (Grohar-Murray and DiCroce, 2002). It has been noted that

- Women tend to use communication to maintain or establish relationships, share ideas and learn about others in a personal way. Quieter and more tentative.
- Men tend to use communication in an instrumental way to reach their goals. More direct and forceful. There is a tendency towards more abstraction and conceptual.

(Wood, 1997: 59)

Recognition of these differences in leadership matters because communication styles are an important element of getting messages through to people, as well as of understanding the needs of people in a team. Chapter 6 will further develop the notion of diversity of communication styles. Managing and leading health care teams involves an underpinning philosophy of the importance of individuals and developing teams who can manage diversity in their everyday work. It is useful to get teams to develop awareness of some of the models of transcultural care and to try and work towards a fully integrated transcultural operation in the health service.

Models of Transcultural Care

Leininger (1997) offers a model that is underpinned by the notion that one's cultural background affects the reactions that are generated by any given situation. The value of a culturally diverse workforce is that patients and clients perceive that health service delivery involves a transculturally sensitive openness. First, the importance of *care as a concept*, within all cultures, should be recognised. However, what is defined as *caring* can be different in different cultures. Second, each culture identifies what it considers to be adequate and necessary care. Transcultural care requires an acute awareness of each culture's

- lifestyle patterns
- values
- beliefs and norms
- symbols and rituals
- verbal and nonverbal communication
- caring behaviours
- shared meanings
- rituals of health, wellness and illness

For example, a few weeks ago when I was looking after an older Asian man with prostate cancer, his son and daughter-in-law asked whether there was any possibility of a single room. They were concerned about their mother, who was sleeping in a chair by their father's bed, with limited privacy in the three-bedded men's ward. Some of the staff felt the request was unreasonable and wondered why the mother did not go home to bed as the father 'had been admitted for symptom control not for terminal care'.

Activity

Jot down what you think about the issues of this ethical dilemma.

It is difficult getting single rooms for all families. However, the caring behaviours within this family needed to be understood. The gentleman expected his wife to look after him and be with him at night, even while he was in a hospice. They had been married for 34 years. Their caring, sharing, togetherness and closeness behaviours were ingrained within this family unit. Neither spoke good English, and preferred to have their children bring them a familiar diet from home. This left them feeling even more isolated from the majority of other families. The mother found sleeping difficult with other men in the room. The outcome was that a single room was eventually found for them until an early discharge plan was organised.

Giger and Davidhizar's (1999) transcultural care model consists of five central concepts underpinning care:

- Transcultural nursing and provision of culturally diverse nursing care
- Culturally competent care
- Cultural uniqueness of individuals
- Culturally sensitive environments
- Culturally specific illness and wellness behaviours.

When undertaking a culturally competent assessment of patients, professionals should recognise the following of every cultural group:

- Communication
- Personal space/touch and closeness
- Social organisation
- Time
- Environmental control
- Biological variations.

A model reflecting a development of competent care is seen in the figure below.

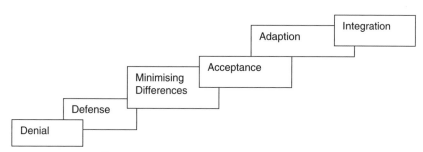

Figure 3.1 Stages of diversity awareness
Source: Bennett, 1986
Reproduced with permission

Diversity of values and beliefs are to be welcomed, but how does this fit with what the public expect from health care staff as a whole? Patients and clients expect some consistency of action and advice from health care professionals. There are now a number of academic, professional standards and benchmarks associated with each professional group. These professional qualifications, codes of conduct and policy drivers invariably influence and shape specific roles in health care.

Leading a Culturally Diverse Team

A health care team featuring diversity of race, culture, age, race, ability and sexual orientation will be one that reflects the breadth of patient diversity, resulting in a beneficial, culturally mirrored partnership of staff and patients. In order to work effectively as a team, leaders could reflect on the following recommendations:

- When problem solving, be sure to examine the diversity of the workgroup so you can get diverse perspectives for the solutions to be more widely accepted.
- Understand how team members respond to conflict and their expectations.
- Work towards understanding the benefits of diversity and appreciate all contributions.
- Avoid assumptions that cultural groups act and respond in the same way.
- Avoid labelling.
- Value everyone's differences and recognise similarities. Seek out different experiences from the majority.
- Play close attention to both verbal and non-verbal communication for cultural cues.
- Ask for clarification to avoid assumptions.
- Assist those in minority groups to be successful. Include them in informal networking within the team culture.

Summary of Key Points

This chapter has examined the issues related to diversity, values and professional care in order to meet the identified learning outcomes. These were:
- ▶ **Examine the breadth of the concept of culture** This was examined in relation to the uniqueness of individuals and the norms, values and beliefs of various cultures.
- ▶ **Discuss the importance of cultural diversity, influencing health and health care** This was also explored within the context of the health service.
- ▶ **Discuss leadership in the context of cultural diversity** Leading culturally diverse teams was examined in the context of diversity and recommendations were made.
- ▶ **Examine the theoretical models of transcultural care** These were discussed in order to manage anti-discriminatory and anti-oppressive behaviour in the health service.
- ▶ **Critically reflect on personal transcultural care** This was examined and related to leading the culturally diverse team.

Further Reading

Bolam vs Friern Hospital Management Committee (1957) 1 WLR 582; (1957) 2 All ER 118

Fletcher L and Buka P (1999) *A Legal Framework for Caring*. Hampshire: Macmillan.

Haddad A M (1992) 'Ethical problems in healthcare', *Journal of Advanced Nursing* 22 (3): 46–51.

Walsh M (2000) *Nursing Frontiers: Accountability and Boundaries of Care*. Oxford: Butterworth- Heinneman.

4   Theories of Leadership

Learning Outcomes

By the end of this chapter you will have had the opportunity to:
- Identify the evolution of leadership theories
- Compare and contrast the various leadership theories
- Critically discuss the application of these theories in relation to health care

Introduction

This chapter highlights the evolution of some of the work of the main leadership writers and the context in which their ideas surfaced. Despite the discipline of leadership being comparatively young and relatively unchallenged, the main theories that are noted here still influence and hold ground today within health care. Attempts will be made to link the theories to the practice setting. It must be recognised that the most effective leaders, however, adjust their style and approach to the prevailing situation. This means that the suggestions made here are just suggestions and not a recipe for immediate success.

Evolving Theories of Leadership

The concept of leadership can mean different things to different people depending on their various perspectives. There have been a range of ways identified to classify leadership theories (Rafferty, 1993; Mullins, 1999; Daft, 2005) but it may be useful to look at leadership in the following forms:

- as a collection of personal characteristics or traits
- as a function within an organisation
- as an effect on group behaviour
- as an influence on forming an organisational culture.

Most of the ideas contained in the above theories can be seen as evolutionary. The emerging production of research is seen to contribute to the greater knowledge base in the area of leadership. It could be argued that some of the ideas are not always based on good quality evidence – particularly the older research where we would now consider the research biases to be transparent. Hewison and Stanton (2003) examined the development of management theory, in order to compare it to emerging nursing theory and identify the implications for health care. They concluded that health care management was based on the 'fads and fashions' of the prevailing theory at the time and questioned whether many ideas were scientifically valid. The complex development of management/leadership theories has been influenced by the prevailing psychological or sociological theories of the time. More specifically, the school of behaviourism *within* the psychology discipline and the school of functionalism *within* the discipline of social science underpin some of the leadership theories. Therefore, most of these ideas and theories relate to both *social science* and *psychology* as relevant perspectives.

Activity

Write a few notes on the following:

- Have you learnt about psychology previously?
- What is the basis of this discipline?
- Have you learnt about social science previously?
- What is the basis of this discipline?

The basis of psychology is the study of how individual people attempt to make sense, through cognitive processes, of their social world, how their social contexts affect their social behaviours and how individuals share the representation of the social world with others (Cardwell et al., 1996). Social science relates to the study of how social groups in society behave. There is an overlap of the two disciplines but the former focuses more on individuality and the latter on group processes. For the purpose of this chapter, four simple perspectives of how leadership is classed have been mapped against the various disciplines and ideas (see Table 4.1).

Table 4.1 Comparative classifications of developing leadership theories (Van Seters and Field, 1990; Crainer, 1996; Sadler 2003)

Leadership classification	Development of leadership theories
1 Leadership as a collection of personal characteristics or traits	• Personality era
2 Leadership as a function within an organisation	• Influence era • Situational era
3 Leadership as an effect on group behaviour	• Behavioural era • Contingency era • Transactional era • Role development
4 Leadership as an influence on forming an organisational culture	• Organisational cultural era • Transformational era • New leadership era

Leadership as a Collection of Personal Characteristics or Traits

Trait or 'Great Man' theory was popularised around the 1900s and focused on the idea of some universal traits of leaders. 'Great man' theory is based on the belief that leaders possess exceptional qualities. It has been argued that trait theory was based around the philosophy of Aristotle (384–322 B.C.), who believed that some are born to lead and others are born to be led, so linking back to the notion of leadership and followership (Chapter 2). It also raises the assumption that some people have specific leadership qualities and others do not. This assumption could be seen as a way to identify potential leaders for the future.

Activity

■   So what do you think about effective leaders?
■   What characteristics do you think they need?
■   Are they different now from those that were needed in the last century?

■   Write down any other leadership characteristics that you think are important from what you have experienced or have heard about.

You may have a list that includes the following:

- Someone who knows what's got to be done
- Gets things done
- Good communicator
- Admirable
- Good persuader
- Good at bringing about change

You may have found this difficult, as the way some people lead others varies in time and place; sometimes it is hard to identify characteristics that they all share. This may be because in different contexts, leaders require different attributes. You are not alone in your difficulties. The literature is still confusing and there is much debate about the value of trait theory in the world of work today. Leadership traits seem to become more noticeable in *retrospect*, alongside recognition of a significant achievement. Bennis (1999) highlighted that past research showed that there were seven attributes essential to leadership

1 Technical competence in one's own field
2 Conceptual, abstract or strategic thinking
3 Track record
4 People skills
5 Taste to cultivate talent
6 Judgement
7 Character

More recently, Marquis and Huston (2006: 50) identified certain characteristics of leaders in terms of their *intelligence, personality* and *abilities*.

Table 4.2 Characteristics of leaders (Marquis and Huston, 2006: 50)

Intelligence	Personality	Abilities
Knowledge	Adaptability	Able to enlist
Judgement	Creativity	cooperation
Decisiveness	Cooperativeness	Interpersonal
Oral fluency	Alertness	skills and tact
	Self confidence	Diplomacy

Source: Marquis and Huston, 2006
Reproduced with permission

Table 4.2 Characteristics of leaders (Marquis and Huston, 2006: 50) (continued)

Intelligence	Personality	Abilities
	Personal integrity	Prestige
	Emotional balance and control	Social participation
	Non-conformity	
	Independence	

However, in the mid-1940s trait theory was challenged, as the research was found to be inconclusive and contradictory; especially as the relationship between leaders and the context of the situation were seen as more important. Trait theory has also been criticised because it does not seem to take account of the organisational culture and may even negate the part that social class, gender and race inequalities play in maintaining the status quo in leadership positions. Indeed, Bennis and Nanus (1985) identified the following myths about leadership:

- Leadership is a rare skill
- Leaders are born not made
- Leaders are charismatic

Senge (1990) and Gardner (1990) both agree that leadership qualities and skills *can* be developed and are not just inherited. This then leads us to ask a number of questions pertinent to the style you might adopt in your quest to become an effective leader.

Activity

- Do you believe you have inherited leadership qualities?
- Do you believe you have developed your present leadership qualities from experience?
- Do you believe you could develop further leadership skills?

The answers you reached will depend on your individual views of what leadership is about and the results you got from the leadership/followership test you completed in Chapter 2. In terms of developing present leadership qualities, for instance, you may have included such influences as observing and emulating senior colleagues in the way they have dealt with specific situations. Similarly, reading about leadership theory may help you to develop but you may also feel that you learn more through workshops, that is 'learning while doing'.

You may subscribe to 'Great Man Theory', first suggested by Carlyle (1841), who said that 'the history of the world is but the biography of great men and that great leaders emerge to deal with specific situations'. However, Great Man theory has largely gone out of fashion today in favour of other theories that discuss the development of leaders through study and experience. As such, the nature/nurture debate is still ongoing. There are signals that trait theory is still valued. In trying to set desirable attributes and competencies for positions in the health service, you will see that essential and desirable criteria for the roles are based on trait assumptions.

These position/role attributes give rise to questions, such as, 'Are leaders born or made?' and, 'Is leadership an art or a science?' Whatever you decide, in the first instance if you are being interviewed for a clinical leadership post you can argue both ways. If you believe leaders are born you could argue for inherited trait theory based on your leadership experience. However if you think leaders are made you could discuss developmental training which could enhance deficits in attributes you have for the post.

Activity

Write 50 words to reflect on how trait theory influences practice in health care today.

You may have considered the fact that potential leaders go 'on courses' that will teach them how to do it, but how many of them come back and deliver what they have been taught? Maybe this is because he or she is not the sort of person who likes to make decisions and direct people, which may mean they do not have the trait required to be an effective leader, according to Marquis and Huston (2006).

I remember well a colleague who was promoted into a post that had 'leader' in its title. Well she would have been unable to lead all the rats out of Hamlin, even with the help of the pied piper! She just didn't know how to lead effectively.

When you are in the clinical area look to see who is the most likely person you would ask for advice. It may not be the person with leader in their title, but someone who is seen to be approachable, knowledgeable and willing to impart knowledge; ... the traits, according to Bennis (1999), of a good leader.

Leadership as a Function within an Organisation

The theories connected with this category relate to social functionalism. The focus relates to *managing integration* and *stability towards organisational conformity* (Lee and Newby, 1983: 262) rather than managing people as individuals within the organisation. Ideas within this category centre on how leadership supports the function of the organisation to carry out its work with attention to:

- Sources of power and influence over others
- How various roles relate to the functions in an organisation to meet its needs

The role that leaders play, in relation to any organisation, highlights the emphasis on not *what they have* but what leaders *actually do, who they influence* and *how this relates to the function* a particular leader plays in an organisation. In examining what leaders actually do, Fayol (1925) first identified the main management functions seen as essential at the time as Planning, Organising, Coordination and Control, whereas Gulick (1937) expanded the scope of these functions to include

- Planning
- Organising
- Staffing
- Directing
- Coordination
- Reporting and
- Budgeting

(Denoted by mnemonic **POSDCORB**).

These functions, however, were set in the context of scientific management and administration, rather than relating to the specific concept of leadership, and is underpinned by the assumption that the 'manager knows best'. In terms of connecting the functions of the organisation to the people, it was Adair (1979) who coined the term 'action-centred leadership' where the group leader, in order to be seen as effective, needed an ability to meet three functions:

- To achieve the required task(s)
- To maintain the team
- To meet the needs of individual team members.

His three-sphere model highlights the overlapping areas of functions (Figure 4.1) that the leader must be aware of in order to achieve the desired outcomes.

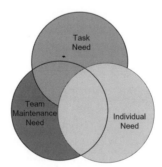

Figure 4.1 Interaction of needs within the group
Source: Adair, 1997
Reproduced with permission

> ## Activity
>
> How could this model of leadership apply in clinical practice?

It can be seen that clinical practice fits with this simple model. When examining patient care the task needs are related to specific aspects of care being undertaken at the time and the resources required to undertake those tasks. Individual needs relates to ensuring staff understand what is expected of them, and have an understanding of the purpose of their task, but it is also to do with ensuring that individuals have their physical needs attended to (food and drink etc., highlighted in Maslow's (1987) Hierarchy of Needs); if these elements and group cohesiveness are achieved then the integrity of team maintenance should follow.

Task Needs

An organisation must undertake various activities in order to fulfil its objectives. In health care, there are a number of tasks that are undertaken by various levels of staff. These tasks often involve overlap of input from members of the multidisciplinary team. The tasks, the required resources and the organisation of skill mix all contribute to the task being completed. For instance, a diabetic patient may require blood glucose monitoring. At first sight this may look easy as it appears to just involve time, the patient and a health care professional to take the blood, but on further analysis it can be seen to be a much more complex process. More specifically, the task may be analysed as set out in Table 4.3.

Table 4.3 Task needs

The individual task	Monitor the blood glucose of patients
The allocation of resources to achieve that task	Calibrated blood glucose monitoring equipment
	Haematology laboratory facilities/ technology
	Time
The organisation of skill mix in order to ensure the quality of performance	Trained health care professionals to judge the level of monitoring required
	Trained health care professionals who can take and test the blood samples
	Trained health care professionals, who can interpret and take action – including advising the patients, referral to other professionals as necessary and documenting the relevant issues

---

Activity

Do you think that the 'task' can be easily learnt by an individual within a team?

In health care, the 'task' relates to not only the delivery of effective and efficient physical care for the patient but should also be about addressing the emotional care required by the patient. All patients are individuals; they have very different needs physically, socially and mentally. Individual staff have to know how to deal with all these aspects of care as they are carrying out the tasks for, or with, patients. Teams also vary, some teams are more effective than others and leaders need to understand how each person works within the team and how their skills and strengths can be best utilised.

Leading out on this complexity is challenging. Leaders in health care have to think about the type of work and jobs that have to be done for the health service to address the needs of patients. For example, there are certain tasks that have to be planned and organised in a surgical unit.

Activity

Can you think of any examples of tasks required, for instance, around midday?

In regard of the Activity, there are patients who will be hungry and thirsty after returning from their surgery and will want to be offered something to eat and drink. Others may have just returned and airway management is required. They or their relatives will expect to see their doctors to discover whether there are any results from the surgery or diagnostic tests, and medical rounds/consultations have to be organised. There may be patients who will need to be prepared for afternoon theatre or other procedures such as X-ray or MRI scans. New patients may be arriving into the area and will need to be 'admitted' and some will be waiting for discharge from hospital. The various patients' needs will have to be addressed in order of priority. In the community there are similar tasks that have to be done, such as the administration of referrals, telephone contacts, visits to book, patient/client visits to make, clinics to run as well as management meetings to attend. Filling the car with petrol is also a task that has to be fitted in!

Managing and leading teams will require leaders to think about *how* the following activities will be achieved:

1 Setting and achieving goals and objectives to get the required work done
2 Communicating goals and objectives to the rest of the team
3 Defining the tasks to meet the objectives
4 Planning the work
5 Bargaining for and mobilising resources e.g., beds, linen, people
6 Delegating the work, organising responsibilities and supporting the team
7 Monitoring performance and quality management
8 Reviewing progress.

Leading from the front in order to ensure all eight elements are addressed is an accepted part of effective leadership, whichever style is adopted.

Hey George, I can hear the sea.......!

The Needs of the Team

When we consider the *team*, we must consider training needs, communication systems and team development in order for the multi-professional teams to function. Teams require leaders and followers (Chapter 2), who may not always be the same people, as various roles change and take shape. The people in a team, however, should have the right skills, knowledge and attitudes for the tasks to be completed, if the team is to be a success. All team leaders must consider:

1 Team development and encouraging a team spirit
2 Encouraging a working cohesive team unit
3 Setting standards and professional behaviour
4 Setting up systems of communication within the team
5 Learning and training within the team
6 Delegating and team growth.

These features may be addressed formally within a Team Meeting as part of the recognised agenda or addressed within an informal situation, say a night out ten-pin bowling, encouraging team growth, team spirit and cohesion. It may be difficult at times to address the needs of the team where there is no one leader identified, e.g.,

- **Job sharing leaders** When one leader has one way of doing things and the other holds a different view

- **Rotational leaders** Where leaders change on a rotational basis or with specific functions and accountabilities within a specific situation
- **Distant leaders** Where the team members are working throughout the geographical community and only have limited face to face contact.

Differing philosophies and styles may affect how the team functions but through open discussion a central path and philosophy can be devised to satisfy all concerned.

Needs of Individuals

This area focuses on a leader giving attention to personal needs or individual problems while giving praise and status to those concerned. Again, professional development and training has to be recognised in order to raise the quality of care delivery. Individuals will have personal as well as professional needs. They will come to work for a variety of reasons, besides financial gain. They will want to be valued and developed within the working team. Leaders may well need to think about the following:

1 Appraising and listening to the needs of individuals
2 Attending to personal issues
3 Giving praise and status to individuals
4 Reconciling conflicts between team needs and individual needs
5 Training and developing individuals
6 Clinical supervision and reflective practices.

Working within the three spheres of Adair's model (Figure 4.1) is challenging for any leading individual. The ideal is, of course, to occupy the position in the centre where all three areas are integrated, the needs are adequately met and the team or group is satisfied. Adair (1990) stated that the future requires leaders with:

- Direction
- Team building capacity
- Creativity.

Leadership as an Effect on Group Behaviours

This category overlaps with 'Leadership as a function' but has a greater focus on the behavioural aspects of people relationships. The Human Relations

Management era greatly influenced the humanistic view of leadership and the importance of people over productivity. The theories that emerged within this category focused initially on how leaders behaved towards their team; but later the importance of the effects of team behaviour *on* leadership was realised. The various *leadership style* and *motivational* theories, which concern how to get the best out of people to get the work done, are seen as wide ranging. The motivational theories of people such as Maslow (1987), McGregor (1987), Ouchi (1981) or Hertzberg (1966) 'fit' within this section but will be discussed in greater depth in Chapter 6.

Leadership Styles

The way an individual leads, within an organisation or a team, has been seen in terms of their style of behaviour and relates to the underpinning behavioural theories. Lewin (1951) and White and Lippitt (1960) identified various types of leader behaviour that signalled different styles. One way of looking at leadership style is in connection to the *power* that a managerial leader exerts over any subordinates in a team and these were situated on a continuum (Figure 4.2).

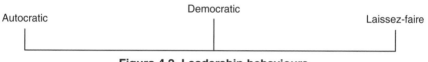

Figure 4.2 Leadership behaviours

- **The autocratic or authoritarian style**. The leader exercises ultimate power in decision making and controls the rewards and punishments for the subordinates in conforming to their decisions.
- **The democratic and participative style**. The leader encourages all members of the team to interact and to contribute to the decision-making process.
- **The laissez-faire style**. The leader *conscientiously* makes the decision to pass the focus of power on to the subordinate members in genuine laissez-faire style. This is distinct from abdication or 'non leadership' when the 'leader' refuses to make any decisions.

A person's leadership style has a great deal of influence on the work environment. For many years, it was believed that leaders employed a consistently dominant style. It was also felt that autocracy and laissez-faire styles were less acceptable than democratic leadership. Later on, it was felt that there was a continuum of styles between autocratic and laissez-faire behaviours and those leaders moved dynamically between styles in response to new situations. Go back to Chapter 2 and look at the results of your Leadership/ Followership quiz to see where you might 'fit' in the following table. The table highlights how this categorising of styles is influenced by situations and is therefore more complex than what was first suggested.

Table 4.4 Comparative elements of leading styles

Comparative criteria	Autocracy style	Democracy style	Laissez-faire style
Situations where valued	Where predictable group action is required to reduce group frustration and develop group security. Useful in crisis situations	Where groups are together for long times and cooperation and coordination are necessary	Where problems are poorly defined and all views can be considered to get solutions
Possible negative outcomes	Creativity, self motivation and autonomy are reduced	Time consuming and frustrating when decisions need to be made in a short time. Less efficient than autocracy	Group apathy, disinterest leading to frustration
Possible positive outcomes	Well defined group actions reducing frustration and producing security	Promotes autonomy and growth in individual workers. Communication flows up and down	Group cohesion when trying to deal with ambiguity
Cultural issues	'You' and 'I' signal the different status	'We' is emphasised	The group is emphasised
	Coercion is used to motivate	Rewards are used to motivate	Motivation by support when requested
	Decision making does not involve others	Decision making involves others	Decision making is spread within the group

The notion of a continuum model from laissez-faire to autocratic leadership has also been challenged. The work of Tannebaum and Schmidt (1958) highlighted that the continuum model is too simplistic, that a mixture of autocracy and democracy is needed, and elements such as leadership skills, the situation, and the abilities of the group are needed for effective leadership.

The ideas of Blake and Moulton (1985), Hersey and Blanchard (1977) and Yuki et al. (2002) are also reflected in this section, concerning the multiple dimensions involved in leadership behaviour.

Table 4.5 Multiple dimensions in leadership behaviour (adapted from Yuki, in Daft, 2005: 84)

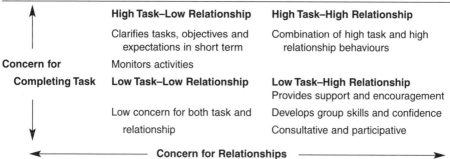

	High Task–Low Relationship	**High Task–High Relationship**
	Clarifies tasks, objectives and expectations in short term	Combination of high task and high relationship behaviours
Concern for	Monitors activities	
Completing Task	**Low Task–Low Relationship**	**Low Task–High Relationship**
		Provides support and encouragement
	Low concern for both task and	Develops group skills and confidence
	relationship	Consultative and participative

Concern for Relationships

Emergence of Contingency Theories

Theories that identified the impact of the situation on the behaviour of a leader highlighted that leadership styles of individuals *could* be changed. From this a range of contingency theories emerged in order to explain the variety of contexts which influenced leadership (Fiedler, 1967; Vroom and Jago, 1988; Vroom and Yetton, 1973). In essence one can think of these theories as being quite fluid and manoeuvrable; an 'if/then' sort of relationship between a number of variables, so that, if a certain situation arose it would be dealt with in the most appropriate manner. Within the clinical situation we work a good deal within the confines of such theory; we rarely know what is going to happen next so we have to adapt to each situation as it occurs.

Fiedler Model

The work of Fiedler (1967) concluded that no one particular style of leadership met the needs of every situation and so developed his leadership contingency model. Fiedler came from a background in Psychology and used the assumption that personality is relatively stable but that *situations* changed the effectiveness of the leadership style. The relationship between the leader and the group was affected by the leader's own ability, the task to be met and the positional power of the leader. Fiedler developed a *Least Preferred Co-worker* (LPC) scale that measured the relationship between the leader and another person whom they would work with, in order to measure the attitudes of the leader. Fiedler's interpretation of his research was that there were leaders who were good in terms of developing interpersonal relationships with the team. Conversely, there were leaders who derived most satisfaction from knowing that a specific task had been completed, rather than considering the implication of relationships within that achievement. However, as a piece of scientific research this has been challenged over the years. Fiedler's work has been subject to much criticism but it is worth recognising the contribution it has made to gauge leader effectiveness and to stimulate further research. Its real value is arguable, as the best style of leadership in any context is a variable in itself and dependent on the environment. From Fiedler's work, a range of theories explored the effectiveness of leadership behaviours. Indeed, many theorists worked together to research various topics and a plethora of models emerged.

The Vroom-Jago Contingency Model (1988)

This model focused on the degrees of people relationships of the leader and its impact on decision making. The starting point is the idea that a solution is needed to solve a problem and the amount of involvement of others depends on the leadership influence. The model is made up of three main parts:

- Leader participation styles
- Diagnostic questions
- A set of decision-making rules.

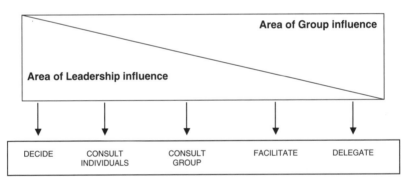

Figure 4.3 Vroom-Jago Contingency Model (1988)

The seven diagnostic questions that accompany this model relate to:

1 The importance of the decision for the organisation
2 The commitment of the group to implement the solution
3 The level of leadership expertise in the decision
4 Likelihood of group commitment to decision
5 The group's support for the organisational goals
6 Group's expertise
7 Competence of the group to team problem solving.

This model is complex but interesting in its view of the relationship between the group, the organisation and the leadership. It has since been integrated into a computer based model to add more complexity. Despite being less than perfect, it is a useful model for learning to make timely, high quality decisions by managers (Daft, 2005).

Leadership as an Influence on Forming an Organisational Culture

Having examined the last three forms of leadership theory, the latest era concerns the different cultures set within the organisation in which the leadership operates. Transactional culture and transformational culture have been differentiated as being part of organisational life. The *transactional era* stems from the work of Bass, who stimulated new management thought around transactional leadership between the 1960s and 1980s. This was a time when there was more employment stability in Britain and transactional leadership was based on the notion of a *contract process* between the leader and the group. Bass (1985) noted that transactional leadership concerned:

- rewards and incentives to influence motivation
- the ability for the leader to monitor and correct subordinates in order to work effectively
- an explicit promise of tangible benefits for followers
- an ideological appeal.

The bureaucracy of the Health Service benefited from the contractual or transactional leadership style in the stable environment at the time. The growth in policies, procedures and employment law started at this time. It was also felt that leaders and groups found mutual satisfaction with these transactional relationships, 'knowing where they stood'.

Marquis and Huston (2006) identified the characteristics of a transactional leader as someone who:

- Focuses on management tasks
- Caretakes
- Uses trade-offs to meet goals
- Shared values not identified
- Examines causes
- Uses contingency rewards.

Transactional leadership has been criticised in less stable environments where creativity is needed to deal with today's more complex business worlds.

However, a culture of 'following the rules' has been noted to be effective, especially where planning, organising and budget management are essential, as in the British NHS. When traditional industry in Britain was changing in the 1980s and 1990s there was a shift away from a culture formed through transactional leadership. We began to lose our manufacturing base for employment and the information revolution started to take a hold on a global basis. Traditional ways of working, where employees had a job for life and were rewarded for their loyalty to the employer, were starting to dissipate. More creative problem solving was required to look for new markets, new products and services and 'fit' within the emerging global economy. This environment also affected the health services, within the public services, and quasi management modelling, based on the private sector, occurred. *Transformational leadership* theories started to surface, in contrast to the transactional leadership theories. Transformational theories of leadership are based on the idea that leaders are people who *motivate* others to perform by encouraging them to see a vision and change in their perception of reality. They are seen as committed individuals with long term vision, a need to empower others and interested in the consequences. They use

- charisma
- individualised consideration
- intellectual stimulation to produce greater effort, effectiveness and satisfaction in followers
- inspiration through symbols (Bass and Avolio, 1990).

Burns (1978) identified that the transforming process is one in which leaders and followers raise *each other* to higher levels of morals and motivation. So values such as liberty, peace, equality and humanitarianism are often emphasised rather than values based on individual benefits. However, it has been noted that transformational leaders can have the potential for accruing a good deal of control and power, which can lead to the exploitation of large numbers of followers. Great leaders can be seen as very positive; however, there may be transformational leaders who are portrayed in a negative light (Table 4.6).

Table 4.6 Positive and negative transformational leaders

Positive	Negative
• Pope John Paul II	• Charles Manson
• Mohandas Gandhi	• David Koresh
• Martin Luther King	• Adolf Hitler
• John Kennedy	• Saddam Hussein
• Nelson Mandela	

Other criticisms of transformational leaders may be that they tend to focus on the bigger issues of life and because of their high visibility are unwilling to spend time facilitating the implementation. Thus, to followers, leaders may be seen as autocratic and that often success is about the detail of getting things done. The old adage that 'The devil is in the detail', might be appropriate.

Activity

- Have you ever been inspired and motivated by someone else's charisma in practice?
- Jot down three reasons why you think they made such an impact on you.
- How do you think these ideas relate to Trait theory?

An anaesthetist I worked with was amazing with children; he was so calm that the parents went away knowing that their child was in good hands irrespective of how ill s/he was. I'm not sure why he made such an impact on me but I think it was the calm, quiet way he went about his work. I believe the fact that he was so positive in his outlook, and encouraging to junior colleagues made him approachable when one didn't quite understand an element of care.

Anti Leadership Era

It is interesting that some management theory from the 1970s recognised the important relationship between leaders and their team workers and although the focus of the time was on leadership styles, the relevance of the team situation was underplayed. Hersey and Blanchard (1977) highlighted that the characteristics of the team ethic *influenced* their leadership behaviour. The readiness of the work-team to take on board the required organisational tasks was reflected in the way their managers/leaders approached them.

Table 4.7 Team readiness and leadership approaches

Team Readiness	Leadership Approach
Low	TELLING
Moderate	SELLING
High	PARTICIPATING
Very high	DELEGATING

This is an interesting perspective for health care work-teams. More recently there has been a developing perspective of *anti leadership* theory moving towards the importance of teams of 'followers'. Servant leadership theories are more recent and may combine views from any of the others above.

Greenleaf (1977), as a Director of the communication company AT&T first raised the idea of servant leadership. He noted that successful managers led in a different way and put 'serving others' as a priority. He noted they had certain qualities:

- Listened deeply to others to try to understand
- Kept an open mind without judging
- Dealt well with ambiguity and complexity
- Shared critical challenges with all and asked for input to solutions
- Shared clear goals and gave direction
- Served, helped and taught first
- Chose words carefully to avoid damage
- Used insight and intuition
- Had a sense of whole and relationships/connections with that.

Howatson-Jones (2004) highlights that understanding the followers' perspective in servant leadership offers a valid way to promote health care effectiveness. The style involves mature mutual trust, collegiality and empowerment of multidisciplinary or multi-agency professionals. Greenleaf (1998) noted that contrary to traditional leadership, the two leadership stages involved in servant leadership are reversed:

1 Serving the needs of followers to empower them to reach their potential
2 Aspiring and maturing into leading.

There seems to be more acceptance of servant leadership in the health industry (Lucas, 1999; Mullaly, 2001) because of the complexity of professional relationships. However, it has been debated whether vision and direction get lost in this type of leadership; as the direction of the NHS is well set within the total goal and governance of quality patient care, this may not be a valid argument here (Snow, 2001). McAlpine (2000), however, challenged the idea of serving in a moral and ethical style and drew an analogy between Machiavelli (1469–1527) and organisational achievement. In highlighting the role of leaders and followers, the principles that are not good indicators for success are that:

- Leaders require the souls of their followers
- Leaders should never fail to express gratitude and appreciation: followers need flattery as a success for recognition
- Leadership loyalty, fairness, trustworthiness in prosperity and adversity are keys to success
- True leaders have a sense of history and awareness of the present position
- Leaders must never blame or penalise followers for their own misjudgement
- Leaders should resist exchanging old friends for new.

Jealousy, competition, skulduggery and treachery keep the power and leadership in place; an interesting idea in politics but when patient care is the centre of the business, these principles could also work against the quality of service provision. How these ideas may influence an organisational culture will need to be evaluated.

Leadership in the context of changing cultures and dynamics has thus emerged, which is especially important within different health care environments, even within the NHS. Schein (1985) felt that leadership needs to be seen in context and the culture of that context is important: 'Leadership is entwined with culture formation.' The type of leadership required in health care is one that therefore fits with the culture of the organisation in which that health care is delivered. Schein (1992: 237) defined organisational culture as

> The pattern of basic assumptions that a given group has invented, discovered or developed in learning to cope with its problems of external adaptation and internal integration ... and therefore taught to new members as the correct way to perceive, think and feel in relation to those problems.

These levels of culture (Table 4.8) can be seen within the organisation of a hospital or community placement and also within University life itself.

Table 4.8 Levels of culture (www.12manage.com/methods_schein_three_levels_ culture.html, accessed 5.01.07)

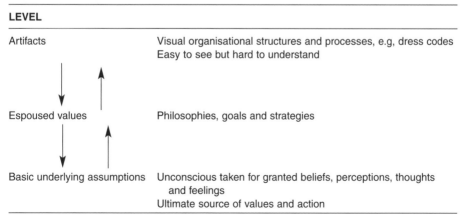

LEVEL	
Artifacts	Visual organisational structures and processes, e.g, dress codes Easy to see but hard to understand
Espoused values	Philosophies, goals and strategies
Basic underlying assumptions	Unconscious taken for granted beliefs, perceptions, thoughts and feelings Ultimate source of values and action

Induction at the start of a new course, meeting up with lecturers, mentors and other students on the course as well as people who have nearly finished their courses integrates us into what is expected in terms of our behaviour within the University. During our induction into new clinical placements we note the way other professionals behave, react to patients/clients and their relatives. This idea will be explored further in Chapter 6.

New Leadership

New roles and expectations are driving health care professionals into a more prominent position. Non medical prescribing, nurse-consultant led clinics, integrated community teams, hospital and community matrons and nurses managing doctors are signs of this challenge for clinicians. Kanter (1991) identifies some specific skills for new leadership.

- Self mastery
- Strategic visioning
- Continual learning
- Creator of partnerships
- Team facilitator.

Multi-agency teams will be a feature of the future and they too will require appropriate leadership. Mintzberg et al. (1998: 588) highlighted vision, shared ideals, creation of organisational pride, developing environments for energies and innovation as essential attributes of leadership. They also identify that a unique and essential leadership function is to build an organisation's culture and shape its evolution. They go on to suggest the leadership roles of designer, teacher and steward were required for contributing to leadership in the past but propose that new meanings will be needed for 'learning' organisations of the future.

Through personal mastery, group synergy, learning and sustainable development, a new leadership theory will emerge. Bennis et al. (1994) and Malby (1994) support this view and identify that the time is right for leading in this way within a framework of increased accountability. Scott (1998) points to the value of improving relationships between settings, process-based skills and professional judgement for the future of clinical leadership.

Daft (2005) indicates that these newer paradigms of leadership, involving change facilitation, creating a learning environment, sharing vision and shaping cultural values are important in the complexity of working life. Daft (2006: 682) notes we are now in a post-heroic leadership era and focuses on the need for leaders to show more humility. He notes the importance of

- Servant leadership
- Interactive leadership
- Moral leadership
- E-leadership and
- Level 5 leadership.

These ideas have connected themes within leadership theories. E-leadership concerns the notion that in many industries, communication is often not on a face-to-face stance but with increasing amounts of e-communication there are thus challenges for leaders. Building trust, maintaining open lines of communication and being open to subtle cues of concern are crucial in what is seen as virtual working environments. Level 5 leadership emerged from a five year study by Collins (2001), where a model of five hierarchical states to top leadership was proposed. Maybe not everybody can climb to be a level 5 leader, but in line with many of the new leadership theories, the ultimate leader is not seen as someone who is egotistical and overly ambitious but someone who works ethically, humbly and gives credit to others.

Level 5: Level 5 Executive

Builds enduring greatness through a paradoxical blend of personal humility and professional will.

Level 4: Effective Leader

Catalyzes commitment to and vigorous pursuit of a clear and compelling vision, stimulating higher performance standards.

Level 3: Competent Manager

Organizes people and resources toward the effective and efficient pursuit of predetermined objectives.

Level 2: Contributing Team Member

Contributes individual capabilities to the achievement of group objectives and works effectively with others in a group setting.

Level 1: Highly capable Individual

Makes productive contributions through talent, knowledge, skills, and good work habits.

Figure 4.4 The level 5 hierarchy model

Source: Collins, 2001a

Reproduced with permission

One of the most important aspects of all of these ideas is the ability to encompass human skills in order to build a culture of performance based on trust and integrity. These ideas will be discussed in greater detail as we progress through this book.

Will clinicians be able to rise to these demands? Hopefully, they will not accept the traditional followship roles of the past. The following quote is a useful ending for this chapter.

> As for the best leaders, the people do not notice their existence. The next best, the people honour and praise. The next, the people fear, and the next the people hate. When the best leader's work is done, the people say 'we did it ourselves!'
>
> Lao-Tsu (604–531 BC), cited in Robertson (1997: 278)

Summary of Key Points

This chapter has briefly looked at various aspects of leadership theory in order to meet the identified learning outcomes. These were:

▸ **Identify the evolution of leadership theories** There is a direct link to psychology and social sciences in the adopted styles of the leader; however, it is generally felt that – depending on the situation – the role of leadership may change.

▸ **Compare and contrast the various leadership theories** Trait theory originated prior to the turn of the previous century and the industrial revolution. It was felt that leaders exhibited distinct qualities or traits in order for them to function effectively. Conversely, what leaders do in terms of Action Centred Leadership to meet the needs of an organisation was discussed. However, it is necessary to be aware of the effects different leadership styles have on the overall behaviour of the group in order for that group to become effective.

▸ **Critically discuss the application of these theories in relation to health care** The wide range of leadership theories that have developed over time have contributed to the drive to make the health service more effective and efficient. However, it has been debated whether these theories are not always scientifically substantiated. The influence of these theories can be seen through the recruitment, work practices and appraisal processes in organisations and these have an impact on the performance of the individual or the team.

Further Reading

Northouse P G (2001) *Leadership: Theory and Practice* (2nd edition). London: Sage.

Prosser S (2002) 'Servant leadership', *Professional Nurse* 18(4): 238.

Van Seters D A and Field R H G (1990) 'The evolution of leadership theory', *Journal of Organizational Change Management* (3): 3.

Part 2

The Team

5   Team Life

Learning Outcomes

By the end of this chapter you will have had the opportunity to:
► Define what is meant by 'group' and 'team'
► Examine the values of team membership
► Discuss the value of group/team unity
► Discuss the importance of group/team formation
► Debate the classification of work groups
► Investigate the application of team leadership
► Evaluate the notion of effective leadership teams and their impact on the learning environment.

Introduction

Over the last four chapters, you have been investigating yourself as an individual preparing for the role of leader, taking into account the expected behaviours, beliefs and values you may hold. It is now prudent to scrutinise the team from the point of view of group/team formation, team dynamics and how you might expect individuals to react within a given situation. It is important to recognise the dynamics of the team to lead effectively for best patient care outcomes. In order to do this we must examine group formation and dynamics prior to studying the effects these elements have on leadership skills. Following this, we will attempt to offer suggestions as to the best method or style of leadership within given hypothetical health care situations.

Group and Team Characteristics

Individuals do not often work in isolation; rather they are members of a group. Indeed, you may well be a member of one or more groups related to both work and leisure activities. Groups are an essential feature of any organisation, their power cannot be underestimated and so the way in which they work together are fascinating phenomena. It is interesting to study children at play to see how they interact with each other. If you watch what is going on in the playground, crèche, or any group of children you will see different behaviours, from leader to subservient member, emerging. The effective leader should consider the impact of diversity such as age, gender and ethnicity (Chapter 3) on group processes and work pressures. These pressures in turn can have a great influence over the behaviour of group members; society expects health care workers to dress and act in a particular way. It is useful to think of other areas where expectations in fads and fashions influence the way groups of people dress and act together – 'Mods and Rockers', 'Teddy Boys', and today's 'hoodies', where group members have to dress in a particular way in order to be accepted into the prevalent teen society.

Activity

What do you think a group is?
Write a definition.
List how many groups you belong to.

Honey (1997: 88) notes that a group is seen as 'a collection of individual people who come together to achieve some purpose'; whatever groups you may have listed, the identified group members share a common purpose with shared norms, values and beliefs. Mullins (2005: 518) offers the suggestion that any number of people who interact with one another; are psychologically aware of one another; and perceive themselves to be a group are therefore a group. Other authors add to this by highlighting the need for a communication network, complementary goals and a group structure. Buchanan and Huczynski (2004: 283) state that 'it has been estimated that the average person belongs to five or six different groups, and about 92% of people are in groups of five people or less'. Humphries (1998: 11) states that:

a *group* is a collection of individuals each with their own thoughts, ideas, abilities and objectives – the sort of gathering you might encounter on a social occasion, or indeed waiting at a bus stop.

He goes on to say that

a *team* is a group of people working together to achieve common objectives and willing to commit all their energies necessary to ensuring that the objectives are achieved.

Honey (1997) distinguishes a group from a team in that the latter evolves from the former and performs at a much higher level of cohesion than a group needs to. Whether we concentrate on work or leisure activities we all have roles to play within a team or a group and we all seem to function better when we work with others rather than working in isolation.

Loyalty within a team or a group is often seen as a requirement. Those who question the actions or decisions of the group may run the risk of being ostracised or subtly made to conform. For instance, within the workplace, allied health professionals may work in directorate groups; standard setting groups, and workplace audit groups to name a few. There are also the Royal College of Nursing (RCN) Forum groups, supporting different professional groups such as theatre, rehabilitation, primary care nursing. If you wish to maintain membership of these groups then you might suppress or restrain your feelings to retain your membership without any loss of face. So it is clear that group and team formation is an important area to understand when endeavouring to lead; it is this knowledge that will help the leader to understand better the ways people behave. If leaders or managers are to avoid the negative aspects of a group, it is important for them to understand the dynamics of work groups and the advantages and limitations of using them to accomplish different types of tasks. Try the self-assessment of your own position in Table 5.1 dealing with people in teams.

If you answered mainly yes to these statements, your role is seen as having a *people focus* within the role of dealing with groups and teams. It is important to realise that a work team strongly influences the overall behaviour and performance of individual group members. Belbin (2000) describes teamwork as being a fashionable term and seems to have replaced the more usual reference to the group; therefore, every activity conducted by a group is referred to as teamwork. Mears and Voehl (1994) are more specific in describing the differences between groups and teams to include skills exhibited by members (Table 5.2).

There were many changes in the way people viewed groups during the twentieth century. However, it appears that for universal purposes the word 'group' is taken to have a general sense, whereas 'team' has a more specific context, so that in order to 'get the job done' a team needs to be formed. In general, we refer to 'group' or 'team' according to the particular focus of attention and the spirit, style and perception of the group/team. Confusion arises due to the duality and interchangeability of the terms and many writers

Table 5.1 Self-assessment of ability to deal with people in teams

I have a position where:	YES	NO
I deal with a variety of people and need to adjust my approach and style accordingly		
I am expected to give people helpful feedback		
I am expected to interview people as a major part of my role		
I am expected to negotiate, give presentations and be persuasive in reaching agreement		
I am expected to attend meetings and participate in different group/team meetings		
I am expected to give 'customer satisfaction/delight'		
I am expected to coach and mentor others		
I need to be innovative and come up with new ideas as well as encouraging others to generate ideas		
I am expected to deal with change management and resistance to change		
I need to use the telephone regularly		
I am expected to delegate		
I am often in tricky/conflicting situations		
I often need to establish a rapport with strangers and get on the same wavelength		

Table 5.2 Differences between a team and a group (Adapted from Mears and Voehl, 1994)

Group	Team
Normally information shared within the group	Collective performance goals
Members may not necessarily accept the common objectives but may exhibit individuality	Objectives understood and accepted by members
Tending to have opposite poles of opinion	Decisions by consensus with members heard and valued
Damaging criticism	Exchange of ideas with resolution
Members hide personal feelings	Free expression accompanied by listening
Little discussion about how the group is functioning	Self-examination about team functioning
Individuals protecting their role or place	Understood roles
Individual accountability	Individual and mutual accountability
Varied and random skills	Complementary skills
Neutral sometimes negative energy	Synergy leading to a result being greater than the sum of the members' individual effects or capabilities
Leadership that is appointed or elected	Shared leadership

do not differentiate between the two. The dynamics of the group are about the ever changing forces within a group to meet specific situations; it is also about the science investigating the action of these forces relating to the strength of the demands of given situations on individual members. Not only does this affect the way in which we interact at work but also when we are in our homes and within our individual communities.

Value of Group/Team Membership

Activity

Why do you think working in a group is so popular?
What benefits does it offer to individuals?

There are both positive and negative aspects to the use of work groups or teams. On the positive side you might have thought about the feedback, support and praise you get from others as you attempt to complete a task. There is also the togetherness and friendships formed that may give you a feeling of selfworth. Look at the success of web sites like *Friends Reunited*, where people are able to reach out to members of groups they have lost contact with, in order to see how they are getting on. On the negative side, group membership may attract pressures for an individual to perform at a certain level due to peer pressure. Similarly, an individual may find the behaviours of the group unacceptable but, due to the power within the group, finds it difficult to rail against the 'norm', which is a form of 'groupthink' (Janis, 1982). This concept will be discussed further in Chapter 7.

Humphries (1998) highlighted specific benefits from teamwork where the team can:

- Achieve goals more quickly and efficiently than individuals working alone
- Support each other to improve skills
- Become more confident and develop interpersonal skills
- Be more creative
- Take more risks
- Be more flexible
- Show commitment to the task and each other
- Share information, knowledge and feelings
- Be self-motivated
- Enjoy their work by being with other people
- Be easier to lead.

Activity

Do you agree with this or does team working seem to take too much time?

It is interesting to read how management theory and research relates to this concept. The classical approach to management and organisational behaviour tends to ignore the importance of groups/teams. Indeed, Taylor (1947), commonly thought to be the 'father' of scientific management, described the concept of the 'rabble hypothesis' wherein he made the assumption that people should carry out their work as solitary individuals, unaffected by others and with no interaction. He may also have thought that allowing people time to mix would only lead to trouble and rebellion! This assumption was challenged by the Hawthorn experiments at the Western Electric Company in America (1924–1932). The experiments were designed to demonstrate a positive correlation between the amount of light and worker productivity. One of the experiments took a group of 14 men working in a bank wiring room. It was noticed that the men formed their own subgroups so that despite financial incentive, the group had decided that 6000 units per day was a fair level of output. The group felt that if they started to produce in excess of the 6000 units then it would ultimately become the 'norm'. Although 6000 units was well below the level the group was capable of producing, group pressure was stronger than the financial incentive not to 'over work', so that the actual output was kept to the perceived 'reasonable' limit.

The four general conclusions drawn from the Hawthorne studies were that:

- **The aptitudes of individuals are imperfect predictors of job performance.** Although they give some indication of the physical and mental potential of the individual, the amount produced is strongly influenced by social factors.
- **Informal organisation affects productivity. The Hawthorne researchers discovered a group life among the workers.** The studies also showed that the relations that supervisors develop with workers tend to influence the manner in which the workers carry out directives.
- **Work-group norms affect productivity.** The Hawthorne researchers were not the first to recognise that work groups tend to arrive at norms of what is 'a fair day's work', however, they provided the best systematic description and interpretation of this phenomenon.
- **The workplace is a social system.** The Hawthorne researchers came to view the workplace as a social system made up of interdependent parts.

The notion of the Hawthorne effect arose from these experiments. The effect can be defined as 'an increase in worker productivity produced by the psychological stimulus of being singled out and made to feel important', hence team or group members experience a boost to their self-esteem when their work was being valued (http://www.nwlink.com/~donclark/hrd/history/hawthorne.html accessed 14.01.07).

Activity

How do the groups you identify with meet your social needs and enhance your social identity?
Do they stifle your individuality and freedom?

It can be argued that better ideas emerge when a number of people work on a problem separately and come together at a later date than when they work face-to-face in a group. This is possibly because group situations can inhibit the generation of ideas from less vocal members. Which begs the question, why form work groups or teams? Groups will often take greater risks (possibly, because responsibility is shared and therefore less threatening) and groups make fewer errors because there may be more rescuers, members who see potential problems and set out to rectify them before they become problems. In a group, there is greater total knowledge and information. By discussing the situation, a more thorough review is accomplished and a particular proposal strengthened. Most importantly, problems require decisions that depend on the participation and support of a number of persons. By forming groups, more members will accept a decision based on the group solving a problem rather than when one person solves it alone. Furthermore, communications relating to the decision can be speedy in the group process; communication breakdowns are reduced when the individuals have ownership.

Group Unity

Group unity is an important aspect of work group dynamics. When establishing a new work group, it is important to cultivate a feeling of unity among the group members at an early stage. Unity in a group develops slowly, as members open up and learn about each other. In the beginning, members are not yet sure if they will be accepted and may hold back until they feel more secure. If the group has an unfriendly atmosphere or there is a chance of rejection, unity may not develop. As a leader, you can help the group to be more unified by providing a safe environment for all. Today, for the most part, groups are usually composed of people possessing some basic idea upon which they are all agreed and which they are trying to express through the medium of their clashing personalities and, frequently, in obedience to someone in a leadership role. Groups also come together in order to exploit and use methods, which are regarded as essential to attaining the prevailing definition of 'successes'. Whatever degree of unity is achieved in such groups is often based on expediency or good manners. Ambition, conflict, hurt feelings and bruised egos are yet the norm in-group experience. A number of factors have been identified which affect the cohesiveness of a group.

Size As the size of a group increases, its cohesiveness tends to decrease.

Achievement of Goals The attainment of goals, especially if the group increases cohesiveness, and establishes them.

Status of the Group Generally, the higher a group ranks in the hierarchy of an organisation, the greater its cohesiveness. A group can achieve status for many reasons, including:

- Achieving a higher level of performance or attaining other measures of success within the organisation.
- Achieving recognition because individuals within the group display a high level of skill.
- Conducting work that is dangerous or more challenging than other tasks.
- Receiving more financial or material rewards than other groups.
- Recognition that members of the group are considered for promotion more often or more quickly than those outside of the group; it should be noted that a sense of 'eliteness' might cause friction with other groups.

Dependence of Members on the Work Group The greater individual members' dependency upon the group, the stronger will be the bonds of attraction to the group. A group that is able to satisfy a number of an individual's needs will appear attractive to that individual. These needs may include status, recognition, financial rewards, or the ability to do his or her job more easily.

Types of Groups

In every organisation, people are assigned to groups to perform tasks that one person could not accomplish alone. Some work groups are formal parts of the organisation's structure, such as departmental teams, e.g., operating department teams, ambulance teams. Some are ad hoc groups established to meet a short-term objective; others may be formed where members operate individually but with equal commitment to achieving a set goal, such as integrated teams/multi-agency teams. Still others are informal working arrangements that evolve to meet the various needs of the organisation. The formal group is one created to accomplish a defined part of the organisation's collective purpose. It has specific tasks allocated to it for which it is officially responsible.

On the other hand, the informal group is a collection of individuals who influence one another's behaviour within the formal group. The informal group normally develops spontaneously and the persons within the group talk and joke with one another, they have 'in jokes', they associate with one another outside of the working environment and may be referred to as 'cliques' or be part of the grapevine system of communication within an organisation.

Formation of Groups

Discussion related to the formation of groups starts with an examination of the members of the proposed group. They are a collection of people who will meet for the first time and then go on to form a group. Tuckman and Jensen (1977) suggest that groups pass through five clearly defined stages of development that they call Forming; Storming; Norming; Performing; and Adjourning (sometimes listed as Mourning). They admit that not all groups go through all the stages, some find that they are stuck in the middle and remain inefficient and ineffective. With others, passage through the stages may be slow, but that passage appears to be necessary and inescapable. To elucidate the stages further:

Forming: This is the orientation phase where individuals have not yet gelled. Each person is busy finding out about the others' attitudes and backgrounds; from this, ground-rules (i.e., codes of behaviour) for the group are established. Members often like to establish their personal identities and a leader is established. Task wise they seek instruction of what they are being asked to do, what the issues are and whether everyone in the group understands the task.

How to Address the Forming Stage: Help team members get to know one another. Make sure the purpose and task are clearly defined and share management expectations of the group. Give the team time to get comfortable with one another, but move the team along as well.

Storming: This is a conflict stage in the group/teams' life and can be quite an uncomfortable period. Members bargain with each other and try to sort out their position within the group and, occasionally, hostility may result as differences in goals emerge. The key element for the leader here is to manage and resolve the conflict.

How to Address the Storming Stage: Do not ignore the Storming stage. Acknowledge it with the team as a natural developmental step. Facilitators should

acknowledge the conflicts and address them. This is a good time to review ground rules, revisit the purpose and related administrative matters of the team.

Norming: In this cohesion stage, members of the group/team develop closer relationships with each other; overall working roles like norms of behaviour and role allocation are established, and group cohesion becomes obvious.

How to Address the Norming Stage: At this stage, the team has process down fairly well. Task will take on new significance, as the team will want to accomplish its purpose. Facilitators should keep this in mind and remind the team of the task. In addition, facilitators should be more diligent in adhering to the road map, providing time for feedback, closure, etc.

Performing: Here the group/team has developed an effective structure and is actually concerned with getting on with the job. Interestingly, not all groups reach this stage with many becoming 'bogged down' in an earlier and less productive stage. Within the performing stage members are equally happy to work alone; in subgroups or as a single unit.

How to Address the Performing Stage: Teams at the performing level are generally self-regulating. Road maps, processes, decision making, and other matters of team management will be handled independently by the team.

Adjourning: In this final stage, the group may disband, as it's work is complete.

In some literature, the final stage (adjourning) is not mentioned because it is thought to be a natural performing conclusion as the purpose of the team has been achieved. Tuckman and Jensen go on to suggest that groups may oscillate between the stages and pass through some stages several times without ever becoming effective.

Activity

Consider the teams you are a member of and think of the following:
- What stage are you at in the formation of your team?
- If you believe you are at the performing stage, did it take you a long time to get there?
- Has there been a change in membership of the team?
- Has it affected the performance level of the team?

Humphries (1998) discusses the need to identify team roles, recognising that each team member will have two roles: their professional role and their team role. He then listed seven team roles: the natural leader, activator, thinker, organiser, checker, judge and the supporter. He suggests that the role undertaken will be related to the personality of the team member but will not be under the control of that person, i.e., you would not be able to select the role you think you would wish to undertake. As each role has some advantages, it is useful to have a mix of the attributes within the team so that as the team leader, you would be able to develop the positive features and reduce the negatives. In an ideal world, a team would have one member from each category together with several supporters. Belbin (2000) lists eight similar roles but gives slightly different descriptions of each role, the overall intent is for the leader to recognise and utilise these roles effectively. It might be useful to go to his website (www.belbin.com/belbin-team-roles.htm) in order to compare and contrast the team roles described. Marquis and Huston (2006: 486–487) similarly identified that tasks within a team are encompassed within 11 roles but agreed that managers and leaders have to be aware of how teams carry out these specific roles and tasks.

1 **Initiator:** person(s) who propose or suggest group goals or redefines the problem in order to make sure all members understand what is to be achieved
2 **Information Seeker:** searches for a factual basis for the groups work
3 **Information Giver:** offers an opinion of what the group's values are
4 **Opinion Seeker:** seeks opinions that clarify or reflect other members suggestions
5 **Elaborator:** gives examples or extends meanings of suggestions and may indicate how they might work
6 **Coordinator:** clarifies and coordinates ideas and activities of the group
7 **Orienter:** summarises decisions and actions, questions departures from original intention
8 **Evaluator:** questions group accomplishments and compares them to the standard
9 **Energiser:** stimulates and prods group into action
10 **Procedural Technician:** facilitates group by arranging the environment *and*
11 **Recorder:** records the group's activities and accomplishments.

Together with this, managers and leaders need to examine the importance of team-building. It is necessary to identify *supportive* roles in order to provide care for the members of the team. They also need to identify roles that negatively affect the team dynamics.

Activity

Look at Table 5.3 and see if you can identify any of these roles you or others play in a regular meeting you attend.

How do you think these relate to conflict and conflict management (Chapter 8)?

Table 5.3 Positive and negative team roles

Team Builder/Supportive role	Team members serving their own needs
Encourager: accepts and praises *all* contributions with warmth and understanding.	**Aggressor:** expresses disapproval of others values or feelings through verbal attacks.
Harmoniser: resolves any conflict.	**Blocker:** persists in expressing negative
Compromiser: gives up his/her position in order to resolve conflict.	points of view and keeps resurrecting old issues.
Gatekeeper: facilitates participation by all members of the team.	**Recognition Seeker:** works hard to be the centre of attention.
Standard Setter: evaluates team processes to ensure maintenance of standards.	**Self-confessor:** uses the team for personal expression.
Team Commentator: records team achievements and provides feedback to the team.	**Playboy:** seems to be uninvolved, disinterested, full of cynicism and nonchalant. Tends to use horseplay unnecessarily.
Follower: listens to and accepts team decisions.	**Dominator:** attempts to control and manipulate the team, 'control freak'.
	Help seeker: attempts to manipulate team in order to receive sympathy from the members.
	Special Interest Pleader: continually speaks for others while hiding personal prejudices and biases.

Source: Marquis and Huston, 2006
Reproduced with permission

It could be that the negative behaviour on the right hand side is not meaningfully destructive but just indicates that the individual has found no other arena in which to convey their work dissatisfactions; leaders need to confront these dissatisfactions in a one to one supportive meeting. These individuals may be seen as helpful in raising creative expressions of the value systems of the team but it must be noted that an individual may feel excluded from the team unless the leader manages this positively. Their behaviour will continue to impact negatively on the team's ability to reach its goals unless the individual feels valued as a member and has their concerns taken seriously.

How to Handle the 'Not Always Helpful' Roles

- Set clear time limits for making decisions and remind people often of the time – jokers are less likely to intrude or delay if they are regularly informed of the time and process.
- Clarify expectations – get team 'buy-in' up-front for the work to be done. Agree by consensus that everyone will accept responsibility for any extra work. If the 'Busier Than Thou' person begins to complain, remind that person of his or her agreement.
- In general – individuals disrupt meetings for myriad reasons. Skilled facilitators will acknowledge the fears or anxieties behind the behaviour, and then move on.

Remember This ...

Team members must commit to the success of the group and promise to participate.

Here is another activity that reflects the interrelationships of individuals within a team.

Activity: The Drawbridge

In the story below, there are six characters. They are (in alphabetical order):
The Baron; the Baroness; the Boatman; the Friend; the Lover; and the Gatekeeper.
Put the characters in order of their responsibility for the death of the Baroness.
There should be 100 per cent agreement between all members of the group undertaking the exercise.

As he left for a visit to his outlying districts, the jealous baron warned his pretty wife: 'Do not leave the castle while I am gone, or I will punish you severely when I return!' However, as the hours passed, the young Baroness grew lonely, and despite her husband's warning, decided to visit her Lover who lived in the countryside nearby. The castle was located on an island in a wide, fast flowing river, with a drawbridge linking the island and the land at the narrowest point in the river.

'Surely my husband will not return before dawn,' she thought, and ordered the servants to lower the drawbridge and leave it down until she returned. After spending several pleasant hours with her Lover, the Baroness returned to the drawbridge, only to find it blocked by a Gatekeeper wildly waving a long and extremely sharp knife.

'Do not attempt to cross this bridge, Baroness. If you attempt to do so, I have orders from the Baron to kill you,' he said. Fearing for her life, the Baroness returned to her Lover and asked him to help. 'Our relationship is only a romantic one,' he said, 'I will not help.' The Baroness then sought out a Boatman

on the river, explained her plight to him, and asked him to take her across the river in his boat.

'I will do it, but only if you can pay my fee of five Marks.'

'But I have no money with me!' the Baroness protested.

'That is too bad. No money, no ride,' the Boatman said flatly.

Her fear growing, the Baroness ran crying to the home of a Friend, and after again explaining the situation, begged for enough money to pay the Boatman his fee.

'If you had not disobeyed your husband, this would not have happened,' the Friend said. 'I will give you no money.'

With dawn approaching, and her last resource exhausted, the Baroness returned to the bridge. In desperation, she attempted to cross to the castle, and was slain by the Gatekeeper.

The above exercise is designed to challenge your attitudes, beliefs and values. In doing so you can see that there is more than one side to an argument with each of the characters feeling that they are correct in what they do to support, or not, the Baron. The exercise may cause a great deal of discussion among your colleagues and it will become extremely difficult to come to the same outcome between different teams.

Clearly, people do not necessarily elect to adopt one of the highlighted roles (Table 5.3) but their individual personality and knowledge will mean that certain people will not be able to avoid working in a particular way. This knowledge can be utilised by an effective leader when allocating tasks but is also of use for the followers when learning to deal with appointed managers.

Activity

Have you worked with people in the clinical area who fit into the categories mentioned (see Table 5.3)?

I well remember a colleague who clearly functioned within the 'dominator' role. I seemed to spend a great deal of time reassuring new members of staff that it was 'just her way' of achieving objectives; that her attention to detail when delegating work was not personal, she did it to everyone irrespective of role or position within the hierarchy. Once they had realised that it was not personal, members of staff were able to function effectively and not take her comments to heart. In this situation, I could be seen as the 'harmoniser', the new staff became effective 'followers' until they took on their preferred roles.

While in the main, diversity within a team may lead to creativity, it can also contribute to a healthy level of conflict. The effective leader must remember that there can be negative effects of teamwork. Sullivan and Decker (1997) highlight the negative aspects of 'groupthink' (Janis, 1982), which is a negative phenomenon occurring in highly cohesive, isolated groups in which group members start to think alike. In turn, this can interfere with critical thinking and may lead to inappropriate decision making.

You may have found that it took you longer to reach the performance level in one group than it did in another; indeed, you may never have reached high performance in one of your groups and found that you remained at the storming stage for most of the time until the group was disbanded. The problem may have stemmed from the lack of effective leadership where the leader may have been unaware of the roles of some of the group members. Dynamic leaders will inspire followers towards participative management by how they work and communicate in groups. Effective leaders will need to keep group members on course, draw out the shy, politely cut off the talkative and protect the weak. At all times leaders must be aware of the team but remember that they should not be 'hung up' on the roles but recognise that all roles are valuable. The longterm consequence of this is 'labelling' a person so leading to the 'halo' or 'hero' effect (Hartley, 1997).

Classification of Work Groups

Mullins (2005) discusses the classification of work groups as being either formal or informal. These groups may coalesce in order to accomplish a specific task or may arise naturally in order to meet the needs of a particular group of people working within the organisation. Understanding the functions of these groups is important in becoming an effective leader.

Formal Groups

These include a variety of groups and teams whose roles can be clearly defined. In the main, they are permanent groupings of personnel specified in the organisational chart. Within the NHS these groupings could be speciality based, e.g., operating theatres, ambulance trust, ward based, community and PCT based. Subordinates report directly to a designated supervisor and the relationships among personnel have some formal basis. This might take the form of duty rotas where there is a rota chart that relates to who is working with whom on what days in order to ensure all care is given to the patients/clients within a specific area. Others may be termed *Task Groups* and are formed by a number of personnel assigned to work together to complete a project. There are different levels of task groups. Task groups may comprise of personnel from two or more departments and, are thus, cross-departmental. A *'Committee'* is a special-purpose task group. The purpose of committees is to:

- exchange views and information
- recommend action
- generate ideas
- make decisions.

Here the term 'committee' refers to a group of people whose job is to define the parameters of tasks, while a 'work group' is assigned the job of accomplishing tasks.

Activity

Go back to the purposes of a committee above where the exchange of views and information, recommending action, generating ideas and making decisions are identified.
What views do you have about the effectiveness of committees you know?

You might wonder about the outcome or output of many committees. One can think of areas where a committee may be necessary in deciding a long term strategy or business plan but it sometimes seems out of touch with reality. Indeed, remember that 'a camel is a horse designed by a committee' (Sir Alex Issigonis 1906–1988) (http://en.wikipedia.org/wiki/Alec_Issigonis). It's an ironic expression, used to show that deciding anything by committee, and therefore by taking too many opinions and wish-lists into account, will result in something that's probably vaguely similar to what was originally planned, but which won't be anywhere near as effective as was wanted. A camel and a horse are both ungulates, but the point is that the camel is both ugly and slow in comparison. Strategic decisions are not always translatable into operational tasks. Leaders should read and try to understand fully any committee documents produced and appraise them for their effectiveness and workability. Often it feels as though nothing ever comes from a committee, we hear of people/managers 'going to meetings' but then go on to ask, What has been achieved? Meetings for meetings sake have to be challenged and there are now more references made to task and finish groups in order to prevent stagnation. However, these may be seen as too 'quick-fix' a solution to a problem that requires more sustainable action. Task groups in the form of unilateral or multidisciplinary teams may also be charged with reviewing policies and procedures governing clinical practices. Here we may think of a project like ensuring all procedures are documented and updating any research that informs practice towards better patient quality care.

Advantages to teamwork include broader experience and wider knowledge, and members may be more committed to implementation if they have the opportunity to share in the decision-making process. Disadvantages might include any decisions that come from a group process being open to social pressures, with decisions made for the wrong reasons, with weaker members being strongly influenced by stronger ones.

Informal groups

Within a work setting, people may band together informally in order to accomplish an objective. This objective may be related to the work of the organisation; for example, a group of people such as nurses, physiotherapists, pharmacists, and dieticians may join up in order to produce a health education poster. Informal groups are likely to develop when the formal organisational structure does not accommodate their joint needs. Another example is where all the paramedics within a shift might get together informally to compare notes, talk about practice, and socialise in the context of clinical support groups. Workers who want to promote a particular interest or point of view also form interest groups within an organisation; these are the most important non-formal groups for the manager to consider.

'Friendship groups' are informal associations of workers developed as an extension of their interaction and communication in the work environment. They are formed for a variety of reasons, including common characteristics (such as age or ethnic background), political sentiment, or common interests. In this book, we will not explore friendship groups in detail. However, managers should be aware that many actions (such as assignment of tasks and the establishment of other types of working groups) influence the interaction and communication patterns among subordinates, causing individuals to affiliate with each other so that interests and friendship groups inevitably emerge. These groups can have both positive and negative consequences for an organisation, and managers should be alert to ways in which these informal friendship groups affect the overall performance.

Team Leadership

Within the management of the NHS workforce, the notion of team and group appear to be interchangeable. Teams emanate from groups. Earlier in this chapter, we were discussing the differences between groups and teams; we highlighted the differences within Table 5.2 and noted that it is important to ensure the team is empowered to do what is necessary to achieve the over-all goal. The complex process of leadership is highlighted by Barge (1996), who sees leadership as 'mediation' and 'coordination'. Owen (2005) also discusses the 3½ Ps of leadership (see Figure 5.1). He states that performance is the odd one out (2005: xvi) as most leaders in his survey saw performance as a symptom rather than a feature of leadership; it therefore achieves only a ½. He then goes on to discuss what good leadership might look like at each level of the organisation (2005: xvii–xix).

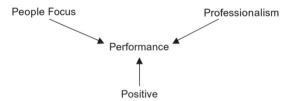

Figure 5.1 Owen's 3½ Ps of leadership (Owen, 2005: 5)

These descriptions draw together factors that have been discussed through-out this chapter in terms of group/team formation and the personalities of people in the situation. Moving on from this we can revisit the application of information from the MBTI® (Chapter 2). From the results of the indica-tor and by learning to know yourself – and how you prefer to work – you can construct your 'style compass'.

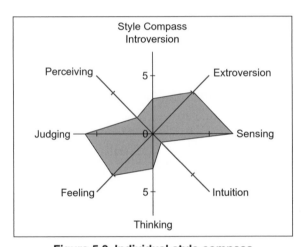

Figure 5.2 Individual style compass

Following this, you can use your judgements of what you know about others to plot their shape over yours (see Figure 5.3).

Now you will see how alike/different you are and note the degree of overlap. Clearly, it would not be of great benefit for us all to be the same otherwise nothing would be achieved; there needs to be a balance so that decisions can be made, thus making it easier to move forward as a team. The style compass is only a quick way of thinking about any style and can be adapted to highlight interactions among people within a team.

Certainly, while we both appear to be extroverts, I appear to be more judgmental than my colleague is but she has more perception of what is required, hence, we work well together recognising each other's differences and building on each other's strengths.

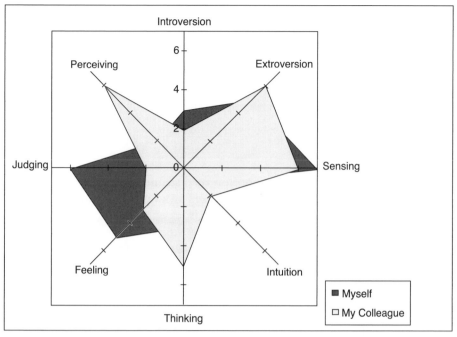

Figure 5.3 An example of a style compass for two people

Activity

Plot your own style compass and that of a colleague.
Highlight where you differ and discus how these differences may enhance your abilities to lead effectively.

Group Conflict

Effective team development can help to resolve conflict. Initially the group needs to plan what they are going to do, identify goals and decide, if appropriate, on a mission statement (Marriner Tomey, 2004: 156). There are techniques that can be utilised in order to do this; the best known of which is *nominal group technique*; alternatives include *consensus, majority rule* and *independent listing,* so that items can be considered in order of importance. This is very similar to nominal group technique, which follows the following pattern:

- First, the group members are asked to list, on paper, what the group wants to achieve and how they will behave in order to reach that identified goal.

- Second, each person will read out one item from their list, which will be recorded on paper or whiteboard for all to see, discuss and agree to.
- Third, discussion will take place to prioritise the items prior to them being typed up for all to have a copy.

By having all members of the group agree to the list of objectives and behaviours then a feeling of identity is engendered and the group should function well.

Leadership Teams

Of late, in general education, the notion of distributed leadership is becoming the 'norm'. It is a notion that has been around for a long time, either as delegated or as shared leadership. It is essentially about sharing out leadership across the organisation. However, we are aware that, while there is a strong belief in the idea, there is not a great deal of evidence about how it works in practice. Therefore, we need to explore the idea in some depth. We know that effective leadership makes a difference so it follows that the caring professions need effective leaders at all levels.

Leadership teams, it is believed, is one way of giving power to everyone. As caring professions and the NHS in general becomes more complex to manage and lead, we need many more leaders than ever before, enabling us to create pools of talent, from which we can grow tomorrow's leaders. A key to successful planning and implementation is the development of teams. Table 5.4

Table 5.4 Three types of team and their relative advantages and disadvantages (www.nsba.org/sbot/toolkit/LeadTeams.html, accessed 21.01.07)

Model	Features	Advantages	Disadvantages
Executive	Small teams of 3–8 All district managers No constituent or stakeholder involvement	Quick, focused, consensus among leaders	Isolated, no district-side ownership
District	Mid-size team of 15–20 Representatives from each key stakeholder group within the 'boundaries' of district staff	Key representatives are involved, sense of district- wide ownership	Representatives can take the narrow view, no community-side ownership
Community	Large team of 25–30 Mix of district staff and community leaders (50:50 preferred)	Key district community leaders involved, sense of community-wide ownership	Slow process, everyone needs to be heard, steep learning curve as citizens become knowledgeable about issues and practices

provides a description of three types of teams and their relative advantages and disadvantages.

When we talk about sharing leadership, we ought to mean sharing learning-centred leadership. We should create and develop many leaders who influence and improve the quality of learning and teaching. Although distributed leadership is not a difficult idea, when put into practice it can take many different forms. For example, you will find that there are assortments of teams within the health service that have powers in a variety of situations (Table 5.5). It is useful to understand how they work in order to function effectively.

Table 5.5 Team and administration responsibilities

Management Team	Governance Team Responsibilities	Administration Responsibilities
Vision (planning)	Creates, reviews and approves	Recommends process, develops and plans (decides what) and implements plans (decides how)
Structure (policy)	Creates reviews and adopts	Recommends and implements
Advocacy (communication)	Represents public interest, seeks public input	Acts in public interest, seeks and provides public information
Accountability (evaluation)	Monitors progress toward goals, evaluates the board standards and personnel in accordance	Implements evaluation of programs

When a unit has leadership in teams, the whole institution can evolve toward becoming a learning organisation. Learning organisations are able to retain staff due to their commitment to those staff. It is, therefore, part of the role of the effective leader to ensure students are supported within their clinical placements, which in turn requires effective mentorship programmes and updating of staff to ensure accurate and professional assessment within that clinical area. The following characteristics define the effective learning environment:

- People feel they are doing something that matters – to them personally and to the larger world.
- Every individual in the organization is somehow stretching, growing or enhancing his/her capacity to create.
- People are more intelligent together than they are apart.
- The organisation continually becomes more aware of its underlying knowledge base in the hearts and minds of employees.
- Visions of the direction of the enterprise emerge at all levels. The responsibility of the administration is to manage the process whereby new emerging visions become shared visions.

- Employees are invited to learn what is going on at every level of the organisation, so they can understand how their actions influence others.
- People feel free to inquire about each other's assumptions and biases.
- People treat each other as colleagues.
- There is a mutual respect and trust in the way they talk to each other no matter what their position is.

All this is led by the effective leader and done within the framework of the team. Staff retention and team morale will be supported and maintained; together with this students will feel that there is a place for them within the organisation and as they complete their individual courses will apply for a permanent post.

Summary of Key Points

This chapter has briefly looked at various aspects of team life in order to meet the identified learning outcomes. These were:

- ▶ **Define what is meant by 'group' and 'team'** The various definitions, and interchangeability, of the two labels were discussed. Ultimately, it seems from the literature, there is ongoing debate related to whether or not there is a need to differentiate between the two.
- ▶ **Examine the values of team membership** Teams are valued because they can achieve cohesiveness and effectiveness within our working environments. The Hawthorne Experiment demonstrated the ability to enhance worker productivity through boosting self-esteem due to work being valued.
- ▶ **Discuss the value of group/team unity** This is an important aspect of work group dynamics. As a leader, you need a unified team in order for the workplace to become effective.
- ▶ **Discuss the importance of group/team formation** It is important to remember that groups and teams form for specific purposes. The stages of formation are important if the effective leader is to encourage the team to meet their final objectives.
- ▶ **Debate the classification of work groups** Here we note that there are two main classification of groups: formal and informal. Each has its own role and responsibility but working effectively relies on all types of groups/teams.
- ▶ **Investigate the application of team leadership** Effective team leadership is vital. In order to achieve this, a number of tools have been developed to identify personal strengths and weaknesses in order to work effectively.
- ▶ **Evaluate the notion of effective leadership teams** In particular, their impact on the learning environment. Learning from general education we can see that employee retention is affected by staff perception of involvement with the decision-making process. The knock-on effect of this may be to enhance the learning environment.

Further Reading

Department of Health (2001) *A Health Service of all Talents: Developing the NHS Workforce*. London: DoH.

Donaldson L (1995) 'Management for doctors: conflict, power, negotiation', *British Medical Journal* 310: 104–107.

Pattison S (2001) 'User involvement and participation in the NHS: a personal perspective'. In T Heller, R Muston, M Sidell and C Lloyd *Working for Health*. London: Sage/Open University Press.

Salvage J and Smith R (2000) 'Doctors and nurses: doing it differently', *British Medical Journal* 320: 1019–1020.

6 Communication and Leadership

Learning Outcomes

By the end of this chapter you will have had the opportunity to:
► Describe various forms of communication
► Discuss the importance of effective communication
► Debate motivational theory and its place in the clinical area
► Consider the benefits of Active Listening
► Consider the benefits of Neuro-Linguistic Programming
► Discuss the legal and ethical issues related to effective communication.

Introduction

Effective leadership means communicating with others in such a way that they are influenced and motivated to perform actions that achieve common goals and lead toward desired outcomes (Daft, 2005); so in order to be an effective leader it is vital to be a good communicator. This chapter will examine various forms of communication to enable you to understand how knowledge and ideas are shared. If you can't get your message across clearly then the message doesn't matter and nothing will happen. Maxwell (1999: 23) stated that 'Educators take something simple and make it complicated. Communicators take something complicated and make it simple.' A statement hinting at the fact that things can be made to sound more complicated than they really are by bad or ineffective communication. So effective communication can be seen to influence the ways in which a team will function by motivating through planning and effective delegation. It must be remembered that leadership and communication are always affected by the overall structure of the organisation. We must then make reference to some management theory, its application and effect on practice, when examining communication within the workplace.

There is much discussion in the academic world of communication as to what actually constitutes communication. Currently, many definitions of communication are used in order to conceptualise the processes by which people navigate and assign meaning. We might say that communication consists of transmitting information from one person to another. In fact, many scholars of communication take this as a working definition, and use Lasswell's (1948) maxim, 'who says what to whom in what channel with what effect,' as a means of circumscribing the field of communication theory. Other commentators suggest that a ritual process of communication exists, one not artificially divorceable from a particular historical and social context. Communication stands so deeply rooted in human behaviours and the structures of society that scholars have difficulty thinking of it while excluding social or behavioral events. Because communication theory remains a relatively young field of enquiry and integrates itself with other disciplines such as philosophy, psychology and sociology, one probably cannot yet expect a consensus conceptualisation of communication across disciplines. Currently, there is no paradigm from which communication scholars may work. One of the issues facing scholars is the possibility that establishing a communication metatheory will negate their research and stifle the broad body of knowledge in which communication functions.

Forms of Communication

It is important that the effective leader is able to adapt their communication to each given situation depending on the needs of the audience. That is not to say that this is always a conscious decision. Communication styles, like leadership styles, are often intuitive. It is useful, however, to understand how communication can be made more effective in order to reduce risks through misunderstanding and unplanned confusions.

A model, as a representation of reality, may help to describe the communication process and consecutive stages through which someone or something has to pass in order to achieve a specified aim (Weightman, 1999). The model also acts as a checklist to ensure each stage has been negotiated successfully. The basic communications model takes the form of a chain of events (see Figure 6.1).

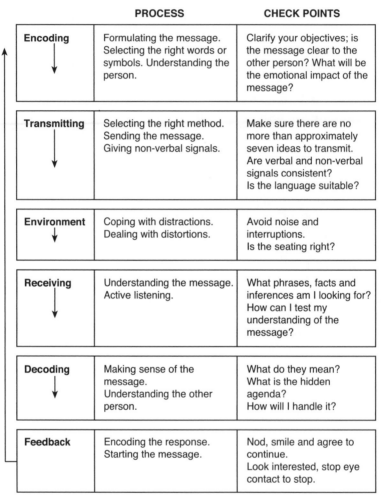

PROCESS		CHECK POINTS
Encoding	Formulating the message. Selecting the right words or symbols. Understanding the person.	Clarify your objectives; is the message clear to the other person? What will be the emotional impact of the message?
Transmitting	Selecting the right method. Sending the message. Giving non-verbal signals.	Make sure there are no more than approximately seven ideas to transmit. Are verbal and non-verbal signals consistent? Is the language suitable?
Environment	Coping with distractions. Dealing with distortions.	Avoid noise and interruptions. Is the seating right?
Receiving	Understanding the message. Active listening.	What phrases, facts and inferences am I looking for? How can I test my understanding of the message?
Decoding	Making sense of the message. Understanding the other person.	What do they mean? What is the hidden agenda? How will I handle it?
Feedback	Encoding the response. Starting the message.	Nod, smile and agree to continue. Look interested, stop eye contact to stop.

Figure 6.1 The basic communications model
Source: adapted from Weightman, 1999
Reproduced with permission

Problems may occur at any of these points so it is worth sitting down and working out where the potential problem might originate so that it can be addressed. This is applicable within all individual or group interactions.

Overall the purpose of communication is to ensure that messages are received and understood in order to make life easier both in working and home environments. Of course the system goes 'pear shaped' at times and communication is not as effective as it could be but if we understand what is happening then we can do something about it.

Another form of this model is one described by Shannon and Weaver (1954) and depicted in Figure 6.2. As a feedback diagram this can be easier to understand than the line diagram in Figure 6.1. However the cycle is depicted it can be seen that there is a purpose and direction for messages to travel in order for effective communication to take place. It can be thought of as being a useful – but too simple – model. It assumes the communicator wishes to influence the receiver and therefore sees communication as a persuasive process. It also assumes that messages always have effects and can exaggerate the effects of mass communication. However you think of them, models are a simplified description of a complex entity or process that allows you to understand the process and so make it work for you.

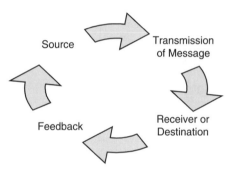

Figure 6.2 Communication feedback loop
Source: adapted from Shannon and Weaver, 1954
Reproduced with permission

Activity

Consider the stages of effective communication and attempt to formulate a message for a patient within your sphere of practice.

- Ask whether the patient can move their right arm up and down.
- Relate this to a patient who is deaf, then for one who is blind, then one who does not speak English.

You might have discussed the need for written material, Braille, or interpreter and also thought of the type of environment you were in to see if it helped or hindered conversation. I am sure we have all tried to carry on a conversation in a night club, or where there is a loud TV where it is difficult to hear yourself think, let alone understand what is being said. Following anaesthesia there may be distortions in understanding due to the drugs. It is important to check

understanding by their response or by asking further relevant questions
following the transmission of a message.

Communication Networks

Leavitt (1951) outlined various communication networks that can be depicted
to demonstrate how messages get passed on from a leader to others (Figure 6.3).

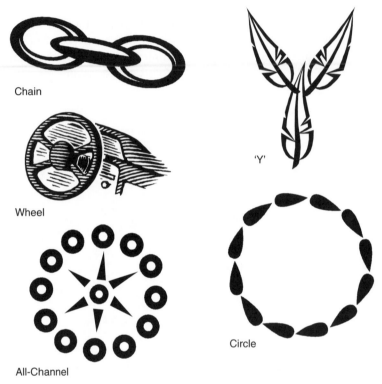

Chain

Wheel

'Y'

All-Channel

Circle

Figure 6.3 Various communication networks
Source: adapted from Leavitt, 1951
Reproduced with permission

Within the *chain* it is the one in the middle of a group that often emerges
as the leader, but the strain in this situation of trying to hold all the messages and communication together may prove too much. They try to ensure
that messages travel in both upward and downward directions. Here,
morale may be low and it may be difficult to be flexible when attempting
to solve communication problems. By comparison, within the Y format the
leader is situated at the centre of the fork and negotiates between numbers
of parties, as is the case with the leader who is at the hub of the *wheel* who

ensures fast, accurate problem solving. The leader who is centrally located will ensure efficiency and effective communication. The *circle* structure of a group does not allow for the emergence of a leader as messages are just passed round and round with no-one taking control and then there is limited decision making and communication is poor. The *all-channel* network allows everyone to talk to one another and the leader is centrally in control; problems are then made simple as everyone can elicit more ideas, thereby coming to a conclusion much quicker. Essentially the right network is the structure that allows the communication necessary to accomplish the task. Leavitt further stated that when the leader was more centralised problems were solved more quickly, there were fewer mistakes and fewer messages were required. Together with this the person in the centre enjoyed himself much more than the other members of the group. In the decentralised network – the circle – performance was slower and more erratic.

Other methods of communication evolved from management approaches are described as being top-down or *downward communication* (Figure 6.4) where the intention is that messages such as instructions or directives are passed down from above, i.e., from the manager or leader downwards. This form of communication is primarily directive and can be linked to scientific/classical styles of management together with the autocratic style of leadership.

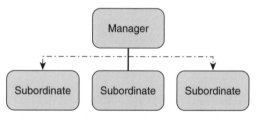

Figure 6.4 Downward communication

By contrast, bottom-up or *upward communication* (Figure 6.5) is encouraged within the realms of humanistic management techniques, whereby the subordinates are encouraged to share ideas with their managers and will be involved with the decision-making process.

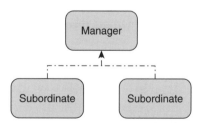

Figure 6.5 Upward communication

Effective Communication

Greenbaum (1974) suggested that there are 4 main areas about which there needs to be effective communication within an organisation. They are:

- Regulation
- Innovation
- Integration
- Information

Each of these areas is designed to ensure that the workforce knows and understands the purpose of the organisation and is able to work effectively within it. Regulation may take the form of a code of professional practice, as with the Nursing and Midwifery Council (NMC) and the Health Professions Council (HPC), where there may be dire consequences for breaking the code. Innovation communications may be seen in policies for new initiatives. Team meetings and away days may help in getting integration among a small group. Information may emerge as emails or memoranda. Dowding and Barr (2002) suggest that you might have thought of many reasons to communicate with others that could have included some or all of the following:

- Ensure that everyone gets the same message (Regulation)
- To change someone's behaviour (Innovation)
- Sort out a problem and raise motivation (Integration)
- Give factual information that people need to proceed efficiently with their work (Information).

Activity

- Think back over the last 24 hours.
- Make a note of how much time was spent in communication with someone else.
- What form did that communication take?
- What purpose did the communication serve?

You might have identified any of the vast number of communication forms that can be used, e.g., speaking/verbal (v), writing (w) and non-verbal (nv). Some of these are formal (f) and some informal (if), e.g., department meetings (f); team briefings (f); saying hello (if); coffee break conversations (if); shift change-over (f); memos (f): eye contact in the corridor (if) and so the list goes on. Effective communication should ensure that messages are received and understood by relevant parties, especially in health care environments whether in an institution, an ambulance, or in a patient's home. It is important we are clear what our message is.

Activity

Have you ever been in a situation where you have asked someone for help only to be 'blanked'?

It may have been that you were not clear in outlining your need, why you needed help or indeed what you expected your helper to do. Tappen et al. (2004b: 20) highlights a situation where this occurred

> Peter has been working on a busy oncology floor for several years. He usually has a caseload of six to eight clients on his shift, and he believes that he provides safe, competent care to his clients.
>
> While Peter was on his way to medicate a client suffering from cancer of the bone, a colleague called him, 'Peter, come with me please.' Peter responded, 'I need to medicate Mr J in Room 203. I will come right after that. Where will you be?' 'Never mind!' his colleague answered. 'I'll find someone who's more helpful. Don't ask me for help in the future.'
>
> This was not the response Peter had expected. He thought he had expressed both an interest in his client and a willingness to help his colleague. What was the problem?
>
> After Peter had given Mr J his medication, he went back to his colleague. 'Sonja, what's the matter?' he asked. Sonja replied 'Mrs V fell in the bathroom; I needed someone to stay with her while I got her walker.' 'Why didn't you tell me it was urgent?' asked Peter. 'I was so upset about Mrs V that I wasn't thinking about what you were doing.' Peter said 'And I didn't ask you why you needed me. I guess we need to work on our communication, don't we?'

This story highlights just how easy it can be to appear disinterested and unwilling to help in a situation when you don't have the full facts; it also tells us of the importance in being clear in what you have to say. Along with this is the need to have an understanding of non-verbal communication. There are times when you might feel that you have something vitally important to say but as you look around your audience, be it the patients or your colleagues, you can see from their non-verbal signs that you have lost their interest. It may be the yawn that gives it away, that far-away look in their eyes, or increased doodling, but clearly whatever it is that is happening there is a need to change your approach in order to attract attention. Communication in whatever form it takes is vital.

Motivation and Communication

There are numerous theories related to motivation, some of the most well known are those of Adair (2003), Maslow (1987), Hertzberg (1966), McGregor (1987), Ouchi (1981) and McClelland (1984). They all believe that the job of the leader/manager is to get the work done. In order to do this they must motivate their team members. Motivational theory is still not clearly understood but McClelland (1984) pioneered workplace motivational thinking, developing achievement-based motivational theory and models, and promoted improvements in employee assessment methods, advocating competency-based assessments and tests, arguing them to be better than traditional IQ and personality-based tests. His ideas have since been widely adopted in many organisations, and relate closely to the theory of Hertzberg (1966). McClelland (1984) is most noted for describing three types of motivational need:

- Achievement motivation (n-ach)
- Authority/power motivation (n-pow)
- Affiliation motivation (n-affil).

The needs-based motivational models are found to varying degrees in all workers and managers, and this mix of motivational needs characterises a person's or manager's style and behaviour, both in terms of being motivated, and in the management and motivation of others.

- The *need for achievement* (n-ach) person is 'achievement motivated' and seeks realistic but challenging goals and advancement in the job. There is a strong need for feedback as to achievement and progress, and a need for a sense of accomplishment.
- The *need for authority and power* (n-pow) person is 'authority motivated'. This driver produces a need to be influential, effective and to make an impact. There is a strong desire to lead and for their ideas to prevail. They also seek increasing personal status and prestige.
- The *need for affiliation* (n-affil) is 'affiliation motivated' and is motivated by friendly relationships and interaction with other people. The affiliation driver promotes motivation and a need to be liked and held in popular regard. These people are team players.

McClelland said that most people possess and exhibit a combination of these characteristics. Some people exhibit a strong bias to a particular motivational need and this motivational or needs 'mix' consequently affects their behaviour and working/managing style. He goes on to suggest that a strong *affiliation* motivation undermines a manager's objectivity, because of their need to be liked, and that this affects a manager's decision-making capability. A strong *authority* motivation will produce a determined work ethic and commitment to the organisation, and while people motivated by *authority and power* are attracted to the leadership role, they may not possess the required flexibility and people-centred skills. He also argues that people with strong *achievement* motivation make the best leaders, although they can demonstrate a tendency to demand too much of their staff in the belief that they are all similarly and highly achievement-focused and results driven, which of course most people are not.

McClelland's particular fascination was for achievement motivation, and this laboratory experiment illustrates one aspect of his theory about the affect of achievement on people's motivation. He asserted, via this experiment, that while most people do not possess a strong achievement-based motivation, those who do, display a consistent behaviour in setting goals: for instance, volunteers were asked to throw rings over pegs rather like the fairground game; no distance was stipulated, and most people seemed to throw from arbitrary, random distances, sometimes close, sometimes farther away. However, a small group of volunteers, whom McClelland suggested were strongly achievement-motivated, took some care to measure and test distances to produce an ideal challenge – not too easy, and not impossible. Interestingly, a parallel exists in biology, known as the 'overload principle', which is commonly applied to fitness and exercising, i.e., in order to develop fitness and/or strength the exercise must be sufficiently demanding to increase existing levels, but not so demanding as to cause damage or strain. McClelland identified the same need for a 'balanced challenge' in the approach of achievement-motivated people.

McClelland contrasted achievement-motivated people with gamblers, and dispelled a common preconception that achievement-motivated people are big risk takers. On the contrary, typically, achievement-motivated individuals set goals which they can influence with their effort and ability, and as such the goal is considered to be achievable. This determined, results-driven approach is almost invariably present in the character make-up of all successful business people and entrepreneurs. McClelland suggested other characteristics and attitudes of achievement-motivated people:

- Achievement is more important than material or financial reward.
- Achieving the aim or task gives greater personal satisfaction than receiving praise or recognition.
- Financial reward is regarded as a measurement of success, not an end in itself.
- Security is not a prime motivator, nor is status.
- Feedback is essential, because it enables measurement of success, not for reasons of praise or recognition (the implication here is that feedback must be reliable, quantifiable and factual).
- Achievement-motivated people constantly seek improvements and ways of doing things better.
- Achievement-motivated people will logically favour jobs and responsibilities that naturally satisfy their needs, i.e., offer flexibility and opportunity to set and achieve goals, e.g., sales and business management, and entrepreneurial roles.

McClelland firmly believed that achievement-motivated people are generally the ones who make things happen and get results, and that this extends to getting results through the organisation of other people and resources, although as stated earlier, they often demand too much of their staff because they prioritise achieving the goal above the many varied interests and needs of their people.

There are interesting comparisons and relationships to be drawn between McClelland's (1984) motivation types and the characteristics defined in other behavioural models.

Table 6.1 Comparative features of McClelland's leadership types

McClelland motivational type	Achievement-motivated leaders (n-ach)	Authority-motivated leaders (n-pow)	Affiliation-motivated leaders (n-affil)
Focus	Task	Individual self	Team and Individual
Favoured style of behaviour Hersey and Blanchard (1977)	1.Telling 2. Selling	3. Delegating	4. Participating
McGregor (1987) style typology	X Theory	X theory	Y theory

Development of Written Health Care Records

Leading on from the motivational aspect of communication, we must consider the impact of written health care records. It is vital that these are accurate and completed as near to the completion of a task as possible. Lumby (1991) noted that caring had it's communication roots built on an oral tradition; indeed Florence Nightingale (1859) felt that writing down one's observations about patients was a mental crutch that would diminish the nurse's capacity to observe and remember. This meant that early nursing knowledge was not recognised or even regarded as credible, possibly because it wasn't written down. Nursing and Midwifery knowledge was seen of lesser value than medicine and merely a part of it; indeed years ago it was doctors that prescribed the nursing care and nurses did as they were told. Emerging professions such as Paramedics and Operating Department Practitioners (ODPs) are currently experiencing similar problems; there are limited materials published for these specialities and so they may not be seen as true professions yet, but as their own referenced literature becomes available so the 'profession' will emerge. It can be argued that the oral tradition was useful in the past when health care was 'simple', but as health care services become more complex, hospitals become more specialised and health expectations expand, written channels are legally required to pass information on to different staff in different health and social care organisations. There is an old saying which stresses the need for written information that goes something like, 'If it isn't written down then it hasn't been done.' We will come back to this when considering legal and ethical issues related to communication.

Activity

Recall the records you keep within your clinical area.

- Are they complete?
- Could you have increased the amount of information given?
- Do they fulfil the needs of a person taking over the care?

At times it may seem to be difficult to complete records immediately after a period of care delivery but they should be completed as soon as possible, otherwise accuracy could be jeopardised. On occasion, for instance, errors in recording have been made which have led to the removal of the wrong limb during surgery. Health care records are generally used to inform others of the needs and progress of patients, clients and families in respect of their overall health. However, they are also used to instruct others of what is expected of them in continuing care. Within the theatre environment, do you always record where a diathermy plate was placed, or the position the patient was in during the operation? Accurate records are a useful learning and motivational aid for students and therefore can keep them focused on 'best practice'.

Medical records have always been centrally stored in GP surgeries but where consultant care was involved the central records departments within a hospital for in-patient or out-patient episodes was utilised. The 'kardex' was a nursing communication system that was introduced to support a verbal 'handover' in a ward office or community health centre. In the 1980s, when the nursing process was being introduced, further paper systems were required to bring in nursing care plans. In true bureaucratic style, more multi-professional paper records were felt to be required rather than streamlining the process of record keeping. The Department of Health is encouraging the use of multidisciplinary protocol-based care (DoH, 2002). In many areas there is much duplication of information and health care workers lose valuable direct patient contact time at the expense of administration. Diversity of clinical care such as day surgery, medium stay surgery, continuing care in nursing homes, outpatient departments, midwifery, community nursing, accident and emergency, operating theatre duties, paramedic services, walk in centres, NHS Direct, as well as public health nursing, reveals a plethora of record-keeping styles. This means that the variety of record keeping methods should reflect the needs of the environment, e.g., minute by minute recording will not be as commonplace in nursing homes as it will perhaps be in theatres or within the ambulance service where things change from minute to minute.

Another important aspect to note is that record keeping is seen in the context of professional standards of practice and within a legal framework

(NMC, 2002). There are ethical issues concerning integrity, truth, respect, confidentiality, consent and informed decision making. Records can be used for the following reasons: legal protection, reimbursement, patient education, quality assurance and research. Records and documentation is the primary communication tool that reflects nursing and care philosophies, models, structure, processes and outcomes. All health care professionals communicate with each other and other agencies through their records of:

- Collection of data to identify needs
- Problems and concerns
- Reactions and responses to existing or potential health needs
- Goals set and planned interventions

Review and goal evaluation should, then, highlight the effectiveness of the professional input by examining the outcomes or responses. Record keeping is an integral part of professional health care practice. It is a tool of professional practice and one that should help the care process. It is not separate from this process and it is not an optional extra to be fitted in if circumstances allow.

Good record keeping helps to protect the welfare of patients/clients by promoting:

- High standards of clinical care
- Continuity of care
- Better communication and dissemination of information between members of the interprofessional health care team
- An accurate account of treatment and care planning and delivery
- The ability to detect problems, such as changes in the patient's/client's condition at an early stage
- The concept of confidentiality.

The HPC (2004), NMC (2002) and DoH (2000b) all agree that members of the public have the right to expect that health care professionals will practise a high standard of record keeping. Good record keeping is a mark of a skilled and safe practitioner, while careless or incomplete record keeping often highlights wider problems with that individual's practice. There is no single model or template for a record. The best record is one that is the product of the consultation and discussion that has taken place at a local level between all members of the interprofessional health care team and the patient/client and fulfils the needs of the situation. It is one that is evaluated and adapted in response to the needs of patients/clients. The record should enable any registrant to care for the patient/client, regardless of where they are within the care process or care environment. It is an invaluable way of promoting communication within the team and between registrants and their patients/clients. Good record keeping is, therefore, both the product of good teamwork and an important tool in promoting high quality health care. The NMC (2002) believes that there are a number of key principles that underpin good records and record keeping. Some of these relate to the content and style of the record. In addition, there are some legal issues that all registrants should be aware of and take into account in their record keeping practice.

The primary function of the Nursing and Midwifery Council (NMC) and the Health Professions Council (HPC) is to 'protect the public' by setting professional standards and giving advice and guidance to registered nurses, midwives and specialist community public health nurses (registrants). The *NMC Code of Professional Conduct: Standards for Conduct, Performance and Ethics* (the Code) is designed either to be used on its own or in conjunction with other NMC guidelines. When used with these other guidelines, the Code is an effective tool that leads to a much greater understanding of the principles of providing nursing and midwifery care. Registrants have a responsibility to deliver safe and effective care based on current evidence, best practice and, where applicable, validated research. The NMC accepts that, until there is national agreement between all health care professions on standards and format, records may differ depending on the needs of the patient or client. The record must, however, follow a logical and methodical sequence with clear milestones and goals for the record-keeping process. The NMC also advises that it is good practice to retain records with reference to the Human Rights Act (2000) and the Caldicott Report (NHS, 1997a).

There are a number of factors that contribute to effective record keeping. Patient/client records should:

- Be factual, consistent and accurate
- Be written/electronically recorded as soon as possible after an event has occurred, providing current information on the care and condition of the patient/client
- Be written clearly and in such a manner that the text cannot be erased or deleted without a record of change
- Be written in such a manner that any justifiable alterations or additions are dated, timed and signed or clearly attributed to a named person in an identifiable role in such a way that the original entry can still be read clearly
- Be accurately dated, timed and signed, with the signature printed alongside the first entry
- Be, as a written record, attributable to a named person in an identifiable role (for electronic records)
- Not include abbreviations, jargon, meaningless phrases, irrelevant speculation and offensive subjective statements
- Be readable on any photocopies.

In addition, records should:

- Be written, wherever possible, with the involvement of the patient/client or their carer
- Be written in terms that the patient/client can understand
- Be consecutive
- Identify problems that have arisen and the action taken to rectify them
- Provide clear evidence of the care planned, the decisions made, the care delivered and the information shared.

Activity

Think back to some records you have kept related to your patients/clients.

- Do you think they accurately reflected the care you offered?
- Could you have made them clearer?
- If they were brought under scrutiny within an audit/inquest would they stand up as being factual and accurate?

Within the acute sector, notes related to a period of care may be written sometime later in a shift rather than immediately a period of care is complete. This may then lead to questions related to accuracy of recall. In the past, kardex records may have contained ambiguous phrases like 'slept well' and 'comfortable day'; neither of these phrases would support care offered within a court. Authors like Dimond (1999; 2002; 2004a; 2004b; 2006), Young (1989; 1994a) and Castledine (1998) have much to say about the need for accurate and precise record keeping, which is applicable to all branches of health care.

Audit

Audit is one component of the risk management process, the aim of which is the promotion of quality. If improvements are identified and made in the processes and outcomes of health care, risks to the patient/client are minimised and costs to the employer are reduced. Audit can play a vital part in ensuring the quality of care being delivered to patients/clients. This applies equally to the process of record keeping. By auditing records, registrants are able to assess the standard of record keeping and identify areas for improvement and staff development. Audit tools should, therefore, be devised at local level to monitor the standard of record keeping and to form a basis both for discussion and measurement. Whatever audit tool or system is used, it should primarily be directed towards serving the interests of patients/clients, rather than organisational convenience. It may prove useful, when auditing, to consider including a system of peer review in the process. The need to maintain confidentiality of patient/client information applies equally to the auditing process as it does to the record keeping process itself.

Rule 10 of the *Midwives Rules and Standards* (2004) permits supervisors of midwives to request that midwives' records be audited. This is primarily to confirm they are being kept as required by Rule 9 and to assist the midwife in making records. Currently, there is a drive for fewer paper records and an increase in the use of ICT, which is supported by the NHS Plan (DoH, 2000a). Indeed this aspect of communication has been incorporated into all training programmes in order to meet the various professional bodies' requirements.

The importance for documentation in all aspects of health care in the future will grow as the culture of litigation appears to be on the increase and health care expectations rise. All this makes redundant Nightingale's view of the need for written notes related to patient care.

Active Listening

Active listening is a way of listening and responding to another person that improves mutual understanding. Often, when people talk to each other, they don't listen attentively. They are often distracted; half listening, half thinking about something else. When people are engaged in a conflict, they are often busy formulating a response to what is being said. They assume that they have heard what their opponent is saying many times before, so rather than paying attention, they focus on how they can respond to win the argument. In order to become more active in the process the listener must take a structured approach to listening and responding that focuses the attention on the speaker. The listener must take care to attend to the speaker fully, and then repeats, in the listener's own words, what he or she thinks the speaker has said. The listener does not have to agree with the speaker, he or she must simply state what they think the speaker said. This enables the speaker to find out whether the listener really understood. If the listener did not, the speaker can explain some more. Elements that tell the speaker that you are listening can be seen in eye contact, posture and gesture.

We can all tell if someone is listening. How many times have you been involved in a conversation and the listener is looking all around the room rather than at you, or they are sitting with their arms folded and leaning away from you. One gets the feeling that they are just not interested in what you have to say and this can make you angry enough that the point of the conversation is lost.

Active listening has several benefits. First, it forces people to listen attentively to others. Second, it avoids misunderstandings, as people have to confirm that they do really understand what another person has said. Third, it tends to open people up, to get them to say more. When people are in conflict, they often contradict each other, denying the opponent's description of a situation. This tends to make people defensive, and they will either lash out, or withdraw and say nothing more. However, if they feel that their opponent is really attuned to their concerns and wants to listen, they are likely to explain in detail what they feel and why. If both parties to a conflict do this, the chances of being able to develop a solution to their mutual problem becomes much greater.

The skills associated with active listening are normally denoted by the mnemonic SOLER, which stands for:

Squarely face the person
Open your posture
Lean towards the sender
Eye contact maintained
Relax while attending

Paraphrasing is a useful tool. By restating a message, but often with fewer words, the listener is encouraged to interpret the speakers' words in terms of feelings. So, instead of just repeating what happened, the active listener might add 'I gather that you felt angry or frustrated or confused when ... [a particular event happened]'. Then the speaker

can go beyond confirming that the listener understood what happened, but can indicate that he or she also understood the speaker's psychological response to it. It tests your understanding of what you heard and communicates that you are trying to understand what is being said. If you're successful, paraphrasing indicates that you are following the speaker's verbal explorations and that you're beginning to understand the basic message.

Clarifying helps you to understand exactly what is being said, it brings vague material into sharper focus so that unclear or wrong listener interpretation is untangled, more information is given, the speaker sees other points of view, and it identifies what was said, e.g., 'I'm confused, let me try to repeat what I think you were trying to say', or, 'You've said so much, let me see if I've got it all.'

Perception Checking again helps you to understand by giving and receiving feedback and checking out your assumptions, e.g., 'Let me see if I've got it straight. You said that you love your children and that they are very important to you. At the same time you can't stand being with them. Is that what you are saying?'

Summarising is about pulling together, organising and integrating the major aspects of your dialogue, paying attention to various themes and emotional overtones, putting key ideas and feelings into broad statements but *not* adding new ideas. By doing this there is a sense of movement and accomplishment in the exchange. It may also establish a basis for further discussion and pull together major ideas, facts and feelings, e.g., 'A number of good points have been made about rules for the classroom. Let's take a few minutes to go over them and write them on the board.'

Primary Empathy is a reflection of content and feelings in order to show that you understand the speaker's experience and that allows the speaker to evaluate his/her feelings after hearing them expressed by someone else. The basic formula for this is 'You feel [state feeling] because [state content]', e.g., 'It's upsetting when someone doesn't let you tell your side of the story.'

Advanced Empathy, by contrast, is a deeper reflection of content and feeling to achive greater understanding, e.g., 'I get the sense that you are really angry about what was said, but I am wondering if you also feel a little hurt by it?'

Active listening intentionally focuses on who you are listening to, whether in a group or one-on-one, in order to understand what he or she is saying. As the listener, you should be able to repeat – back in your own words – what they have said, to their satisfaction. This does not mean you agree with, but rather understand, what they are saying.

Neuro-Linguistic Programming

Linking to the ability to actively listen is the notion of being able to understand and 'read' how people are reacting to any form of communication or situation. Interestingly, the notion of Neuro-Linguistic Programming (NLP) may help with the ability to 'read' how people are reacting within a given situation and, thus, what course to follow to achieve the best outcome. NLP was advocated in the mid-1970s by a linguist (Grinder) and a mathematician (Bandler) who had strong interests in:

- Successful people
- Psychology
- Language
- Computer programming.

It is difficult to define NLP because those who started it and who are involved in it use such vague and ambiguous language that it means different things to different people. While it is difficult to find a consistent description of NLP among those who claim to be experts at it, one metaphor keeps recurring. Neuro-linguistic programming claims to help people change by teaching them to programme their brains. Furthermore, consciously or unconsciously, it relies heavily upon:

1 The notion of the unconscious mind as constantly influencing conscious thought and action
2 Metaphorical behaviour and speech, especially building upon the methods used in Freud's *Interpretation of Dreams* (1911)
3 Hypnotherapy as developed by Milton Erickson.

A common thread in neuro-linguistic programming is the emphasis on teaching a variety of communication and persuasion skills, and using self-hypnosis to motivate and change oneself. Most NLP practitioners advertising on the internet make grand claims about being able to help just about anybody become just about anything. The following is typical: *NLP can enhance all aspects of your life by improving your relationships with loved ones, learning to teach effectively, gaining a stronger sense of self-esteem, greater motivation, better understanding of communication, enhancing your business or career ... and an enormous amount of other things, which involve your brain* (www.nlp3. co.uk/personal.htm (accessed 21.08.2007)).

Some advocates claim that they can teach an infallible method of telling when a person is lying (in Australia they often have an NLP practitioner in court to identify which aspects of evidence could be lies!), but others recognise that this is not possible. Some claim that people fail only because their teachers have not communicated with them in the right 'language'. Another (false) NLP presupposition is that 'If someone can do something, anyone can learn it'. This comes from people who claim they understand the brain and can help you reprogramme yours. Indeed, recently on television a NLP practitioner attempted to cure 40 people of their fear of flying – he succeeded in 38 cases. Was this due to NLP or some other phenomenon? They want you to think that the only thing that separates the average person from Einstein or Pavarotti or the World Champion Log Lifter is NLP.

NLP is said to be the study of the structure of *subjective* experience, but a great deal of attention seems to be paid to observing *behaviour* and teaching people how to read 'body language'. I am not aware of signalling my feelings because the message is coming from my subconscious mind, so how might we test these kinds of claims? Probably the answer is that we can't test them with any degree of reliability and there is no empirical evidence to back up the claim. Sitting cross-armed at a meeting might not mean that someone is 'blocking you out' or 'getting defensive'. S/he may just be cold or have a back ache or simply feel comfortable sitting that way. It is dangerous to read too much into non-verbal behaviour. Finally, NLP claims that each of us has a Primary Representational System (PRS), a tendency to think in specific modes: visual, auditory, kinaesthetic, olfactory or gustatory. A person's PRS can be determined by words the person tends to use or by the direction of one's eye movements. Supposedly, a therapist will have a better rapport with a client if they have a matching PRS. None of this has been supported by the scientific literature.

The BAGEL Model specifies the five elements (in mnemonic form) that purportedly comprise the behavioral cues that indicate an individual's internal processes. The BAGEL Model is predicated on the notion that internal processes are subjectively represented in sensory terms: visually, auditory, kinesthetically and, least likely, olfactory and gustatory.

Body posture (e.g., leaning back, head upwards and shallow breathing indicates visual representation)
Accessing cues (e.g., fluctuating voice tone and tempo indicates auditory representation)
Gestures (e.g., gesturing below the neck indicates kinesthetic representation)
Eye movements (see eye accessing cues and the representational systems below)
Language patterns (specifically sensory based, e.g., 'I see!', 'Sounds right!' or 'I feel that ...')

Most of the cues we already know about and use within a meeting situation. A leader can tell when members of the meeting have started to lose interest because they fidget or fiddle with their pen, the worst case scenario would be that the person goes to sleep. However, the eye accessing cues of NLP, normally outlined for the natural right-handed person, are interesting and mainly unused. They are the core for NLP training exercises and involve learning to calibrate eye movement patterns with internal representations. According to NLP developers, this core tenet loosely relates to the VAK guidelines below:

Visual: eyes up to left or right according to dominant hemisphere access; high or shallow breathing; muscle tension in neck; high pitched/nasal voice tone; phrases such as 'I can imagine the big picture'.
Auditory: eyes left or right; even breathing from diaphragm; even or rhythmic muscle tension; clear mid-range voice tone, sometimes tapping or whistling; phrases such as 'Let's tone down the discussion'.
Kinesthetic: eyes down left or right; belly breathing and sighing; relaxed musculature; slow voice tone with long pauses; phrases such as 'I can grasp a hold of it'; 'I feel that ...'

NLP theory explains this breathing and mental processing according to the varying levels of chemical composition in the blood that affects the brain. 'Visual' people tend to be fast visual thinkers and can seem untrustworthy to 'kinesthetic' thinkers because thinking by feeling is inherently slow. So by using judgments from your style compass together with observing others you can become effective leaders, although most effective leaders will say that they continue to learn as leaders and are open to new situations and new opportunities. Some authors use internal verbal/auditory/kinesthetic strategies in order to categorise people within a thinking strategies or learning styles framework, for instance, that there exist visual, kinesthetic or auditory types of manager. Certainly it is worth being aware of this but without empirical evidence it is difficult to say, with any degree of certainty, that it is an effective practice.

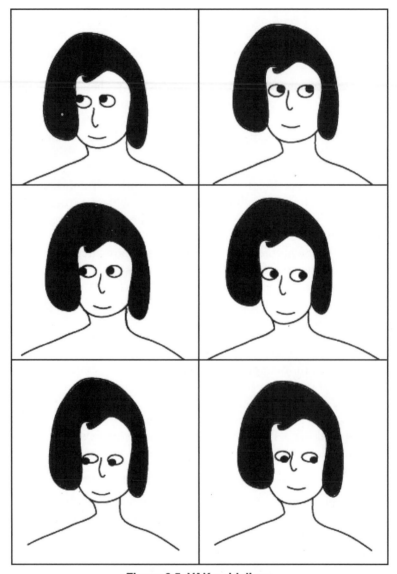

Figure 6.5 VAK guidelines

Legal and Ethical Issues

Another important aspect to note is that record keeping is seen in the context of professional standards of practice and within a legal framework. There are ethical issues concerning

- **Integrity**: The quality of possessing and steadfastly adhering to high moral principles or professional standards.
- **Truth**: Something that corresponds to fact or reality.
- **Respect**: Consideration or thoughtfulness.
- **Confidentiality**: Entrusted with somebody's personal or private matters.
- **Consent**: To give permission or approval for something to happen.
- **Informed decision-making**: Based on a proper knowledge and understanding of a situation or subject.

The importance of documentation in future will grow as the culture of litigation increases and health care expectations rise. Paper records are beginning to be overtaken by computerised records so that, while in the past there has been a need to retain records of care delivered for some time before they are destroyed, it will become a thing of the past as giant computer mainframes store information electronically. This then brings into the discussion the continued vigilance required to maintain confidentiality. Similarly, the notion of explicit (if someone signs a consent form) and implicit (if someone arrives for a blood test) consent has to be dealt with in keeping records safe and that allows them only to be shared with the people who need to know about the medical history, treatment and any other factors regarding health care.

Accountability within the health service is influenced by employment, criminal, civil and professional action. Legal and ethical issues are therefore important professional considerations. Ethics is the study of what our conduct and actions *ought to be* (rather than what it actually is) with respect to others, the environment and ourselves. It is sometimes difficult to separate out ethics and legal issues.

It is interesting to note that health care professionals, once held in high esteem, are now less trusted and are held to account more than before as cases where individuals who have abused their autonomy for personal satisfaction and criminal activities have become more visible. The health care industry is also facing the ethical problem of trying to meet infinite demand with finite resources. Financial, physical and human resources are being allocated on a priority basis. This has been the case previously but there is more openness than before. The implications for these points are that ethical considerations form an important component of health care management. Ethical dilemmas also face clinical staff daily. Haddad (1992: 46) defines an ethical dilemma as a novel, complex and ambiguous problem that does not lend itself to programmed or routine problem solving for which a precedent has been set. In other words, ethical dilemmas are forms of 'messy' problems.

Activity

Can you make a note of any recent clinical problems where you felt ethics played a part?

It may be that you have thought about resuscitation decisions made in your area or maybe decisions about withholding medical treatment for certain groups of people such as the elderly, those with a disability or those who have problems considered self inflicted. You may have identified that screening for certain abnormalities may also pose ethical decisions.

The use of *ethical principles* is useful in examining the issues within any ethical dilemma. Marquis and Huston (2006: 79) identify the following:

1 **Autonomy**: This infers freedom of choice or accepting the responsibility for one's choice. Legal items around the right to self-determination support this moral principle.
2 **Beneficence**: This refers to the point that actions and decisions should be taken in order to promote good.
3 **Non-maleficience**: This goes further and states that if one cannot do good, then at least one should make every effort to avoid harm.
4 **Paternalism**: This principle is related to the positive good that could occur when one individual makes decisions on behalf of another individual. This has to be balanced with the issue where paternalism may limit freedom of choice for another as one individual makes judgments and decisions for another. Paternalism is possibly only justified to prevent harm to others.
5 **Utility**: This principle reflects a belief in utilitarianism, where common good outweighs what is good for an individual. This justifies paternalism in also restricting the choice of the individual.
6 **Justice**: This principle is based on the point that equals should be treated equally and 'unequals' should be treated according to their differences.
7 **Veracity**: There is an obligation to tell the truth.
8 **Fidelity:** There is a need to keep promises.
9 **Confidentiality:** Priviledged information must be kept private.

Legal issues stem from the statutes and the law of the land. As a health care professional, you should be aware of the legal controls surrounding your practice. Professional negligence in health care concerns any form of malpractice. Malpractice is the failure of a professional with a body of knowledge to act in what is considered a reasonable and prudent manner. This would imply a manner expected of the average health care professional in that discipline, based on expected judgments, foresight, intelligence and skill. Health care professionals hold their own personal liability concerning practice. Fletcher and Buka (1999: 53) identify that it is a professional code of conduct that will enable a judge to decide whether a practitioner was acting within the expectations of their particular profession. This point is known as the Bolam Test from a notable legal test case (Bolam vs Friern Hospital Management Committeee, 1957). Issues such as the position of trust afforded to the professional and the action taken to protect patients' or clients' best interests will be of particular interest in the eyes of the law.

Employers have no legal right within a contract of employment to ask you to account for your professional action. They could, however, bring a disciplinary case against you if you failed to account for care, which was deemed poor, and this could thus lead to redundancy. It is only when there is a legal enquiry (criminal or civil) that a professional may need to go to a Court of Law, e.g., child protection, murder or assault/harm cases and that a health professional may have to account for their action. In legal enquiries, the health profession may have to account for any breach in their 'duty to care'.

The NMC or HPC may also ask professionals to account for their actions but they have no statutory right to force an account. They can, however, through their disciplinary procedures make certain decisions concerning registration; it is obviously important that accurate records of care are kept if one is to maintain registration and practise safely. As role models leaders should be exemplary in their conduct and accurate in their communication and record keeping.

Summary of Key Points

This chapter has briefly looked at various aspects of communication in order to meet the identified learning outcomes. These were:

- **Describe various forms of communication** Here we examined the notion of chain, wheel and all channel communication recognising that there are models that depict a phenomena of effective communication.
- **Discuss the importance of effective communication** Without effective communication it has been shown that nobody would know what they were supposed to do within a given situation.
- **Debate motivational theory and its place in the clinical area** Motivational theory must be recognised in the clinical area, because without motivation people will not work to achieve the common aims of clinical care.
- **Consider the benefits of Active Listening** This is an essential tool of caring, as without it we may not really hear what our patients/clients are telling us. On occasion we know that even though someone is telling us that everything is OK there is something about the way they say it that indicates that it isn't really the case.
- **Consider the benefits of Neuro-Linguistic Programming** This is debatable. On occasion NLP has been shown to work, it is used within the court systems of some countries but it is still necessary to be sceptical.

▶ **Discuss the legal and ethical issues related to effective communication** It is vital that legal and ethical issues are understood and adhered to. Being an exemplary role model, and using all elements of legal and ethical perspectives helps one to become an effective health care professional.

Further Reading

Bavister S and Vickers A (2004) *Teach yourself NLP*. London: Teach Yourself.

Fiske John (1982) *Introduction to Communication Studies*. London: Routledge.

Pierce J R (1980) *An Introduction to Information Theory, Symbols, Signals and Noise*. New York: Dover Publications Inc.

7 Problem Solving

Learning Outcomes

By the end of this chapter you will have had the opportunity to:
- Discuss the concept of problem solving
- Critically review the models of problem solving
- Critically examine the theory and skills associated with decision making
- Critically explore the importance of clinical decision making within the context of problem solving for health care practice.

Introduction

Health care practitioners spend a good proportion of their clinical and management time involved in dealing with patient needs and problems as well as dealing with professional decision making. Leadership therefore involves the need to have experience and skills in problem solving and effective decision making. Having examined the team, it is prudent to now focus on some of the relevant theoretical perspectives associated with problem solving and decision making for both the health care professional and from a patient perspective.

The chapter will offer possible solutions and explore the clinical decision making process. Muir (2004) notes the importance of clinical decision making, its effect on patient health care and also the impact on the health care professional. Due to the complexity of health care, and the constant need to keep up to date, the professional is faced with a multitude of problems that require their attention. Professional accountability in the context of clinical governance and evidence-based care (Chapter 10) has also made health care professionals aware of the need to understand the nature of problems and the need to recognise the rationale for the professional judgments they make (Nursing and Midwifery Council (NMC), 2002; DoH, 1997b; Muir Gray, 1997).

What is Problem Solving?

Problem solving is a key management skill that involves complex cognitive processes. It was VanGundy (1988: 3) who noted that a problem could be defined as 'any situation in which a gap is perceived to exist between what is and what should be'. On the other hand, Armstrong (1990) noted ambitiously that there were no real problems – only opportunities.

Activity

What do you think?
Think about a recent problem you have faced and decide which of the above ideas you feel fits the situation.

Armstrong offers a useful 'half-full glass' perspective but in terms of life events, patient experience and finite health care resources, this can appear an unrealistic interpretation for all health care problems or issues.

Problem solving and decision making are often seen as the same activity. Problem solving assumes a

fuller analysis of issues than pure decision-making issues because it relies on trying to discover the *root cause* of the problem. Decision making, however, may not address these issues in depth and can mean that decision making will not take the same amount of time and energy in the process (Tappen et al., 2004b). In some of the literature you may find that decision making involves problem solving and in others, decision making is seen as part of problem solving. For the purposes of this chapter we will assume the latter model.

Neither is wrong but is just a different perception of the link between the two concepts. The reality of focusing in on problems may present a negative aspect of our professional work so care is needed to balance this leadership activity with a proactive stance seeking solutions to potential problems.

Problem Management

Problem management can be considered using the main four-fold organisational management approaches:

- Classical Management
- Human Relations
- Systems
- Contingency.

The scientific (classical) approach, where the need for optimum productivity is sought in an organisation, will relate to how problem management influences the goal. The Human Relations approach focuses on the impact and implications of work-based problems on people and the importance of their human values. A Systems approach highlights the impact and implications of problem management on the interdependency of relationships within an organisation. Finally, a combination of these ideas is seen in the Contingency approach (Dowding and Barr, 2002: Chapter 7). It was VanGundy (1988) who suggested that success in problem management relied on two elements, the approaches used and the nature of the problem.

The notion of successful problem solving relates to how organisations or individuals address the following issues:

- Recognition of the nature of the problem
- Assessing the intelligence, implications and impact concerning the problem
- Identifying success criteria in problem solving
- Decision making for solution generation
- Communicating solutions.

Simon (1977) identified decision making as 'management itself'. He was also concerned with how decisions are made and how problem solving could be improved. This has real relevance for the health care industry if leaders are to learn how to do things better and smarter. The novice practitioner often looks for the 'quick fix' idea in order to solve a problem, using a 'blueprint' approach, whereas the effective leader uses a reflective approach, considering the wider perspectives or implications. Robotham and Frost (2000) highlight the work of Benner (1984) and describe the *proficient* practitioner as someone who perceives situations as wholes rather than in terms of specific aspects.

Traditional and Contemporary Approaches to Problem Solving

Traditionally, problem solving and decision making used a rational model as a basis. One perspective, known as the 'Economic Man' approach has underpinning assumptions that rely on two notions:

- That individuals are all working towards the same organisational goals
- Rationally, they use the best methods to achieve these goals.

This model has been criticised because of its unrealistic nature of the assumptions. There is another approach to compare with the 'Economic Man', which is based on the real or actual behaviour of the problem solvers/decision makers (Simon, 1960a; Cyert and March, 1963). Linstead et al. (2004) highlight the differences between 'Economic Man' and the more realistic 'Administrative Man' (Table 7.1).

Table 7.1 Economic vs Administrative Man

Economic Man	Administrative Man Simon (1960a); Cyert and March (1963)
• Rational approach • Complete knowledge of the problem • Complete list of possible choices • Decisions based on maximising effect	• Solves problems that are 'good enough' • Complete knowledge not possible, knowledge is always fragmented • Impossible to predict accurate consequences due to their futuristic nature • Choice is usually from few alternatives • Choice is based mainly on satisfying

In recent years feminist writings have rejected this patriarchal approach as being politically incorrect and 'man' would be replaced with 'person'. Either way leaders of both genders need to understand the nature of problem solving.

The Types of Problems

In straightforward terms, there are two types of problems, there are the *simple* problems that face us every day and that are fairly easy to solve in terms of time and energy spent on them. Then, there are more *complex* problems that need a good deal of our time and often create internal and external tensions. There are many ways in which health care professionals manage the problems they face. It is often much easier to try and position a problem in the 'simple' category, particularly when we face a new situation, where we think a quick solution is desirable and valued by others. It is therefore easy to jump to conclusions about the type of complexity of some problems.

Ackoff (1981) ascribed simple problems as *difficulties* or *hard* problems with clear boundaries.

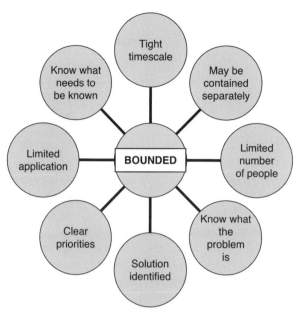

Figure 7.1 Bounded problems

The more complex ones were referred to as 'soft, messy problems'. These messy problems are seen as unbounded (see Figure 7.2), connected to mess or chaos theory. There is uncertainty and there are no straightforward

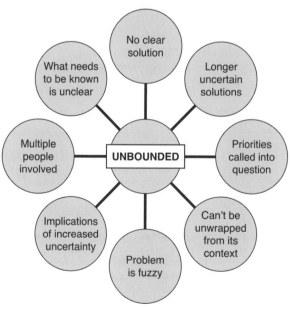

Figure 7.2 Unbounded problems
Source: The Open University, 1996
© The Open University. Reproduced with kind permission

Table 7.2 Hard and soft problems

Hard problems or difficulties	'Soft, messy' problems
➢ One clear problem	➢ Complex problem
➢ One clear solution	➢ No one clear solution
➢ Know what needs to be done	➢ Answer can be one of many
➢ Clear methods for working out solution	➢ Uncertainty about the problem
➢ Problem is structured	➢ No obvious way of working it out
	➢ Problem is unstructured

Source: Ackoff (1981)

answers to these problems (Table 7.2). It is all too easy to try and solve messy problems quickly, like simple problems, without really thinking what the real problem is all about and who the problem concerns. The real trick is to recognise the type of problem, the stages of solving it, and how to make the process look and feel simple. Leaders unconsciously select an approach in managing problems most closely related to their personal leadership style. There is a continuum of approaches related to problem solving from a rational approach to a more creative approach. Both approaches have their place depending on the situation being dealt with.

Scientific Rational Approach

It has generally been accepted in the *rational approach* that there are several stages to problem solving that may help us to understand the concept. Marquis and Huston (2006: 71) illustrate a more traditional Problem Solving Seven Step Model. This can be compared to the handy Six Is (Table 7.2) model depicted by Stott (1992), which emphasises the need to involve relevant people when making decisions.

Table 7.3 Traditional vs six Is framework

Traditional Problem Solving Process	Six Is: A framework for a staged problem solving
1 Identify the problem	1 **Identify:** Try to understand the problem and its causes
2 Gather data to identify cause and consequences	2 **Isolate:** Separate the details of the problem and further define the criteria for successful solution
3 Explore range of alternative solutions	3 **Involve:** Involve necessary and helpful people
4 Review range of alternative solutions against evaluation criteria	4 **Investigate:** A range of possible solutions and evaluate their application to problem
5 Select solution	5 **Implement:** Make a decision, action and communicate decision
6 Implement	6 **Inquire:** Ask into effectiveness of decision and reflect on process for future learning
7 Review success	*Adapted from Stott (1992: 206)*

These stages seem like a useful way of logically looking at problems, but it must be said again that human minds do not always work in such a rational, sequential and logical fashion. We do not always work out solutions in a one-to-seven step process. We may look at any of these steps and move through various stages at the same time when dealing with complex problems. However, this traditional problem solving approach is useful to see some of the elements involved and to have some remembered structure to work with. Indeed, this type of problem solving approach has been modified to a four-stage process and utilised as the Nursing or Health Visiting Process in addressing the needs and problems of our patients/clients. Midwifery does not have a named midwifery management process because most of their clients and patients are not generally seen as having problems, but are undergoing normal physiological changes during pregnancy and childbirth. There are also some three-stage models that offer the simplest way of approaching problem solving (Table 7.4).

Table 7.4 Simon (1977) vs VanGundy (1988)

Simon (1977)	VanGundy (1988)
• Intelligence	• Problem analysis and redefinition
• Design	• Idea generation
• Choice	• Idea evaluation and selection

Intelligence or Problem Analysis

As stated earlier, there are a variety of problems – from simple to more complex ones. There are lots of problems facing health care professionals on an hourly basis, which are dealt with quickly and intuitively because

the solutions are clear. Ackoff (1981) felt that there was a need to use many different approaches when dealing with messy problems.

From these rational frameworks, there is more emphasis on analysing the type of problem presented, rather than reaching a quick solution. It is also important to look at who should be involved with the problem analysis as there may be many stakeholders in the context of the problem and the impact of the solutions (Stott, 1992). Stakeholders may be those who have an interest in the problem and possible solutions due to two factors: relevance and expertise.

The problem/solutions may have relevant implications for stakeholders. Other stakeholders may have expertise in supporting the decision making, for instance, a team of health professionals are aware of an isolated group of new mothers and their babies in a rural area who have difficulty accessing the health centre/GP provision in the city. The team leader wants to explore the problem with relevant stakeholders such as GP, midwifery and health visiting team, social workers and the voluntary sector. It may not be possible to get all these people physically together but if they can set up a communication network they will be able to explore the issues and reach a range of choices for solution. The team leader may well engage with other stakeholders who can help because of their expertise, e.g., a financial expert, charity organiser or legal representative.

In some instances stakeholders may be very few. For example, there may be time to work through health care goals and therapies with just you and your patient/client. In other cases there may be the need to work through the problems with a variety of other professionals and the quality of the solutions may arise out of a period of reflection and collaboration with others. It is useful, therefore, to identify who might own or be affected by the problem, or even be affected by any solution proposed; these are the problem owners. Remember, then, that the *problem itself* needs to be analysed and separated from the *symptoms*.

A staged approach to problem solving may offer guidance for complex issues and help you to resist coming up with a *quick fix* solution that has no value in the long term. However, this notion of a staged progress to finding successful solutions is still not without difficulties – or debate – as the approach is still based on the notion of several assumptions, that:

- the problem solving process is a rational one
- there are no conflicting objectives within the process
- there is perfect knowledge which can be shared
- all possible solutions and consequences will be acknowledged.

Role of Creative/Intuitive Approach in Problem Solving

Against the backcloth of the debate concerning the scientific approach is the value put on the creative or intuitive approach. Benner and Tanner (1987) signalled that intuition relates to being able to understand phenomena without any rationale. *Answers.com* (2006) define intuition as 'The act or faculty of knowing or sensing without the use of rational processes; immediate cognition'.

Activity

Can you recall any decisions you made in the last month, where you were not aware of why you made the decision?

I remember recently dealing with a daughter whose father was terminally ill. When she asked whether it was advisable if she went home for a short rest, I made a decision to encourage her to stay a while longer. She was present when her father died about an hour and a half later and was pleased she had stayed with him. Intuition has been linked with personal experiences influenced by prior patterns of knowledge. Having experience in dealing with many people who have died in your care, there are physiological and psychological patterns of events that are not always easily internalised and can be communicated to others.

Activity

Another view on intuition is one of *heuristics*, or rules of thumb, whereby large amounts of stored knowledge are bypassed using procedural shortcuts.

It is often used to solve problems at a subconscious rather than a conscious level (Buckingham and Adams, 2000). More recently, the work of de Bono (1990) and others has allowed more creative problem solving approaches to become accepted and allows for fresh idea generation, lateral thinking and innovation, especially where the complexity of the problem may be over-whelming to the team. Creative approaches are often used in leadership courses for health care professionals, for example, Leading an Empowered Organisation (LEO) courses.

Idea Generation or Design

There are a huge number of management tools that can help in unpicking a complex problem in more detail. These tools can be shared among any of the problem stakeholders at any part of the process. VanGundy (1988) provides a wealth of ideas for problem solving techniques:

- **PEST/STEP:** (Political, Economic, Societal and Technological context) analysis of problem
- **Six honest serving men:** Kipling (1902) *The Elephant Child*

> I Keep six honest serving-men:
> (They taught me all I knew)
> Their names are **What** and **Where** and **When**
> And **How** and **Why** and **Who**.
> I send them over land and sea,
> I send them east and west;
> But after they have worked for me,
> I give them all a rest.

I let them rest from nine till five.
For I am busy then,
As well as breakfast, lunch, and tea,
For they are hungry men:
But different folk have different views:
I know a person small–
She keeps ten million serving-men,
Who get no rest at all!
She sends 'em abroad on her own affairs,
From the second she opens her eyes–
One million Hows, two million Wheres,
And seven million Whys!

- **Why** method
  - The problem statement is written down and team are asked to keep asking 'Why?' to the responses in order to get to the root of the problem.
- **Input and output** framework
  - The input and output factors are uncovered to review the contributing elements and results on a situation.
- **Cause and effect** or **Fishbone** (Ishikawa, 1985)
  - The cause and effect factors are uncovered to review a situation. An Ishikawa analysis can use brainstorming to identify possible causes or effects of an issue. The fishbone may involve looking at elements such as man, materials, 'mother nature', machines, measurements and methods related to a problem. (www.matrixprojects.ltd.uk/Pages/matrix_projects_Ishikawa_analysis.html)
- **Thought-showering** or **thought-writing,** which can use a verbal or written word method
- **Checklists**
- **Six Thinking Hats** (de Bono, 1990) Where six coloured hats (with specific characteristics) can be used for individuals in a group to allow them to abandon their own personalities
- **Six Action Shoes** (de Bono, 1990) This is a similar approach to the above, but allows people to have 2 personalities/roles
- **Metaphors** or **analogies** These can allow you to see the problem in another context, for instance such as a game, an animal, event or a journey
- **Visualisation** This may help in providing a reflective internal environment in thinking through a problem
- **Reversals** This is where problem statements are made and the wording is reversed. For example:
  - How to deal with relatives of patients parking, when there are limited spaces, can become how to provide relatives of patients available parking spaces. This could lead to more provision of park and ride facilities where there is ample parking provision.

- **Superheroes and heroines** This is where a hero or heroine is seen as the problem solver and you are asked to identify how they might see the situation.

Activity

Some of these ideas may be useful within your work teams and others may be useful in helping patients to work through their own problems.

Which of these do you think lends itself to patient support?

You may have thought of a superhero type person, the one you can always go to when you have a problem at work, the one who will offer suggestions while not making you feel small in asking for help. There may also be a person who looks on the good side all the time, looking for positives. I remember being on placement once with a Sister who was always on my back, to the extent that I used to look at the duty rota to see if I was on with her. If I was I would consider throwing a 'sicky'. I didn't and a colleague pointed out that although I had another six weeks on placement it could be broken down into 30 days and as I only worked with her once or twice every five days that was only another six to ten shifts I had to do with her. That made it all far more acceptable to me so I survived! Clearly reflection on the situation made sure that I would not inflict a similar experience on students when I became a Sister.

Groupthink

Caution must be taken when involving groups of people in identifying problems and solutions. Janis (1982) identified that when groups of people make decisions they are more likely to conform to the majority decision because they do not feel comfortable being an outsider; meaning less creative solutions may be offered up. It is the result of group pressure that prevents members' testing the reality and using individual judgment to decide whether something is good or not. The outward signs of groupthink present themselves in different ways; members of the group may be less likely to challenge the judgment of the majority as they don't want to be seen to be rocking the boat. Also, when suggestions within the group are asked for, there is a reluctance to voice their ideas. Janis further suggests that the following are key characteristics of groupthink:

- Illusion of invulnerability
- Belief in integrity of the group
- Negative views of competitors
- Sanctity of agreement
- Erecting a protective shield.

The consequences that flow from groupthink are synonymous with those of poor decision-making processes. As leaders need to bring out diversity of ideas to address problem solving they should perhaps work towards counterbalancing the possibility of groupthink within their team.

Choice and Decision Making

The skill of decision making, within the context of health care, alludes to the presence of natural cognitive and learnt abilities. We learn to make decisions in our early days, as a child, through identifying how to connect with the environment and learn to deal with more complex decisions as we develop through to adulthood and even into the role of the health care professional.

Activity

Have you ever had an experience where you felt something was wrong with a patient during your training but didn't actually know what decision to make about that feeling?

I well remember a time when I was a very junior nurse on my first surgical placement during my first week. I completed a task and noticed that the last patient in the ward didn't look very well. I didn't feel I had enough knowledge of what could be wrong to make a decision about his care. I was unsure what I should do but when the staff nurse told me to go to break a few minutes later I made the decision to mention my concerns to her. The decision-making process took place but I have little recollection of the for-mality of recognising the various stages in a conscious manner. The staff nurse responded by going to see him and when I returned from my break she told me that he had unfortunately passed away (this episode took place prior to the introduction of Cardio Pulmonary Resuscitation).

Definitions of Decision Making and Research

There are many definitions associated with decision making. Linstead et al. (2004: 489) note it could be regarded as a commitment to a course of action, rather than the action itself. An example of making a decision could be when a nurse decides to administer a specific dose of a drug from the range that has been prescribed, e.g., if one or two tablets are ordered then the nurse must decide how many to give. It is not necessarily their visible action that constitutes the first stage of the decision-making process but the cognitive activity prior to this. A google search (www.google.com) reflects these inconsistencies and uncovers the link with dealing with finite human and other resources, psychology, law and sporting events (see Table 7.5).

Table 7.5 Definitions of decision making

- The act of making your mind up about something. (wordreference.com/definition/decision)
- A decision is the commitment to irrevocably allocate valuable resources. A decision is a commitment to act. Action is therefore the irrevocable allocation of valuable resources. (en.wikipedia.org/wiki/Decision)
- A formal, written judgment or verdict. (www.nfa.futures.org/basicnet/glossary.aspx)
- One step in the long process of problem solving. (www2.uta.edu/ssw/trainasfa/glossary.htm)

Decision making may be seen as a mental systematic and sequential process of making choices from a number of alternatives and putting that choice into action (Lancaster, 1999). Malloch and Porter-O'Grady (2005: 145) identified that good decisions require insight, creativity and methodology where there is uncertainty and a number of alternative choices are available. Stott and Walker (1995) note that the idea of decision making is within the context of overcoming problems or barriers to achievement of goals.

The importance of decision making is thus critical to everyday health care work. It is about giving patients/clients the best care to meet their needs. Bucknall (2000) undertook an observational study of decision making of critical care nurses in Australia and found that they made, on average, patient care decisions every 30 seconds and the three main decision-making areas were:

- Intervening – to modify the patient situation
- Communicative – to give or receive information.
- Evaluative – to review patient data to evaluate their status.

This shows how critical decision making is within the sphere of everyday health care, and often relates to critical episodes and patient outcomes. Table 7.6 gives you a comparison of how some management theorists have classified problem and decision types.

Table 7.6 Problem/decision types

Drucker (1989)	Simon (1980)	Stott and Walker (1995)
• Simple or generic decisions – decisions are based on using principles • Unique or complex	• Programmed • Non-programmed (novel, unstructured, consequential)	• Standard • Crisis • Deep (involving generation of alternatives)

There are similarities between all these ideas but Stott and Walker's (1995) idea appears to offer a little more relevance in the real world of health care with the inclusion of crisis decisions. It was Stott (1992: 203) who highlighted that not all decisions are of equal importance and thus will involve greater or lesser time commitment, skills needed, who might be involved and what resources you may need.

- **Standard decisions** are those we make on an everyday basis and tend to be repetitive. Solutions are usually found by rules of thumb, procedures or policy, e.g., deciding to offer patients or relatives tea when you encounter them in stages of emotional upset.
- **Crisis decisions** arise from unexpected situations and need an immediate response with little or no time to negotiate and plan with others. A quick, precise response is required, e.g., in the case of severe haemorrhage or other life threatening situations.
- **Deep decisions** require more intense planning, reflection and consideration. They may concern forward planning as part of change management and often incur debate, disagreement and conflict. They require a substantial amount of time and networking with a range of people, e.g., you may encounter a patient with complex needs that requires a greater understanding of their lifestyle and attitudes to health. At other times a case conference will need to be called to make decisions with a number of health care professionals as well as the patient and carers.

Column 1: Develop a list of decision situations you have faced this last week and fit them into the three categories.	
Column 2: Write the name/names of people you believe should have been involved in the decision making.	
Column 1	**Column 2**
Standard	
Crisis	
Deep	

Activity

Jot down some thoughts related to decisions that go along with patient prescribing.

Medical and non-medical prescribers often have to think through the complexity of the patients' assessment and the match of the correct treatment to deal with a single patient need. Deep decision making is required for these examples.

Styles of Decision Making

There may be a need to use a variety of skills to solve problems from logical thinking, intuition or trial and error, depending on the type or the context of the specific problem. The kind of management skills and styles you have may affect the outcome of the solution and decisions made. Vroom and Yetton (1973) identified different styles of problem solvers depending on their position on a management style continuum. The style of problem solving will depend on who and how other people are involved in the problem-solving process (Table 7.7).

Table 7.7 Types of decision makers (Vroom and Yetton, 1973)

A1	Solve problems and make decisions using available information
A11	Get information from subordinates and solve problem themselves
C1	Share problem with individual subordinates, generate solutions, then make their own decisions
C11	Share problem with subordinate groups, generate suggestions then make their own decisions
G11	Share the problem with subordinate groups, generate ideas and come to a consensus on a solution.

The quality of decision making may depend upon a variety of factors. Vroom and Yetton (1973) noted the following

- Values and personal beliefs
- Life experience
- Individual preference
- Willingness to take risks
- 'Our' way of thinking
- Critical, collegial culture.

Buchanan and Badham (1999) concurred with these ideas but noted important principles for being considered a successful political decision maker. These were to be able to develop liaisons, appear conservative, clear the air, ally with power, use trade off's effectively, strike when the iron is hot, ape the chameleon, limit communication, involve research and know when to withdraw.

Activity

What do you make of these principles?
How could you apply them in your everyday work?

At first sight the principles appear to be interesting, but they may be part of a double edged sword. They imply networking is essential but there is a need to be careful and wary of the power within the environment and keep on the right side of it. Good decision making is therefore seen to be about awareness of the environment, learning from past experiences, wanting and forcing things to happen and looking for new ways to solve problems while possibly taking risks.

Application of Research

Doherty and Doherty (2005) looked at patients' preference for involvement in clinical decision making. Using an interpretative phenomenology/triangulated approach to look at patients' preference of allowing the health care professional full decision making rights, to the other end of the continuum scale of allowing the patient full control and decision making rights. The researchers conducted semi structured interviews of 20 patients in one British acute Trust; there were equal numbers of medical and post surgical patients. There were 9 men and 11 women. Seventeen of the group were above 60 and the youngest was 18. The researchers categorised the patients into active, collaborative and passive, based on their responses (Table 7.8).

These are interesting, patient focused results as most of our research has related to health care professionals dealing with their own problems and decisions. However, more research may be needed concerning patients' roles in this activity. From these results it is suggested that most of the research participants experienced a paternalistic health service and never thought to challenge it.

Table 7.8 Active vs collaborative vs passive role of the patient

Active role of patient	Collaborative role of patient	Passive role of patient
• *Active decision making role* 15%(3) medical and 5%(1) surgical with 10%(2) noted the importance of personal autonomy e.g., requesting GP to prescribe steroids. However, they did not know about their discharge plans. • *Patient knowledge* The surgical patient felt he disagreed with his surgeon's opinion that he needed more surgery but he consented based on the fact that he wasn't asked for his opinion. • *Communication issues* Concern noted regarding the need for better communication.	• *Share decision making* 40% (8) believed they could make their own opinion but still required the professional knowledge to help in decision making. • *Specific barriers*: 1 noted pain was a barrier to taking an active role 1 noted Doctor interpersonal skills 2 noted limited opportunity to being involved 1 noted there were 'too many on ward round.' 'Sometimes I find the doctors talk to the nurse and they don't consult you. You're the last one to know'	• *Passive role* 40% (8) - mainly because they felt 'Doctors had greater knowledge of illness' than they did. Some felt they were powerless

---

Activity

How will this research change your practice?

You may have considered becoming a better patient advocate. You need to think about the perceived powerlessness of your patients and how you help to avoid their passive role developing. This could be achieved by ensuring that the patient was fully cognisant of the facts about their treatment and any alternatives there might be in order that the patient has an involvement in the clinical decision making process. It is important that whatever your discipline your patients/clients are able to use informed consent for any treatment or intervention offered.

Summary of Key Points

This chapter has briefly looked at various aspects of problem solving and decision-making theory in order to meet the identified learning outcomes. These were to:

▸ **Discuss the concept of problem solving** Only a small number of the many theories have been explored, but it is noted that problem solving is a key leadership skill that involves cognitive processes.

▸ **Critically review the models of problem solving** Traditional and contemporary approaches to problem solving were addressed highlighting the notion that there is more than one way to solve problems.

▸ **Critically examine the theory and skills associated with decision making** Here we examined two models of problem solving, the traditional and the 'Six 'I's', together with comparing the three stage models offered by Simon (1977) and VanGundy (1988).

▸ **Critically explore the importance of clinical decision making within the context of problem solving for health care practice** Clinical decision-making was explored by the examination of research to support the need for patient involvement in the process.

Further Reading

Dowding D and Thompson C (2004) 'Using decision trees to aid decision-making in nursing', *Nursing Times* 100 (21): 36–39.

Dowding D and Thompson C (2002) 'Decision analysis'. In C Thompson and D Dowding (eds) *Clinical Decision-making and Judgment in Nursing*. Edinburgh: Churchill Livingstone.

8   Managing Conflict

Learning Outcomes

By the end of this chapter, you will have had the opportunity to:
▸ Discuss the concept of conflict
▸ Critically review a range of models associated with conflict management
▸ Critically explore the importance of conflict management within the context of problem solving
▸ Recognise the importance of cultural diversity on leadership during conflict.

Introduction

This chapter explores the notion of conflict management within the context of health care. Marquis and Huston (2006: 524) note that conflict involves discord brought about by differences in ideas, values or feelings between two or more people. However, internal conflict can also occur within the individual. It is perhaps expected that within the health industry, where there are huge numbers of people with different backgrounds and interacting with each other daily, that conflict is an everyday occurrence. With infinite demands being put on the health service, conflict can be seen as a result of competitiveness of different groups for scarce health resources. Results of conflict may be poor team behaviour, time wasting, poor productivity, absenteeism, stress and ill health. Leadership, therefore, has to be interested in managing conflict, leaders have to try to foresee as well as make sense of conflict situations, and plan solutions before patient care is compromised. McElhaney (1996, cited in Valentine, 2001) identified that probably about 20 per cent of managerial time is spent dealing with conflict. It is also seen as equal to, or even higher than, communication, motivation and decision making as a leadership skill.

The Concept of Conflict

In the twentieth century, conflict was considered in a negative light. In terms of organisational life it was even seen as a result of poor leadership and as being dys-functional to the objectives of an organisation. Everything was meant to run smoothly and harmoniously and so conflict was pushed underground or accepted passively. The *Collins Thesaurus* (1986) defines conflict in terms of clash, collision and contention. Huczynski and Buchanan (1991: 547) heralded the point that conflict was a state of mind perceived by the parties involved. Pondy (1967) noted, however, that conflict in organisations, more specifically, reflected a dynamic process. A variety of organisational behaviours, which was influenced by differing goals and relationships of individuals, could be seen as a result of conflict.

Activity

Think about a recent episode where you experienced a conflict situation. Write down ten words that come to mind when you think about this situation.

Look back on your ten words. Would you say they are negative or positive words? Conflict is now seen as neither bad nor good so you may have written both negative and the odd positive-sounding word. Good conflict management can bring about organisational growth whereas poor conflict management can bring about destruction. Handy (1985) notes the two disparate views regarding conflict. The negative unitary and traditional view of conflict is that it gives rise to deviant, dysfunctional behaviour resulting in emotional and physical stress where a win–lose situation occurs. The outcome is seen as the dominance of the one party over another.

Activity

Make a note of whether this was seen as a feature of what happened in your situation.

The other side of the argument is that 'well managed conflict' can be ener-gising and vitalise forces that produce constructive group life, which is more of a positive, pluralistic approach and can result in a win–win situation (Handy, 1985; Covey, 1990). Figure 8.1 reflects on how conflict can affect the performance of an organisation both positively and negatively.

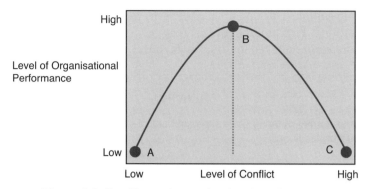

Figure 8.1 **Conflict and organisational performance**

A concept analysis using an evolutionary approach was undertaken by Almost (2006) concerning conflict in nursing environments. She found that conflict was a multidimensional notion with both detrimental and beneficial effects. The antecedents to the concept related to individual and organisational issues as well as interpersonal relationships.

Levels of Conflict

It is useful to understand the three levels of conflict when leading teams in health care. These levels are *intrapersonal*, *interpersonal* and *intergroup* conflict. A good leader should recognise these as different but also recognise how to attempt to manage conflict competently.

Intrapersonal conflict This takes place *within* an individual who has difficulty managing contradictory felt needs or wants. It may involve role conflict or confusion or it may be about balancing work and home life. Discord and unhappiness might occur before the situation is resolved. It is valuable to turn these internalised felt needs and wants into expressed needs. This can be achieved through self awareness, peer and leadership support.

Interpersonal conflict This takes place between two or more people with different values and beliefs. It is becoming a significant issue in health care where the conflict may bring about bullying and harassment, causing discontent, stress and grievance. Farrell (2001) identifies the phenomena of 'horizontal violence' in nursing where some nurses are left squashed and deflated by more powerful members of their own profession. This situation has been widely documented in other countries (Thomas, 2003; Marquis and Huston, 2006: 528).

Intergroup conflict This takes place between two or more groups, departments or organisations. This kind of conflict may be the result of jealousies of others getting more resources, recognition or favourable rewards.

Activity

Jot down examples of these three types of conflict you have experienced as a health care professional.

From a personal perspective, my own intrapersonal conflict example relates to the dislike of driving to work and back along the motorway with lots of road-works. I try and leave home very early or later in order to avoid the rush hours. Recent interpersonal conflict related to confronting staff workload in a team, when one member was not happy helping another member of the team, because they felt they had enough to do. Last week, I experienced intergroup conflict when the teachers on the post-registration programmes felt the teachers on the pre-registration programmes got the first choice of classrooms in the University building. It sounds as though I have had a very difficult time but really I see it as everyday working life, however, it can cause stress and disruption if not dealt with.

Stages of Group Life and Conflict

How conflict emerges is important, because if a leader can identify the early stages they can deal with them appropriately. Indeed, in terms of developing a team (Chapter 5), the principles of leadership are related to two main ideas:

1 Diagnosis of the group stage
2 Intervening in order to help 'move the group on'.

It is interesting to relate the stages of group development and where these fit with emerging conflict. Tuckman's (1965) notion of a natural sequence for small groups offers a simple way of identifying with group life.

Forming   This is where there is a period of uncertainty
Storming   This is where a period of conflict and hostility between members may arise.
Norming   This is a settling down period and the group starts to pull together
Performing This is where performance is at an optimum.

Tuckman, on reviewing this, added a fifth stage, **adjourning**, where the group breaks up as a natural activity. Hartley (1997) compared a number of other models about stages of group life which have been proposed through research over the years. Bennis and Shepherd's (1956) work suggested another conflict stage between Norming and Performing and Bales and Strodtbeck's (1951) three stage model of *orientation, evaluation* and *control* was closely linked to a problem-solving model. Hartley (1997), however, paid regard to the more recent research-based model of Wheelan (1994), characterised by fluctuating stages where some groups may get stuck at one stage, resulting in conflict and self destruction.

Dependency and Inclusion	Reliance on leader; polite, tentative communication; group members are anxious and shy away from tasks.
Counterdependency and Flight	Conflict may occur between leader and members or just between members; there may still be a shying away from tasks and individuals try to work out their roles.
Trust and Structure	Conflict resolution. Norms and roles are agreed; more open communication; members feel more secure.
Work	Group works effectively.
Termination	The group disbands having completed the task. (Adapted from Wheelan, 1994)

Activity

Can you see any problems with these models of group life?

One of the difficulties in working with staged models is that in reality it can be very difficult to identify the transition from one stage to another. Hartley (1997) hints that chaos and disharmony is more prevalent in reality than some of these models suggest. Do you agree? When conflict arises, it can also be seen in terms of another four-staged model (Pondy, 1967):

- Perceived conflict is where there is a feeling of unease
- Felt conflict is where the unease is internalised and agreed as a real conflict of interests
- Manifest conflict is where the conflict is externalised and expressed
- Conflict aftermath is where the outcome of the conflict episode effects the individual(s) and group(s) concerned.

While there are many different models it is important to remember that they are just a simple representation of a complex situation. You may find yourself preferring one model to another or use an eclectic approach to leadership during conflict.

Causes of Conflict

The causes of conflict may be associated, as briefly suggested above, to individual differences but may relate more specifically to differences in ideology and personal objectives. The causes of conflict may relate to the following:

- Differences in perception at various levels of the organisation
- Concealed objectives

- Limited resources
- Departmentalisation and specialisation
- Nature of work processes and design
- Role conflict
- Inequitable treatment.

Here are a few examples of conflicts in health care. Do these sound familiar?

Differences in perception at various levels of the organisation The senior manager believes staff should change their practice in Accident and Emergency to get work done quickly. In order to get patients transferred to home, the right department or to another provision within the government's required target time staff need to work in a more efficient manner. The A&E staff are trying to effectively care and treat patients within a given timeframe, recognising that there may be fluctuating patient numbers and varying dependency needs.

Another example may be that the staff on a medical ward perceive that 'management' are trying to reduce their budget and will not allow bank staff to be taken on when there is staff sickness. The directorate managers have had to put a freeze on bank staff and are also trying to change the sickness culture of the organisation, which has reached excessive high rates.

Concealed objectives The ward sister was told in July that her rehabilitation ward will close in October and the staff will be relocated to another ward area. She has been told that she must not discuss this with the staff as they will be duly informed at the beginning of September, when plans are in place. Staff become concerned that the ward sister is reluctant to discuss any staffing issues. Rumours from an unknown source start to emerge that the ward will be closed.

Limited resources A medical ward and a medical admissions unit (MAU) would like to send a number of staff on a clinical update. Due to the turnover of patients in the MAU, the staff numbers have been curtailed.

Departmentalisation and specialisation A renal ward is introducing a new outreach service into the community. Selected staff will be supporting patients and district nurses in keeping patients at home as much as possible. Some of the senior staff will continue with their in-patient work but those chosen will be given new titles of renal specialists.

Nature of work processes and design The general surgical theatre nursing staff have been divided into two teams and their theatre coverage has been allocated between the two theatres. One team, however, appears to complete their elective work by 4:30 while the other team are faced with elective work until 5:30.

Role conflict The District Nurse has been sent a referral from the hospital to visit a patient. When she gets to the patient's house, the rapid response team is there already and she is told that she will not be required. Here there is confusion about the complexity of community roles and an overlap of role expectations.

Inequitable treatment The night staff in a particular clinical area cannot get access to educational updates while on duty. They have to try and 'fit their professional development' sessions in and around their working hours, which often means they get to the sessions after only a couple of hours sleep or in the middle of their annual leave. The day staff can get to their updates for these sessions during their working time.

Activity

Can you identify similar examples from your own clinical experience?

Symptoms of Conflict or Collision

From the above examples it can be seen that conflict can be a result of the multiple competing demands we have in health care. Leadership is required to help deal with past, present and even anticipated conflict situations. There are underpinning symptoms of conflict; these can help us to identify situations before the conflict becomes too oppressive.

These symptoms can be seen as:

- Territorial issues
- Poor communication – laterally or vertically
- Intergroup jealousy
- Interpersonal friction (personalities)
- Escalation of arbitration
- Increasing rules, norms and myths
- Evidence of low morale

Make some notes of these symptoms related to the following:

- Your past work life experience
- Your current work life situation
- Possibly future work life issues.

You will probably recognise that these symptoms are constant in all work life experiences. An interesting issue can be considered when applying for a new position in health care. The need to question why the vacancy has occurred and why the position looks so glamorous should form part of your SWOT analysis. You must also understand how the organisational culture deals with symptoms of conflict when people are joining or leaving a workplace. You need to get a sense of the quality of leadership, past and present, together with histories of conflict so that you are fully aware of the environment you are applying to work in.

Consequences of Conflict

Almost (2006) noted that the consequences of conflict related to those highlighted in Figure 8.2.

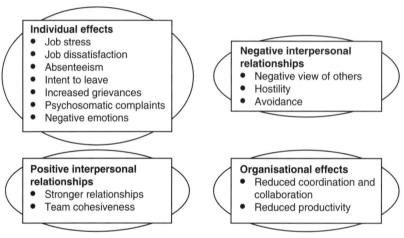

Figure 8.2 Consequences of conflict (Almost, 2006)

From these ideas you can identify both positive and negative outcomes but unless it is managed effectively, negativity can dominate the situation.

Management of Conflict

The Royal College of Nursing (RCN) (2005) highlighted that most people experience negative and positive colleague relationships. They note the importance of good working relationships and support within teams and have produced an excellent tool to explore relationships on an individual and team basis through observable behaviours. You might like to try this first exercise (Table 8.1), which is based on a self awareness exercise.

Table 8.1 Common positive behaviours

	Strongly disagree	Disagree	Neither agree/ disagree	Agree	Strongly agree
I try to say 'thank you' whenever a colleague is helpful					
I praise colleagues when I think they have done a good job					
I try to smile at colleagues when I pass them					
I try to make sure that no one is left out of informal discussions or social occasions					
I offer to make/ fetch coffee/ tea etc for other members of the work team when they are very busy					
I make a point of welcoming new members of the team, helping them to know systems and pro- cedures, and to get to know staff					
I regularly offer to help others when they are overworked or are having some difficulty					
I often ask for other people's views and try to show that I value those opinions					
I always look out for the safety of other colleagues					
I respect other colleagues' jobs and the tasks that they have to carry out and I always try to cooperate when those tasks affect me					
When problems occur, I always try to assume the best about all my colleagues, that is, I give them the benefit of the doubt					
I always try to respect the cultural differences and religious beliefs of my colleagues					
I always try to be helpful to more senior colleagues and carry out what they ask as well as I can					
I try to be considerate to more junior members of staff and respect their abilities and willingness to learn					
I try to help or make allowances for staff who have particular problems to overcome, such as physical limitation or a language problem					
I try to support colleagues whom I know are having personal difficulties					

Table 8.1 focuses on five aspects of leadership:

- Creating a friendly atmosphere (Qs 1 and 3)
- Helping everyone to feel part of the team (Qs 4 and 6)
- Looking after colleagues (Qs 5, 7 and 9)
- Showing appreciation of the work that people do (Qs 1, 2,10,13,14 and 15)
- Demonstrating respect and consideration (Qs 8,11,12,14,15 and 16).

Obviously, you have all scored well as we always have a better perception of ourselves than maybe others do! Now try to think about negative behaviours (Table 8.2) in the workplace and tick whether you have had any experience of these.

Go through these issues and make a decision as to whether you see these as bullying or harassment?

Bullying normally involves overt or covert behaviour to another individual who cannot defend themselves effectively and involves an imbalance of power. This power may involve status, information, knowledge, skill, access to resources and social position.

Table 8.2 Common negative behaviours

	Strongly disagree	Disagree	Neither agree/ disagree	Agree	Strongly agree
Blaming/criticising someone without having all the evidence, that is, assuming the worst					
Not acknowledging the good work that colleagues have done					
Belittling colleagues' work when talking to others					
Voicing doubt about the integrity of a colleague without very good reason					
Making sarcastic or insinuating remarks to or about colleagues					
Verbally threatening a colleague					
Deliberately damaging the property of another member of staff					
Deliberately withholding information from another member of staff who needs it					
Ignoring another member of staff or excluding them from the conversation					

Table 8.2 Common negative behaviours (continued)

	Strongly disagree	Disagree	Neither agree/ disagree	Agree	Strongly agree
Pressurising other members of staff to do a task or produce work despite knowing that they have too much else to do					
Setting very tight deadlines despite knowing they are almost impossible for staff to meet					
Refusing applications for leave, training or promotion without giving the member of staff a good or valid explanation					
Removing a responsibility from a member of staff without consulting with them first					
Using disciplinary or competence procedures as a threat to a member of staff					
Changing the requirements for staff performance ('shifting the goalposts') to keep staff on their toes					
Making rude comments or derogatory gestures to other members of staff					
Making jokes or negative comments about another member of staff's gender, sexuality, race, religion, age or disability					
Requiring a member of staff to act inappropriately to their personal, cultural or religious beliefs					
Showing favouritism to one member of staff or a small group at the expense of others					
Joining in or laughing if other colleagues are teasing or making negative comments about someone					
Shouting or criticising when under pressure					
Using swear words or expressions that others might consider blasphemous					
Making comments of a suggestive or sexual nature to other members of staff					
Using your charm or charisma to persuade someone to do something that should not be their first priority					

Three types of bullying behaviours are identified:

- Downward bullying (superior to subordinate)
- Horizontal bullying (between peers)
- Upward bullying (subordinate to superior).

Conflict Management Styles

There are thought to be a number of styles of conflict management which people use in organisations. Blake and Mouton's (1985) grid for differentiating conflict management styles along two axes stems from their 1960s model and relates to people's motivation in two dimensions:

- Concern for production
- Concern for people.

Thomas (1976) reshaped this model and focused on:

- Desire to satisfy one's own concern
- Desire to satisfy others' concern.

While Rahim (1983) relabelled the dimensions more simply:

- Concern for self
- Concern for others.

Five styles of conflict management have been identified that reflect a degree of how well conflict can be managed.

Avoidance Seen as a passive activity where there is a withdrawal from a difficult situation. Complaints are ignored and there is a closure put on open discussion. This reflects a lack of concern for a healthy team life.

Competing Seen where power is used to dominate the situation for self interest and ignores the needs of the team. This is generally a win–lose situation and the style reflects a high concern for self but low concern for others in the team.

Accommodating Seen as a style to minimise differences as an obliging act and there is surrender to the stronger party. This reflects a low concern for one's self but high concern for others in the team.

Compromising Seen where there is negotiation and an attempt to meet on middle ground so that all sides win. There reflects a moderate degree of concern for one's self and team life.

Collaborating Involves exploring and examining each of the differences in order to find a solution that is acceptable and of benefit to all involved. Openness and exchanges of information with good communication and problem solving are evident. This style reflects a high concern for one's self and those of the team.

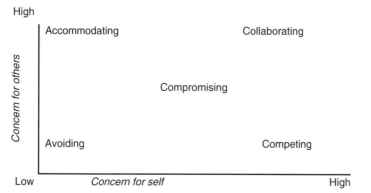

A two-dimensional model of conflict management styles (adapted from Thomas, 1976 and Rahim, 1983)

Figure 8.3 Conflict styles

The model which depicts these styles along the two axes is depicted in Figure 8.3.

It appears that the research points to both positive and negative conflict management styles. However, Thomas (1977) indicated that there were occasions when each conflict management styles were required.

Occasions when conflict management style is active

Avoiding
- Issue is trivial or more important issues have priority
- Perception that your concerns will not be valued
- When outcome of confrontation outweighs benefit of resolution
- To allow a 'cooling down' period to regain perspective
- When resolution is best effected by others
- Issues are seen as symptoms of bigger issues

Competing
- When quick decisions/actions are vital
- Important issues where unpopular actions need implementing
- On issues necessary to the organisation's welfare
- Against people who take advantage of non-competitive behaviour

Accommodating
- When you find you are wrong – to allow a better position to be heard, to learn and reflect reasonableness.
- When issues are more important to others than yourself – to satisfy others and maintain cooperation

- To build social credibility for later issues
- To minimise loss when defeat is evident
- When harmony and stability are paramount
- To allow subordinates to develop by learning from mistakes

Compromising
- When goals are important but not worth the effort or potential disruption of more assertive modes
- When opponents with equal power are committed to mutually exclusive goals
- To settle issues temporarily where there is complexity
- To reach expedient solutions under time pressure
- As a back-up when collaboration or competition is unsuccessful

Collaborating
- There is a need to get an integrative perspective
- When there is a need to learn from others
- To merge insights from people with different perspectives
- To gain commitment by incorporating concerns into consensus
- To work through feelings that have interfered with a relationship

(Adapted from Thomas, 1977)

Barzey (2005: 62) notes the importance of being aware of behaviour that causes problems and suggests that difficult people elicit negative behaviours to gain control over situations. She suggests there are the following difficult behaviour types:

- **Complainers**: they are quick to find problems but offer no solutions
- **Negatives**: refuse to involve themselves in change
- **Insecure**: they throw tantrums and are critical of others
- **Bull in a china shop**: they are always right and must win, stamping all over others
- **Know it alls**: they are usually valuable to the team but give off a superior attitude and override others
- **Timidly pleasant**: they are quiet, pleasant but are often unresponsive to requests for help
- **Passive aggressive**: they are indecisive in not wanting to disappoint others
- **Oblivious**: they have little regard for the way they come across

---

Activity

Do you think we categorise people into these typologies?
Are these behaviours difficult to cope with?

It is important that these behaviours are seen as real but care should be taken not to stereotype individuals. These behaviours happen because of circumstances and indeed may have developed to protect individuals from their external world because of past experience. It is very difficult to change these behaviours overnight. A philosophy for overcoming future conflict in a team may relate to the following points:

- Participative and supportive leadership for a trusting and respecting climate
- Clarifying higher order goals, objectives, roles and standards

- Know when to confront, how to diffuse aggression and reduce risk of aggression
- Careful attention to Human Resources policies and procedures
- Focus on problematical systems and processes (rather than individuals) i.e., communication, structural
- Attempt to use initiative/ innovation to overcome resource limitations and use of non-monetary rewards
- Attend to factors affecting group dynamics.

In terms of effective strategies to handle conflict, Barzey (2005) suggests that to prevent escalation of any conflict situation, the following actions may prove useful:

- Keep calm
- Remain positive
- Protect privacy
- Be direct and objective
- Address the problem not the person
- Maintain eye contact and be aware of body language
- Be aware of the tone of your voice
- Know when to involve a third party such as your line manager or Human Resources.

Cultural Influences

The method of conflict management by individual leaders may be influenced by their own cultural background. Hofsted (1980) used a cross cultural study to identify cultural similarities and differences between 116,000 employees in a large multinational company. He identified four cultural dimensions that could affect conflict management and mapped out 40 cultures into eight categories according to the following dimensions:

- Power distance (PD)
- Uncertainty avoidance (UA)
- Individualism–collectivism (IC)
- Masculinity–femininity (MF)

Power distance (PD) This related to the degree in which inequality of power was accepted by the culture. Argentina and Spain ranked as high power cultures where leaders were expected to use their full power over subordinates, resulting in low mutual trust and preference for leaders to be more directive in order to avoid disharmony. Australia and Canada ranked as low power cultures, where a more collegial relationship existed with mutual trust being demonstrated.

Uncertainty avoidance (UA) This dimension related to the extent to which each culture encouraged or discouraged risk taking. Japan, Iran and Turkey were high on uncertainty avoidance and disliked ambiguity and risk taking. Hong Kong and Taiwan were seen as low uncertainty avoidance cultures.

Individualism–collectivism(IC) Britain and the USA were seen as individualistic cultures as opposed to collectivist cultures such as Philippines and Singapore, which required loyalty to the family and wider social structures.

Masculinity–femininity (MF) Some cultures, such as Italy and South Africa, were considered masculine, with an emphasis on material possessions such as money, status and ambition. In contrast, in feminine countries such as Scandinavia and Holland, emphasis was placed on the environment, quality of life and caring with greater equality between the sexes. The eight cultures and their typologies were defined as outlined in Table 8.3.

Table 8.3 Cultural typologies

1 **More developed Latin** *e.g., Belgium, France, Argentina, Brazil, Spain*	↑ PD, UA and Individualism Medium masculinity
2 **Less developed Latin** *e.g., Columbia, Mexico, Chile, Yugoslavia, Portugal*	↑ PD and UA ↓ Individualism Mostly masculine
3 **More developed Asian** *Japan*	Medium PD and individualism ↑ UA High Masculinity
4 **Less developed Asian** *e.g., Pakistan, Taiwan, Thailand, Hong Kong, India, Philippines, Singapore*	↑ PD ↓ UA, individualism Medium masculinity
5 **Near Eastern** *e.g., Greece, Iran and Turkey*	↑ PD and UA ↓ Individualism Medium masculinity
6 **Germanic** *e.g., Austria, Israel, Germany, Switzerland, South Africa, Italy*	↓ PD ↑ UA Medium individualism High masculinity
7 **Anglo** *e.g., Australia, Canada, Britain, Ireland, New Zealand, USA*	↓ PD and low to medium UA High individualism High masculinity
8 **Nordic** *e.g., Denmark, Finland, Netherlands, Norway, Sweden,*	↓ PD and low to medium UA Medium individualism Low masculinity

From Hofsted G. (1980) *Culture's Consequences*. Beverley Hills, Sage Publications in Open University (1985) International Perspectives Unit 16, Block V Wider perspectives, *Managing in Organisations*. Milton Keynes: Open University Press

What are your thoughts on this research 20 years on? Do you think each culture based on a country can be simplistically broken down like this or do you think that gender, age, social class of individuals as well as the growth of multiculturalism negates these ideas when we think about dealing with conflict?

Despite the question, it appears that the way leaders manage conflict has probably been influenced by the nurtured culture in which they have been socialised and the work by Hofsted offers some explanation of the diversity in the way people manage and lead their teams.

Summary of Key Points

This chapter has examined various aspects of managing conflict in order to meet the identified learning outcomes. These were to:

- ▸ **Discuss the concept of conflict** Here we explored the negative and positive perceptions of conflict and its importance to organisational performance.
- ▸ **Critically review a range of models associated with conflict management** Models that underpin conflict levels, conflict causes and conflict management were offered in the context of the leadership role in developing positive collegial relationships and recognising negative behaviours in the team.
- ▸ **Critically explore importance of conflict management within the context of problem solving** Conflict management styles were positioned against concern for self and others in dealing with problems faced by leaders in health care.
- ▸ **Recognise the importance of cultural diversity on leadership during conflict.**

Further Reading

Barton A (1991) 'Conflict resolution by nurse managers', *Nursing Management* 22 (5): 83–86.

Cavanagh S (1991) 'Conflict management style of staff nurses and nurse managers', *Journal of Advanced Nursing* 16: 1254–1260.

Cox K B (2001) 'The effects of unit morale and interpersonal relations on conflict in the nursing unit', *Journal of Advanced Nursing* 35 (1): 17–25.

O' Grady T P (2003) 'Conflict management special, part 2', *Nursing Management* 34 (10): 34–40.

Part 3

The Organisation

9 Theory of Organisational Life

Learning Outcomes

By the end of this chapter you will have had the opportunity to:
▶ Understand the importance of the overall organisation
▶ Discuss the importance of strategy, structures and systems within the organisation
▶ Critically explore the notion of organisational culture
▶ Reflect on the nature of organisational roles

> ▶ Critically examine professional responsibility and accountability as well as the notions of authority and delegation
> ▶ Develop an overview of Human Resource processes in organisations.

Introduction

Over the last eight chapters, you have been encouraged to examine the individual as a leader and within the dynamics of the team. It is now useful to scrutinise the management of an organisation and its top leadership. The Health Industry has many different types of organisations, some lie within the 'not for profit' public sector, some organisations are run 'for profit' and some organisations are a combination of both of these models, such as in General Practice. Other organisations are run through charity finance and the public purse, such as hospices or establishments for serious long-term conditions. This chapter will unravel the theoretical aspects of organisational life in order for you to learn more about the context in which health care delivery operates.

What is the Purpose of an Organisation?

Organisations can be a simple, collective group of people such as in a small General Practice or can be more complex, reflected as enterprising entities like the National Health Service. Organisations are integral to our social, cultural, political, economical, technological and physical environment. Smith (1995: 11) defines an organisation as a 'group of people who invest something … in the expectation of getting something out'. An organisation can more precisely be defined as:

> A social arrangement for the controlled performance of collective goals with a boundary controlling the relationships, the organisation has with its environment.

Organisations exist for the following reasons:

- Groups overcome the limitations of time, the environment and human biology which would overwhelm an individual acting alone
- They offer companionship
- They increase productivity because people can specialise in what they do best and combine their efforts synergistically (i.e., the whole is greater than the sum of all the parts)
- They can produce economies of scale.

(Huczynski and Buchanan, 1991: 7; CIMA, 1998)

Activity

Do you feel these ideas reflect the policies of the health organisation in which you work?

The NHS is a statutory organisation that is governed by the statutes in the UK and the direction of the government party that is in power. Over the last 20 years, the NHS has been driven by the following policy issues:

- The introduction of market-based mechanisms to allocate and distribute its finite resources to meet ever-growing health needs and demands
- 'Contracting out' of some of the peripheral services to the private sector
- Notions of private initiatives to support the fixed budget of the NHS

This is, however, not so very different for any other international health care organisation across the developed market economy; therefore it has been seen as a way of dealing with the complexity and increased demands placed on health care provision today. The study of organisational life is a specific discipline that is pertinent for leadership and requires knowledge from the social sciences, psychology, economics and possibly political science. Leaders need to have an awareness of how their own organisation works and the extent of its effectiveness and success. Leaders also need to be able to work towards moving the organisation towards this, on a continuous basis, whether that organisation is a small team, a clinical ward, a directorate, a hospital or Primary Care Trust or even the whole NHS.

Strategy, Structure and Systems

For an organisation to be regarded as effective and efficient, many elements have to be coordinated and managed, which means that leadership is vital. The McKinsey 7's model suggests the elements required are

- Strategy
- Structure
- Systems
- Skills
- Shared Values
- Style
- Staff.

Leavitt's (1965, 1978) simple model (Figure 9.1) helps leaders to reflect upon the interdependency of organisational elements. These interdependent elements are crucial and a good leader should be able to recognise the importance of all these elements, especially when it is thought that the organisation is becoming less effective and efficient.

The Weisbord (1976) Six Organisational Model (Figure 9.2) offers another perspective but highlights the central importance of leadership.

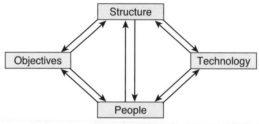

Figure 9.1 Leavitt's (1965, 1978) simple model of interdependency of organisational elements

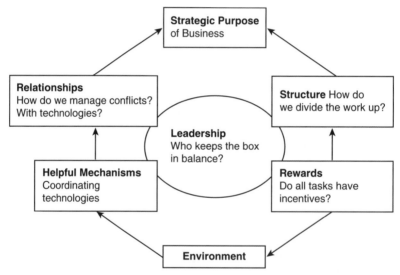

Figure 9.2 Weisbord's (1976) Six Organisational Model

Activity

Write down what you think about the strengths of these three models.

It is useful here to note the importance of strategy, structures and systems in all three models. Although other elements are relevant they have been covered elsewhere in the book.

Strategy

The concept of strategy is complex because it has various meanings. It could be seen as 'a course of action to achieve specific objectives' (CIMA, 1998). Mintzberg et al. (1998) noted it could also be used to mean

- A plan
- A position
- A pattern of behaviour
- A perspective.

These ideas illustrate that a strategy is not always considered as rationally and proactively planned. Leadership requires strategic thinking; what does this mean for clinical leadership? Strategic decisions are seen to be based on the values, beliefs and expectations of those in power in an organisation. Clinical leaders need to be aware of their own power base but also that there is no *one* way of strategically thinking.

Rational Strategy

If strategy has a rational basis, the strategic decisions should relate to:

- The scope of the organisation's activity
- The long term direction of the organisation
- The organisation's environment
- The available resources and resource allocation
- Present climate of change.

The rational approach involves strategic analysis, strategic choice and implementation. The basis of strategic analysis should come from a review of the organisational mission and goals followed by *internal* and *external analysis*. There is a wide range of analytical tools available for this activity. Iles and Sutherland (2001) point to a number of internal and external analysis tools that can be used in health care:

- SWOT (Chapter 11)
- Process Modelling, for example a 'patient journey'
- PEST (Political, Environmental, Sociological, Technological factors) (Chapter 11)
- PESTELI (Including features above but also Ecological, Legislative and Industry factors).

Iles and Sutherland not only looked at rational strategic tools but also highlighted a number of creative analysis tools (Chapter 7). The rational approach to strategy formation has been criticised because of the need for futuristic fore-casting, planning being separated from the operational side of the organisation and the formalisation of the activity. Health policy could be seen as a rational form of strategy. Simon (1960b) felt that the best strategic decisions were not always made (optimisation). Strategic decisions were more likely to be based on least effort (satisficing). This was seen as 'muddling through'. In terms of change, small-scale adjustments are the usual strategic focus in order to avoid major errors (Lindbolm, 1959).

Emergent Strategies

Emergent strategies arise from patterns of behaviour, which are exhibited, and strategically significant operational episodes. For instance, there may have been no conscious overall plan to utilise European hospitals for surgical care but, through marketing of their services, it was felt by some British health care managers that this may have been a useful solution to reducing waiting lists. The 'logical incrementalism' strategy is seen as a compromise between the rational approach, 'muddling through' and emergent strategy. Strategy is seen as a process of learning within an overall organisational direction and small-scale ideas are seen as experiments or projects within a learning culture (CIMA, 1998).

Vision, Mission and Goals

Organisations need to identify what is their future vision, what is their mission statement and what are the goals and objectives in order to drive their people through to the same outcome to meet demand. Health care organisations now need to set annual goals and objectives that can be regularly measured or evaluated. In the past it was usual to set five-to-ten year aims and goals in the NHS but it appears that today, the political and external pressure for change is too dynamic; the difficulty of communicating and driving through annual organisational goals for change is one for debate. In terms of the variety of goals there are probably four basic models (see Table 9.1):

Table 9.1 Four models of organisational effectiveness (CIMA, 1998)

	Human Relations Model	Open Systems Model
Flexible Structure	Goals: People orientated skills of people	Goals: Growth Focus Good environment relationship
	Internal Process Model	**Rational Goal Model**
Stable Structure	Goals: Stability, efficient communication Change avoidance	Goals: Productivity Efficiency

Source: Chartered Institute of Management Accountants (CIMA), 1998 Reproduced with permission

According to Mintzberg et al. (1998) there are seven types of forces that drive the vision, mission, goals and objectives of an organisation:

- Direction
- Efficiency
- Proficiency
- Competition
- Concentration
- Learning
- Cooperation.

Mission statements are formal statements that communicate the vision of the organisation. They are usually brief and cover the following areas:

- The purpose of the organisation
- The strategic intent
- Policies and standards
- Organisational values.

Activity

Has your Health Trust communicated their mission to you? Try to find out where this is and check whether you feel this represents what is happening in your health industry. What about your own clinical area – do you have an identified mission statement? Does it need revising? Do your team members know about it?

Leadership and Health Policy

Health policy can be seen as a rational strategic plan to distribute scarce resources. There are two main economic issues concerning the health service industry in all countries:

- Rising expectations and demands for health care – infinite demand
- Finite resources to deal with these needs, demands and wants.

Health policy reflects how political leaders shape the distribution of these finite health funds and resources to deal with the presenting infinite health service demands. Policy also denotes the strength of belongingness within a society to achieve solutions and a commitment to trying new ways of coping with the underlying issues.

Palfrey (2000) suggests health policy is therefore about:

- A desire to improve people's quality of life
- An attempt to improve a nation
- A perceived need to reduce costs/save money
- perceived need to stabilise expenditure but improve the standard of services
- A practical concern to retain power/authority.

However, not all world governments have the same commitment to health care as each other. The amount of money put into a system varies widely across the world. However, it is not an indication that a higher percentage of funding to a health system equates to healthier populations. New health policy focuses on changing and challenging the status quo. These can relate to the following:

- Changes to the perception of health needs
- Changes to health care structures and systems
- Changes to health care processes
- Changes to roles and responsibilities
- Changes to power bases.

It is important to understand the shifting powerbase and the effect this will have on leadership strategies. The power base of community and primary care was again flagged up as an important purchasing and designing role to address local health needs. Within this health policy, focus lay on the modernisation agenda and a drive to change radically the NHS. Leadership was seen as key to this.

Recently the Health Professions Council stated that 'holders of public office should promote and support ... principles by leadership and example'. This Council states:

> We are a regulator and our job is to protect the health and wellbeing of people who use the services of the health professionals registered with us. At the moment, we register members of 13 professions. We only register people who meet our standards for their professional skills, behaviour and health. (www.hpc-uk.org, accessed on 21. 08. 07)

Similarly, *Making a Difference* (DoH, 1999a) explained the government's strategic intentions for nursing, midwifery and health visiting and its commitment to strengthen and maximise the professions' contribution. In essence it talked about eight areas that required attention. They were to:

- Recruit more nurses
- Strengthen education and training
- Develop a modern career framework;
- Improve working lives
- Enhance quality care
- Strengthen leadership

- Modernise professional self-regulation
- Work in new ways.

The document clearly set out the need for leaders with personal motivation, self-awareness and social skills in order to move the NHS in general, forward. While the document focuses on nursing, midwifery and health visiting it is fair to say that similar essentials would be seen as relevant to other health care professions. However, when financial issues are raising their head in all health care organisations, maybe altruistic sentiments may not always be the first priority.

There is still a case for strong and effective leadership in order to maintain set health care standards. Recently, the National Leadership Network (NLN) was formed (to replace the NHS Modernisation Board) as a body of representatives from 150 areas across the NHS. This body includes members from local government and social care, the independent sector, other government departments, academic organisations, charitable and voluntary organisations representing patients, users and carers, and organisations representing staff and the professions who are now able to meet together and play an active part in shaping the direction of health and social policy and ensure reforms deliver lasting improvements for the NHS (Hewitt, 2005). From meeting with these people, Hewitt hoped that any future changes will come from the bottom up and not be imposed from the top down. This means that the aspirations and expectations of the public about their health service should be a starting point for the next stage of reforms, and that it is leaders from the 150 areas who will influence the way forward.

Government Strategy

The overall strategic plan of New Labour for the NHS emerged from the NHS Plan (DoH, 2000a) and improving the quality of the health service was high on this agenda and the white paper, *A First Class Service* (DoH, 1998), was also launched that informed the parliamentary statutes culminating in The NHS Act (2001).

Activity

Before reading on, jot down the strategic points suggested by *The NHS Plan* (DoH, 2000a) and *A First Class Service* (DoH, 1998).

Table 9.2 Features of *NHS Plan* (DoH, 2000a) and Quality Agenda

The NHS Plan conveyed the following messages in 2000 for the new, modern, dependable NHS

- Commitment to the 10 Core Principles of the NHS
- Commitment to modernisation
- Funding options
- System changes
- Staff changes
- Patient changes
- Address 'waiting' for care
- Address inequality: national inequalities targets; improving health
- Clinical priorities and targets for cancer, heart disease and mental health
- Care issues in old age
- Develop patient power
- 7000 extra hospital beds and intermediate care
- 3000 GP premises modernised
- 250 new scanners
- Clean wards, modern matrons, better hospital food
- Modern IT systems in hospitals and GP surgeries
- Investment in staff

A First Class Service (DoH, 1998) contained the following features that were to address the expectations for a new health service

- Focus upon quality guaranteeing excellence
- Enhance fundamental aspects of care
- Clinical practice benchmarking
- The implementation of clinical governance realised
- User involvement strategies informing service delivery

It also suggested the importance of the following new structures

- National Institute for Clinical Excellence (NICE)
- National Service Framework for Quality (NSFs)
- Primary Care Groups
- Clinical Governance in Trusts and primary care
- Commission for Health Improvement (CHI)
- Health Action Zones

To some extent, these issues are still at the forefront of our health service today. Primary Care Groups have been replaced by Primary Care Trusts (PCTs) and Health Action Zones no longer feature as a separate entity outside mainstream health and social care services. However, as usual there are still the difficult tensions between increasing the services provided to patients, getting more throughputs in hospital care, keeping infection low and keeping within a budget – as well as the introduction of new technology. Wanless (2002, 2004) highlighted the role of technology in the NHS. He noted that the following needed to be considered:

- The initial replacement cost, with running costs, of technology such as scanners, over time
- The pace of technology in the UK (in comparison to other countries)

- That new technology may tend to result in an increase in activity and widening population access
- The importance of the role of NICE to review the impact of technology on patient outcomes
- The possibility of seeing some key diseases (such as cancer) being managed as chronic diseases
- Use of genetics and stem cell technology.

The development of an assessment process for health service evaluation of technologies is an important feature of the effectiveness and efficiency of NHS treatments and it is recommended that you access the web site to see the work of this agency (www.hta.ac.uk).

Public Health, Health Promotion and Policy

Public health as an aspect of overall health policy is an important feature of the health service in Britain in recent years. This is deemed as the 'new' public health as opposed to traditional public health which was more focused on eradicating infectious diseases and social welfare. The World Health Organisation set out the 1977 'Health for All' strategy and went on to draw up the Ottawa Charter in 1986, which has set the scene for the new public health ideology.

Recent UK public health policy in the shape of *Our Health, Our Care, Our Say* (DoH, 2006a) identified the importance of people getting access to good health care, particularly those who are considered as socially marginalised, i.e., those in prison, poverty, disabled or housebound. This policy reflected the importance of patient power and participative and inclusive health care as well as the need to address the inequalities of health as illustrated in the Acheson Report (1998). However, it is important to note that new public health policy is not just about health services but housing, education and employment and there is a plethora of policy emerging to attempt to address inequalities. Whether these are recognised as 'joined up', health policies have long been debated.

It appears that as one health strategy is brought into focus, there is a tendency for others policies to be marginalised. For instance, a focus on people who are more likely to get heart disease or cancer may take precedence over those who have learning disabilities or those susceptible to childhood accidents. It is debated whether health policy is seen as a planned strategic activity or whether it is as a result of lobbying from various sections in society, where whichever lobby 'shouts' the loudest gets most attention. The products of raised consciousness and community action are often seen as the essential building blocks to force the legislators and regulators to act.

Activity

- What would you consider as the most important elements of healthy public policy?
- Suggest ways your own team could influence public health policy.

The team might want to get together with others to campaign for a smoke free staff room. Protests at a Birmingham supermarket, by parents and health professionals, led to a change of policy of having sweets and crisps stacked at exits.

It has been suggested that health care professionals are generally good at health education with patients but rarely are able to make their voice heard in policy making related to health promotion (Whitehead, 2006). As a leader, it is important to try to help your team understand that other groups (e.g., the homeless, the unemployed, those in prison, people with mental health problems) in society currently find it difficult to influence policy making themselves. Getting them to be aware of the valuable ways in which they could influence health and health services on a broader basis can be very powerful in bringing a team together, whatever clinical area they work in.

Policies are formulated at various levels and it should not be assumed that influencing overall health policy at government level is what is always expected. Policy at ward, clinical or Trust level is also important for leaders to support and encourage staff to get involved with their own local policy making clinical groups.

Involvement in the Policy-Making Process

There are four main stages that staff teams can get involved in. Leaders could make their teams aware of these areas and the need for utilising evidence or research-based information.

- Agenda setting: problem identification and issues recognition for policy.
- Communicating the development of health care options by appraisal: setting of alternatives, forecasting, cost-benefit analysis.
- Helping in choosing policy and implementation of this.
- Evaluation and review of policy.

Policy is often concerned with getting the right messages over and setting up the right structures for implementing the policy. It is now useful to look at the issue of structures within an organisation.

Structure

The way an organisation structures its people or functions is important in order to understand the communication flows through from one organisational area to another. Another perspective concerning structures may be that the way an organisation plans its structure relates to the way it plans to *constrain* and *control* its people. Generally, a hierarchical organisational structure is seen within the health service. Task allocation, supervision and coordination generally are undertaken through the organisational structure.

Activity

Can you briefly draw your own immediate structure within your organisation?

Drucker (1989) suggests that organisational structure should satisfy the following tests

- The structure should be geared for *future performance* not on a historical basis
- The structure should have the *minimum number of management levels*
- The structure should reflect *upward training and development* towards the top of the organisation.

Types of Structures

The most usual structure that is represented is the hierarchical vertical structure (Figure 9.3).

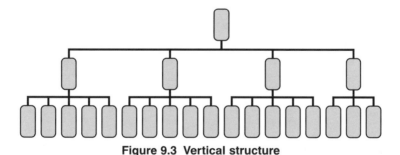

Figure 9.3 Vertical structure

This hierarchy can be quite 'flat' but it can also contain many more levels – a 'tall' hierarchy. This is true within the NHS. Another structural form may be seen as a cross functional team under several project managers (Figure 9.4).

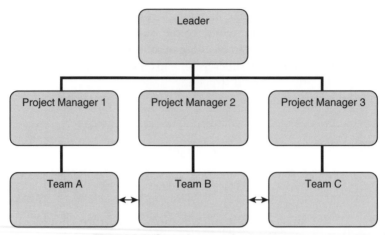

Figure 9.4 Complex matrix structure

This is usually seen as a complex matrix form of structure. Smaller matrix forms of project teams may be less hierarchical, such as those community teams who work together depending on the needs of specific patient groups. Generally, however, within the health service most professionals have a hierarchical structure of accountability as well.

There are many other shapes and forms of structures influenced by international and historical factors. The European Community as an organisation is a highly complex structural entity that bears no resemblance to a hierarchy. However, Leavitt (2005: 2) argues that hierarchies pervade all life, 'in democracies, theocracies, oligarchies, monarchies and autocracies'. He even went on to note that there were even heavenly hierarchies. In rank order these are:

1 Seraphim
2 Cherubim
3 Dominations
4 Thrones
5 Principalities
6 Potentates
7 Virtues
8 Archangels
9 Just plain Angels.

Leavitt (2005) suggested that human hierarchies were far from being angelic and we do not always like what they do to people and productivity. He went on to argue that hierarchies are, however, inevitable. Within each level of the hierarchy, job and role descriptions and span of control are important elements of the organisational structure. Leaders need to recognise the boundaries of job descriptions and the ability of some people to expand these. For others there may be difficulty in fulfilling all the elements of their job description. The span of control reflects the number of subordinates who report to a single supervisor. The 'flat' hierarchy may mean that a supervisor may have a broad span of control whereas a 'tall' hierarchy may reflect a very narrow span of control.

Organisational Roles

In order that an organisation may meet its goals, the work of individual people must be achieved by the variety of roles. A 'role' is regarded as 'expected pattern of behaviour associated with members occupying a particular position within the structure of an organisation' (Mullins, 2005: 538). Role expectations change and develop from the time someone takes on a new role until they leave that role. Most *health care students* are allocated to clinical placements in order to learn their professional role during their training and it is here that they become socialised to their own sphere of work. Learning outcomes, aims and objectives, as laid down by the professional benchmarks, will drive this learning. The management of learning for their professional role is dependent on the learning environments, the place where learners interact with clients, patients and practitioners. Students will then qualify and take their turn in teaching, mentoring and assessing students.

Buckenham (1988) found that the perceptions of students changed during training, in that first year students thought more about the actual delivery of health care whereas third year students thought that the clinical aspects of the job were less important than the effective management aspects. Whatever course you undertake, it appears that many qualified practitioners still felt unprepared for the management aspect of the role. Back in 1974 Kramer called this feeling the 'reality shock', the feeling of dread, terror and fear abound. Schmalenburg and Kramer (1979) further identified four phases of role transition from student to practitioner:

- Honeymoon
- Shock
- Recovery
- Resolution.

Duchscher (2001) used qualitative research to show the frustrations of newly qualified graduates in America when coming to terms with their new professional roles. It is important that leaders and experienced staff recognise the difficulties that face novice practitioners and help to set up formal and informal support mechanisms. It is through exposure to management

knowledge and supervised exposure to practice that new health care professionals are assisted in coming to terms with being able to lead out in the clinical area.

Whenever you take up a post as a new staff member, the expectation from your employer will relate to your ability to engage in and maintain high standards of health care. There will be an expectation to develop excellent communication skills, both verbal and written. In addition, you are expected to keep yourself up to date with your evidence base elements of care delivery. Feedback on your professional, managerial, educational and administrative skills will help to develop you through an appraisal system. These are often carried out yearly and a Personal Development Plan (PDP) is agreed between yourself and your supervisor.

The care delivery expectations of your role will be dependent on the philosophy and culture of the organisation and the particular type of health care activities that your course has prepared you for within that context. You will be expected to assess, plan, implement and evaluate care within the standards and philosophy of the organisation. Therefore, it will be important for you to be familiar with those issues, policies, procedures and systems that are operationalised in the workplace. There is an expectation that you will contribute to a high standard of care and develop effective relationships at all levels including those with clients/patients and relatives.

In another part of your role you will be responsible for the care management of a group of patients or clients. However, there should be support from senior colleagues. In your role, your decision making and problem solving skills will be applied and tested. You will have to decide on priorities of care and on the use of resources within your control and disposal. The organisation and management of the care of a group of clients/patients is going to be your direct responsibility. In that pursuit you will be expected to cope with some aspects of change as well as being able to delegate, monitor and supervise junior staff who are working in your team. You may also be invited to participate in clinical audit and other activities, which involve collecting information and reviewing care.

There are some expectations which all employers expect from their new recruits. Therefore, they have been categorised as general. These include the following behaviours: punctuality, reliability, responsibility, accountability and showing enthusiasm for the post. The importance of authority, accountability, responsibility and delegation is seen within the formal job or role description. This formal contract reflects the ability of the organisation to achieve its mission.

Accountability, Responsibility, Authority and Delegation

It is useful at this point to distinguish between the terms 'accountability,' 'responsibility', 'authority' and 'delegation' and what this means to you and your team.

Activity

See if you can define the following:
Accountability
Responsibility
Authority
Delegation

It is important to recognise the various definitions of these concepts, which often get confused. Here are some suggestions of meanings.

- **Accountability** means being able to explain and justify actions or non-actions for a responsibility given to you. This is seen as an important part of a quality system.
- **Responsibility** involves an obligation to perform certain duties or make certain decisions and having to accept any reprimand from the manager for unsatisfactory performance.
- **Authority** is the right to take action or make decisions that legitimises the exercise of power within an organisation.
- **Delegation** means the conferring of a special authority from a higher authority. It involves a two-part responsibility. The one to whom authority is delegated becomes responsible to the superior for doing the job, but the superior remains responsible for getting the job done.

Marquis and Huston (2006: 689) give a broad moralistic view of the term when they define accountability as: 'Internalised responsibility whereby an individual agrees to be morally responsible for the consequences of his actions'. This definition implies a personal thought process, which is more than just an expectation of a job or a position. Martin (2001b) confirms that accountability and responsibility go together. In leading or managing team activities, you may be asked to account for the areas of work for which you are responsible. Accountability is thus more than responsibility. In being accountable, it is now assumed that evidence can be provided for the way the responsibility has been carried out. Manthey and Millar (1994) highlight the relationship between responsibility, authority and accountability as:

Responsibility + Authority + Accountability leads to a decentralised organisation

where the latter is valued as an effective, efficient, proactive and developing organisation. Accountability within the health service is influenced by professional regulation and civil, employment and criminal law (Table 9.3).

Table 9.3 Features of responsibility, authority and accountability terms

Responsibility	Authority	Accountability
• Allocated and accepted	• Right to act in areas of given and accepted responsibility	• Ability to reflect and evaluate actions/ non-actions/decisions
• Implies ownership	• Levels of authority:	
	1 Gathers data / information	• Aids learning for future events
• Implies outcomes	2 Gathers data/ information and makes recommendations	
• At least a 2-way process	3 Gathers data/ information, makes recommendations and initiates action	
	4 Informs others how to act/delegates	

Accountability to the Public

We have seen that, over the years, the public's expectations of their health service have been raised. Improved health technology, media coverage and the available use of the Internet has meant that the public has had more information on medical and therapeutic advances. Accountability in a civil sense must be seen within this context.

Martin (2001b) identifies that public health and social care services must be held accountable to the public as they carry important responsibilities in relation to the mental and physical health and the protection of individuals and communities. Health authorities, NHS and primary care trusts, general practices, independent sector management committees/trustees and local authorities all have specific responsibilities for which they are accountable. In small health organisations like a single-handed General Practice, it may only be the doctor who is totally accountable for the service he/she provides. However, the health service is made up of many larger organisations where there are numerous people who manage others. The chief executive of a large health Trust is seen to be *accountable* for the total performance of his/her organisation. Clinical Governance forms part of this accountability framework and will be discussed in Chapter 10.

Activity

Why do you think it is important to have a stringent level of accountability in health care?

Patients may not actually know whether they are receiving good or poor care, particularly when they are very ill or disabled. The public have now become very aware that they have particular rights and expectations from their health service. They are now demanding more accountability for public health services. Health care professionals, in particular, work in a very privileged position of trust and need to respect confidences and privacy and use their integrity when managing the care of individuals. The public put a great deal of trust and value in health care personnel when they encounter them in the health service and are often vulnerable when they are in a highly dependent state.

Duty of Care

The concept of 'duty of care' is also important. Young (1995: 13) defines this term in the following way:

> [A] person must take reasonable care to avoid acts or omissions that he can reasonably foresee would be likely to injure a person, directly affected by those acts.

Professional accountability on an individual level is laid down within the requirements of each health professional's regulating and registering body, such as the General Medical Council, Nursing and Midwifery Council or the Health Profession's Council. The term 'professional' is used in this context to convey the notion that health care workers who have a specific qualification that includes registration with a statutory body, are expected to display behaviours that are consistent with their specific code of conduct. In this sense professional behaviour, which would be expected of you, will include being courteous, non-judgmental, respectful and objective with patients and relatives all the time. In addition to your behaviour, there is also an expectation that your knowledge base and practice will be supported by evidence derived from research and good practice.

Activity

Look at the following dilemma where professional accountability and responsibility feature.

Mr P, a patient in a ward is very anxious the evening before his operation. The doctor has prescribed Mr P's usual night sedation but unfortunately, there is no stock of this drug in the drug trolley for the 10 PM drug round.

- What could be done?
- What action should the nurse on duty take, remembering she is accountable for acts of commission and omission?

The nurse would take a reasonable period to try to locate the drug from another ward. If she has no staff to send to look for the drug, she could ask the nurse manager. If the drug was considered 'non-urgent' she may have to make a decision whether the drug could be safely omitted and ordered the next morning and whether it was important to contact the House Officer. Can you think of some 'non-urgent' drugs? Some bowel preparations such as Lactulose may be considered to be non-urgent. However, as night sedation is important, the nurse should telephone the doctor if the drug cannot be found in the hospital. The doctor may wish to prescribe something else to ease the patient's anxiety.

Employment Accountability

Employment accountability is set out under a contract of employment, so all employees will be held accountable to their employing organisation. This is true even for the top person in an organisation, like the Chief Executive. However, in order to be held accountable for managing large organisations it is necessary that the top people are effective, so effective delegation is necessary, right down the hierarchical line. Registered practitioners are accountable to their line manager for their own actions and the actions of their subordinates in getting the 'job done to the expected standard'. Their subordinates, such as physician's assistant or health care assistants are responsible for doing the job required of them while on duty and will be contractually accountable to the registered practitioner. Students may also be held to account for their 'professional' behaviour to both a University and the NHS Trusts involved but unless they have an employment contract, they will not have a specific line manager. Leaders need to be fully aware of the accountability, responsibility and authority issues that are interrelated to the teams of staff they work with.

Organisational Culture

The culture of an organisation has an important part to play in the success of an organisation. It is a concept that is difficult to define but Handy (1985: 186) defined organisational culture as 'sets of values and beliefs – reflected in differing structures and systems'. Mullins (2005: 891) defines an organisational culture as 'the collection of traditions, values, policies, beliefs and attitudes that constitute a pervasive context for everything we do and think in an organisation'.

Cultures are affected by:

- The past
- The climate of the present
- The involved technology
- The type of work
- The aims
- The kind of people who work there.

Activity

Can you make some notes about the culture in your own clinical area, paying attention to these aspects.

The hospice area I work in has a relatively short past; it has only been about around 30 years, it is a well-respected and valued organisation in the community and it's foundations lay on the charity that started it and contributes to its maintenance today. The climate of today is one of expansion; day centre, hospice at home and new hospice provision in another city and town reflect a changing organisation. The technology involved is one of palliation, medication, doctoring, nursing and allied health care, in-patient technology of beds, mattresses and home comforts as well as therapeutic alternatives such as counselling, aromatherapy and reflexology. The type of work is generally of a slower pace than an acute hospital. There is very little rushing around. Work centres on drug rounds, medical rounds, meals and choices that the patients make – be it activities such as bathing, talking with visitors or other patients and a range of activities in the day centre. The aim of the Hospice is to provide palliative care for those who have a progressive deteriorating health condition. The kind of people who work there have to be particularly able to cope with the difficulties of bereavement but also be active in rehabilitation skills to empower patients to take as much control of their lives as possible. There is a kindness and caring personality of staff that I have seen that is in-built and they demonstrate care throughout the whole ororganisation, be they doctors, nurses, catering staff or volunteers as though they are all potential 'hospice customers'.

An organisation culture is important in the way it influences the process of socialisation for team members and shapes the organisational behaviour. French and Bell (1990: 19) have modelled organisational culture to that of an iceberg where there are formal (above the sea) and informal (below the sea) (Figure 9.5) aspects of the organisation.

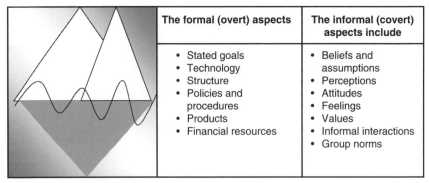

	The formal (overt) aspects	The informal (covert) aspects include
	• Stated goals • Technology • Structure • Policies and procedures • Products • Financial resources	• Beliefs and assumptions • Perceptions • Attitudes • Feelings • Values • Informal interactions • Group norms

Figure 9.5 Formal (above the sea) and informal (below the sea) aspects of the organisation

There are many models of types of organisational cultures. We will reflect on three models (Handy, 1985; Schein, 1985; and Johnson and Scholes, 1989). Handy (1985) identified four types of organisational culture (Table 9.4).

Table 9.4 Handy's (1985) four types of organisational culture

Role	Task	Power	Person
• Based around job • Hierarchical structure • Predictable and stable • Inflexible • Rigid • Barriers between different departments • Impersonal • Suppresses individuality • Change is slow, brought about by fear	• Central figure for strength • Communication radiates from the centre • Dominance from the centre – responds to change quickly • Small organisations • Politics important, 'knowing what the boss wants' • Can exert strict internal control • Conform or GO	• Successful solution to problems • Performance judged by results and problems solved • Flexible • Decisions made at junctions • More loosely bound than role culture • Power influenced from various positions • Respect and power from individual knowledge	• Focuses solely on the individual • Not common for the entire organisation • Usually in small areas of large companies • Culture of educated articulate individuals • Specialists with common interest, research, solicitors • Operate independently

---

Activity

Can you give an example of each of these types that may be seen in health care?

The NHS as a whole may be seen as a role culture. Small project teams may be working in a task culture. Research teams, high dependency, theatres or educational units may be seen as having a power culture and consultancy may be one of person culture.

Table 9.5 Schein's (1985) relationship between leadership and culture formation

◄───►

Operate independently	Ideas valued from older, wiser and higher
Ideas valued from any individual	status individuals
People are responsible, motivated and capable	People are capable of loyalty and discipline
of governing themselves	in carrying out directions
Conflict is OK and can be sorted out through	Relationships are lineal and vertical
groups	Each individual has a place in organisation
Group members will care for each other	The organisation is responsible for taking care
	of its members

Another model of culture types is from Schein (1985), who identified two continuums. One is not better than the other: they are just different. Schein noted that leadership should be seen in context and in the culture of that context highlighting the relationship between leadership and culture formation (Table 9.5).

The third model is that highlighted by Johnson and Scholes (1989) (Figure 9.6). It is one of an organisational cultural web, which portrays the complexity of organisation culture in reflecting how the different components all influence each other.

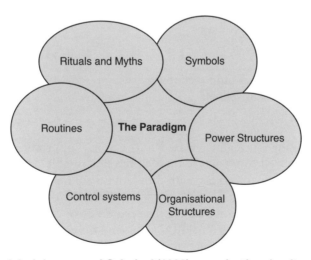

Figure 9.6 Johnson and Scholes' (1989) organisational cultural web

---

Activity

Can you write five words about each of the components seen in the web and your organisation?

You may have thought about many elements within your practice area. Coming from a nursing background my thoughts are:

- **Rituals and myths:** community staff using newspaper as a barrier to infestation
- **Symbols:** wearing a uniform
- **Power Structures:** visibility of Modern Matron, Ward Sisters or Charge Nurses
- **Organisational Structures:** 'A–H' grading system; Agenda for change structures
- **Control Systems:** appraisals; Personal Development Plans
- **Routines:** bathing everyone before 11AM.

Health Service Systems

There are many systems within a health care organisation such as the NHS and a variety of ways of looking at the nature of different systems. An organisational system is said to be concerned with flows of processes through the organisational structure (Handy, 1985). The NHS systems could refer to

- Strategic controlling system
- Marketing system
- Financial system
- Information, research and technology system
- People management system
- Operational system.

All of these systems are interrelated and are as important as each other. Clinical leaders need to recognise these different valuable parts of the organisation and work at networking with different personnel within these systems so they can seek clarification and advice as necessary on a broader scale to help with their own decision making. The relevance of collaboration with the human resource management (HRM) system, however, cannot be understated. If leaders are responsible for dealing with and influencing people, the skills of the HRM should offer the best support.

Human Resource Management (HRM)

Foot and Hook (1996: 4–5) identify the breadth and function of HRM (Figure 9.7) through a space ship model proposed by the Employment and Occupational Standards Council (EOSC). They note that the way to enhance the performance of people in an organisation is through standards of employee relations, staff development, staff reward and employer relations. Leaders need to be able to identify the importance of having the right staff to provide health care delivery and how they are formally managed within their employment contract. So the skills and knowledge are centred around

- processes of workforce planning
- recruitment and selection
- induction, training and development
- performance management
- employer wellbeing and support
- outsourcing.

Figure 9.7 Elements of HRM
Source: Foot and Hook, 1996
Reproduced with permission

These are all seen within the context of legislation relating to health and safety, equal opportunities, discrimination and rights of the individual. From a leader's perspective, it may be important to end the focus of this chapter on the induction, training and development needs of their team members.

Induction of New Staff

Induction is seen as an important process in helping new staff and students settle into a new culture, such as a clinical environment to help them to understand what is expected from them. It is the first part of a staff development process for new employees. In the health service, important health and safety information needs to be conveyed, such as where the fire alarms are, how the fire alarm system works, emergency resuscitation and accident procedures. Induction, however, is more than just passing on procedural rules. It is seen as an important part of *socialising* people into an organisation. Marquis and Huston (2006) even suggest that induction is the first part of the *indoctrination* process and highlight the link with induction, retention and productivity.

Activity

Can you relate to the feelings you had as a newcomer to an established team?

It is difficult to try to 'fit' into an already socialised work team and the structure of that organisation. It is, therefore, important that new individuals get a sense of support and friendship when they first join a new team as well as knowing how to deal with procedural emergencies. Cable and Parsons (2001) found that informal rather than formal types of socialisation had more effect on helping people settle into a new area. The importance of culture is an important aspect in induction. Due to the difficulty recruiting health care staff, solutions to recruit from abroad have meant there have been extra challenges for induction programmes as well. There have been discriminatory stories of the difficulties facing our international recruits who have come in to support our own health service. The variations in practice abroad, the language and jargon differences as well as the non-verbal messages that relate to acceptance of staff from abroad have been barriers to integration of our internationally trained colleagues.

Training and Development and the NHS Framework for Skills and Knowledge

Once staff have been recruited, it is important to value their contribution and motivate them towards achieving a sense of belonging and progression. The Department of Health has produced a framework (DoH, 2004) to highlight the variety of levels of skills and knowledge that health care staff reach within the hierarchy of the organisation. This is a useful framework, which can help leaders work with their teams to develop higher order skills and knowledge. The use of regular appraisal, yearly individual performance reviews (IPRs) and training and development plans is essential in order to help staff to move 'upwards' in the organisation. This ultimately can only enhance better patient care that will fit into the clinical governance perspective of the organisation (Chapter 10).

Summary of Key Points

This chapter has briefly looked at various aspects of organisational life in order to meet the identified learning outcomes. These were:

► **Understand the importance of the overall organisation** By understanding the organisation in terms of structures and processes you can more easily see an overall picture rather than just a small functioning part.

► **Discuss the importance of strategy, structures and systems within the organisation** From a broad NHS policy to practice perspective we have seen how the health service sets about achieving its goals. Strategies are vital in order to cope with the pressures of effective service provision. Varieties of strategies were highlighted in order to demonstrate organisational direction and its communication through mission statements and policy.

► **Critically explore the notion of organisational culture** This highlighted overt and covert aspects of any organisational climate, be it the NHS as a whole or a small team organisation.

► **Reflect on the nature of organisational roles** This involved examining the expectations of staff and students in a health care organisation and the importance of effective leadership in helping people attain their full potential.

► **Critically examine professional responsibility and accountability as well as the notions of authority and delegation** Effective leadership requires an understanding of these aspects in terms of supporting boundary management for team members.

► **Develop an overview of Human Resource processes in organisations** By examining the importance of human resources leaders should be able to manage effective recruitment and retention strategies. This is seen as being in the context of the NHS Skills and Knowledge framework, within the health service.

Further Reading

Department of Health (2005) *A Patient-Led NHS*. London: DoH.

Easterby-Smith M, Burgoyne J and Arunjo L (1999) *Organisational Learning and the Learning Organisation*. London: Sage.

Schein E (1997) *Empowerment, Coercive Persuasion and Organisational Learning: Do They Connect?* Henley on Thames: Henley Management College.

Senge P (1992) *The Fifth Discipline*. London: Century Business.

10 Quality

Learning Outcomes

By the end of this chapter you will have had the opportunity to:
► Identify the importance of quality in the health service for better patient outcomes.
► Discuss the historical developments that lead to the present quality agenda.
► Discuss the importance of clinical governance, audit, effectiveness and risk management.
► Compare a variety of quality models to inform effective leadership for continuous improvement of health care delivery
► Relate the importance of leadership in clinical supervision as a method of developing professional learning.

Introduction

The white paper *A First Class Service: Quality in the New NHS Health Services* (DoH, 1998) demonstrated the commitment of New Labour to providing quality health services. We are concerned about quality in health care because it ultimately affects patients and staff. There is also an assumption that a quality health service will improve the health of the nation. This chapter will examine what is meant by the concept of quality and how the concept has developed over time. Models such as EFQM© Excellence Model (1999), total quality management (TQM) and clinical governance will be highlighted. The impact of quality on staff within the health service will also be examined in the context of how this enhances the overall quality of care delivery to patients/clients. There will be limited reference to the idea of cost effectiveness for leaders but it is seen as an important aspect in quality management.

Historical Context of Quality Movement in the National Health Service (NHS)

In the 1970s and early 1980s, the concept of quality became more important in industry. Quality as a valued commodity began to be associated with the manufacturing industry, where products were inspected for their worth. Dowding and Barr (2002) noted the development of quality from the 1960s until the beginning of the twenty-first century (Table 10.1).

However, this emphasis on quality was rarely associated with the service industries and not particularly in health care. Health care was felt to be in the business for the good of society, not profit, and thus closed to quality scrutiny. The British Government launched the National Quality Campaign in 1984 for both private and public industries and the NHS was strongly encouraged to put a quality control system in place. There was initial resistance and scepticism from professionals who felt that they already gave a quality service. From these initial developments, the NHS worked through concepts such as quality assurance (which assured a quality) then moved through to the Total Quality Management concept (which focuses on meeting and satisfying the needs of customers) towards the idea of continuous process improvement. The latter idea focuses on an active journey of not only meeting customer needs but on 'delighting the customer.' Whether this phrase can be seen as appropriate in health service delivery is debateable but at least it reflects that quality is not just about complacency and 'standing still'.

The Health Act (DoH, 1999c, 2003) integrated the themes of the *First Class Service* (DoH, 1998) and set out a statutory 'duty of quality' for all providers of NHS services. The statutes introduced the National Performance Framework, clinical governance and quality structures such as the National Institute for Clinical Excellence (NICE) and the Commission for Health Improvement (CHI). Specific plans were launched to improve the health service, especially in terms of effectiveness, efficiency and excellence, through Primary Care Trusts and technological communication networks. The drive for

Table 10.1 Development of quality

	Traditional pre-1960	Technocratic 1960s and 1970s	TQM 1980s and 1990s
Definition	La crème de la crème	Fitness for use Meeting requirements	Satisfying and delighting the customer
Who defines quality?	Everybody knows what it is	Experts	Customers
Nature of quality	Attributes of product or service	Attributes of product or service	Process and outcomes
What produces good quality?	Good people and materials	Good people and materials	The right processes
Relationship to cost	Top quality is the most expensive	Quality can be found at all prices but improving quality implies raising costs	Quality is free

quality was seen through the indicators of partnership and performance. NICE, as the agency for establishing which overall treatments and interventions work best, have the remit of making sure clinicians know about them. CHI is responsible for monitoring clinical governance in the NHS and is able to investigate organisations that fall short of providing adequate care (Garbett, 1998). Leadership and innovation is seen as an important feature of modernising the health service in order to bring in a better service delivery that is more responsive to the needs of the public.

Total Quality Management (TQM)

Total Quality Management is a business philosophy based on customer satisfaction and the notion of continuous improvement. TQM is a strategy aimed at the whole organisation in order that resources are better managed, people cooperate so that the organisation is more flexible and responsive to what are seen as internal and external customers. It was Deming who first introduced this quality model very successfully to manufacturing in Japan in the 1950s. One feature concerning the importance of 'customer focus' meant that organisations started to think very differently about their products and how they met with buyers' expectations. The notion of 'customers' as a feature within the health industry creates a difficulty. In business, customer growth is seen as an ideal and healthy. If patients are seen as customers in the NHS, their growth would infer greater cost to an already stretched service. However, this aside, the use of 'customer' within the concept of quality has got a wider interpretation.

Customers are seen as individuals or groups of people who have the need of a product or a service. The breadth of this definition means that customers can be our patients and clients, or *external customers*, as they are outside the organisation. In broader terms, it could also relate to any external agency that purchases a service from any health provider such as a Primary Care Trust or a Strategic Health Authority. There are also internal customers within an organisation, which reflects the interdependent relationships between organisational departments. All internal departments are affected by the quality of each other and that no department/discipline works in isolation. If the X-Ray department did not come up with their services on time, then this would affect surgical and medical decisions. Similarly, if there was a poor catering service, medical and therapy staff may feel more disgruntled and this may influence the quality of interpersonal communications with patients.

Concept of Quality

Quality is a relative concept and although we all have some idea what is good and what is bad it is not so simple to identity what is acceptable.

Quality could be seen as being effective and efficient. Drucker (1967) defined efficiency simply as 'doing things right' and effectiveness as 'doing the right things right'. The questions to ask though are 'what is right?' and 'how do we know we are doing the right things right?' It may be very difficult to know what is right in emotional support, for instance, so we can only 'best guess' initially and then later reflect on the outcomes in order to see how well the patient reacts. In other cases, we know that using an ABC approach to first aid is the right approach to use based on evidence and research. So, effectiveness and efficiency may not tell the full story of quality within health care. Health care quality could be seen in terms of meeting the health needs and expectations of the population at the lowest cost (Øvretveit, 1992). The question of defining quality is difficult and it is probably more important to focus on the elements of quality.

The World Health Organisation (1983) identified the four main principles of quality assurance in health care:

- Professional performance (technical quality)
- Resource use (efficiency)
- Risk management
- Patient satisfaction with the service provided.

More recently, Moullin (2002: 13) examined health and social care quality in terms of 'meeting customer requirements and expectations at an acceptable price'. This was set against three other notions of quality:

- Fitness for purpose
- Conformance to specifications
- Conformance to requirements.

Fitness for purpose originated from the work of the quality guru Juran (1986), in asking whether a treatment or intervention is appropriate. For instance, some new technologies may give very accurate health data but if the technology is difficult for patient attachment, causes them discomfort, or is difficult for health professionals to read and interpret then it is not fit for purpose. *Conformance to specification* originates from the work of another quality guru, Levitt (1972), where customers set the specifications of the health service they require and how well it is addressed and measured. However, it is unusual for patients to get involved in this activity. It is more likely to be PCTs or GPs and although it is hoped that they try to reflect the ideas of patients, it is not necessarily easy to represent all patient views. *Conformance to requirements* arises from the work of Crosby (1984) and involves looking at meeting needs, demands or requirements of the customers. However, this does not address the infinite patient needs and the costs of meeting these health needs. Moullin's (2002) idea of quality in 'meeting customer requirements and expectations at an acceptable price' addresses the relationship between requirements of customers and costs. There is still some question, however, between customers who may not be the ones who pay the financial price, i.e., patients.

Models of Quality in the Health Service

There a number of ways of looking at what quality means in the health service. There have been some differentiated quality models (Table 10.2) in primary health care put forward (Toon, 1994; McSweeney, 1997)

Table 10.2 Quality models characteristics

Model	Characteristics
Biomedical	Addressing biological dysfunction
	Appropriate relief of symptoms and ability to cure diseases
Teleological	From the perspective of patient's holism. Offering dignity, privacy, empathy, confidentiality and information to help them understand their needs and health choices
Preventative	Offering services which prevent ill health
Business	Offering a growth in services in primary care with more convenience, acceptable waiting times and clinical environments

Source: McSweeney, 1997
Reproduced with permission

In reality, we probably see all these models merging into the eclectic model communicated by government policy today, but depending on the audience, one will enjoy more emphasis than the others. The European Model of Excellence (EFQM©) (1999) is helpful in offering a 'whole system' overview (Figure 10.1) of the health service and is valuable because it recognises that people and leadership are so much a part of success and getting good results.

On the research side, there has been an exploration of what quality dimensions would be important to the health service. The research work of Berry et al. (1988), who used in-depth interviews with a number of 'customer' groups, concluded that the groups highlighted several dimensions of quality (Table 10.3).

You may feel that these are very important dimensions to all of us as patients. In a way, they point to the expected standards of a good service delivery whether we are looking at buying a second hand car, a home or a piece of jewellery. In terms of the NHS, there can be difficulties in always reaching the standard required by patients, a professional body or by health service managers; it is important to identify how well a service measures up to each of their standards. So what are standards? What do they mean for

Table 10.3 Dimensions of quality

Quality dimension	Best practice	Poor practice
Reliability	Good IT health information	Failure to contact service user if that was agreed
Responsiveness	Staff who are able to address issues that arise unexpectedly	Long waits without direct action / explanations from issues that arise unexpectedly
Competence	Skilled staff	Staff inadequately trained for tasks required
Access	Ease of access to facilities or staff. Good signposting and attention to those with disabilities	Poor signposting / limited parking
Courtesy	Polite and helpful staff	Patronising and unhelpful staff
Communication	Staff who explain a diagnosis and alternative treatments/ -interventions without jargon	Lack of information about what is happening or what could happen
Credibility	Staff you can trust and depend on	Staff who don't appear to have the full information about individuals
Security	A feeling of safeness/ confidentiality	Unlit access to facilities
Understanding	Staff who make an effort to understand them as individuals	Staff who don't recognise a regular service user
Tangibles	Pleasing physical appearance of facilities	Poor / out of date equipment/ accommodation

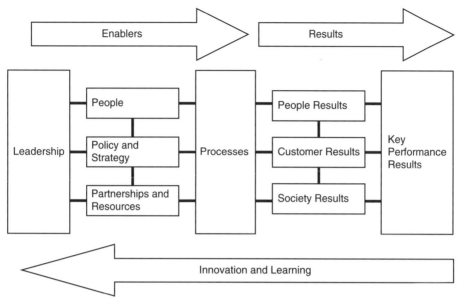

Figure 10.1 Whole system overview (EFQM© Excellence, 1999)

health practitioners? The setting of local standards of all kinds of profes-sional care is seen as vital to assuring quality. The Royal College of Nursing (1988) defined a standard as a 'professionally agreed level of performance appropriate to the population'. Standards should:

- describe the desired quality of performance
- have been agreed
- be clearly written
- contain one major thought
- be measurable
- be concise
- be specific
- be achievable
- be clinically sound.

There are eight prerequisites for a successful standard:

- A philosophy
- The relevant skills and knowledge
- The authority to act
- Accountability
- The control of resources
- Organisational structure and management style

- The professional relationships
- The management of change.

Standard statements should be related, descriptive, free from bias, suitable for quantification, valid and reliable so that they are unambiguous. There have been several Quality Assurance models for standard setting proposed. Donebedian's (1966) approach to quality evaluation has been regularly used within the NHS and serves as a reminder of the different domains that affect health care.

Table 10.4 Donebedian's approach to quality evaluation

STRUCTURE
The factors within the organisation that enable work to be carried out. These may be environmental facilities, equipment, staffing, educational facilities and management factors.

PROCESS
The performance or activity required to achieve the outcome, i.e., the care given to an individual, group or community.

OUTCOME
The result of care and performance or the effect of care on an individual, group or community.

Kitson (1988) proposed a cycle of Quality Assurance that involved three stages:

- **Describing Phase**
    1 Select topic for quality improvement
    2 Identify care group
    3 Identify criteria (Structure; Process; Outcome)
    4 Agree standard.

- **Measuring Phase**
    1 Refine criteria
    2 Select or construct measuring tool
    3 Collect data
    4 Evaluate results.

- **Taking Action Phase**
    1 Consider course of action following results
    2 Plan action
    3 Take action
    4 Re-evaluate results.

This fits in with the 'plan, do and check' cycle that is linked to TQM theories. However, Keighley (1989) argued against the Donebedian approach and identified two elements of a quality standard, the technical performance and the expressive performance. *Technical performance* is something that the customer expects the NHS to deliver consistently. Good technical performance is achieved through knowledge that is required in training, in the use of supplies, the use of facilities and, most of all, dependent on the number of staff available to deliver the service. In contrast, *expressive performance* is concerned with attitudes of staff with their relationships and interactions with customers, each other, and with the manner in which the staff deliver the service. This 'fits' well with the findings proposed by Berry et al. (1988) but it is also true to say that it is more difficult to qualify what constitutes 'good expressive performance', as this can be quite subjective to the individual giving or receiving it. In terms of measuring quality in the NHS as a whole, Maxwell (1984) first introduced a framework of the dimensions of quality in health care:

- **Acceptability:** Services are provided such as to satisfy the reasonable expectations of patients, purchasers, providers and the community.
- **Equity:** A fair share for all the population. The service or procedure is what the individual or population actually needs.
- **Efficiency:** Resources are not wasted on one service or patient to the detriment of another.
- **Effectiveness:** Achieving the intended benefit for the individual and the population.
- **Accessibility:** Services are not compromised by undue limits of time or distance.

Activity

Think about your own clinical care delivery. Jot down how each of these aspects can be applied to your service.

Maxwell's model, although useful as a checklist, has largely been encompassed into the modern NHS quality initiatives through the NHS performance framework.

Clinical Governance

The notion that public services had a responsibility for monitoring and improving their provision, in the context of health care, was coined clinical governance. Scally and Donaldson (1998) noted that clinical governance was to be the main method of improving the quality of patient care in the NHS.

They stated that it needed organisation-wide transformation, clinical leadership and positive organisational cultures. They highlighted the need for learning from past failures such as variations in standards of care, particularly with respect to breast and cervical screening programmes. They also noted that poor quality is often detected through complaints, audit, untoward incidents or routine surveillance. They proposed the key to success being a more open, participative and shared culture, good leadership, team training and working as well as evidence for good practice.

The Government defined clinical governance (DoH, 1998) as

A framework through which NHS organisations are accountable for continuously improving the quality of their services and safeguarding high standards of care by creating an environment in which excellence in clinical care can flourish.

Bassett (1999: 5) suggests clinical governance can be best summarised as:

A protective mechanism (umbrella) for both the public and healthcare professionals, ensuring that their hospitals and community trusts are actively developing structures to improve the quality of care in the hope of preventing any recurrence of the Bristol Case 1998.

Lilley (1999), as the Director of the Clinical Governance Research and Development Unit at the University of Leicester, concurred that clinical governance is:

- Everyone's business
- Involves patients and service users
- Ignores departmental and service boundaries and works across them
- Involves everyone in developing their professional capabilities
- Continuous and evolving in its quest for improvement
- About finding out what works best and doing it every time
- Based on evidence
- Transparent and open.

He highlighted that the responsibilities of NHS Trusts were to

- Establish leadership, accountability and working arrangements
- Carry out quality assessments
- Formulate action plans
- Clarify reporting arrangements.

Health practitioners have to accept responsibility for developing and maintaining standards of care within their local service. Ultimately, health care needs to be evidence based and professionals need to identify the rationale for treatment and care being effective as well as efficient.

In terms of clinical practice, Crinson (1999) noted five key components for a system of clinical governance:

- Clinical audit
- Clinical effectiveness
- Clinical risk management
- Quality assurance
- Staff development.

More specifically, the National Audit Office (NAO) (2007), in reviewing clinical governance progress in primary care, noted the components of Clinical Governance in improving quality and safety as relying on

- Improving services based on lessons from patient safety incidents/near misses
- Improving services based on lessons from complaints
- Ensuring the quality of patient experiences
- Involving patients and public in the design and delivery of health services
- Involving professional groups in multiprofessional audit
- Collecting 'intelligent' information on clinical care
- Proactively identifying clinical risks to patients/staff
- Measuring the capacity and capability to deliver services
- Ensuring effective clinical leadership.

The NAO made future recommendations to strengthen clinical governance for the Department of Health, Strategic Health Authorities and PCTs with respect to guidance, monitoring, better systems of accountability and development of staff for evidence-based care, audit and service involvement.

Clinical Audit

Dunitz (1995) identifies audit as a measuring, evaluation or study process, which should improve the medical care a patient should receive. There have been many attempts to do more than set standards. The idea of measuring quality implies that there will be some benchmark of quality acceptability. BS5750 or the ISO9000 were examples of awards (or reaching a certain quality benchmark in organisations but are often seen as quite administratively mechanistic). However, all health practitioners have a responsibility in making sure audit of key benchmarking policy is on their agenda. The *Essence of Care* (DoH, 2001b) set out standards for the quality of fundamental or essential aspects of care.

Activity

What do you know about the benchmarks set out in the *Essence of Care*?

There is developing work on the *Essence of Care* themes. The *Essence of Care: Patient Focused Benchmarks for Clinical Governance* (DoH, 2003) set out eight benchmarks for patient care:

- Continence and bladder and bowel care
- Personal and oral hygiene
- Food and nutrition
- Pressure ulcers
- Privacy and dignity
- Record keeping
- Safety of clients with mental health needs in acute mental health and general hospital settings
- Principles of self care.

More recently, in 2006, the *Essence of Care* set out nine benchmarks for best practice in promoting health.

Table 10.5 *Essence of Care*

1	**Empowerment and Informed Choice**
	Individuals, groups and communities are helped to make positive decisions on personal health and well-being
2	**Education for Practitioners**
	Practitioners have and use their knowledge and skills to promote health
3	**Assessment of Health Promotion Needs**
	Individuals, groups and communities are able to identify their health promotion needs
4	**Opportunities to Promote Health**
	Every appropriate contact is used to enable individuals, groups and communities to find ways to maintain or improve their health and well being
5	**Engagement**
	Individuals, groups and communities are actively involved in health promotion planning and actions
6	**Partnership**
	Health promotion is undertaken in partnership with others using a variety of expertise and experiences
7	**Access and Accessibility**
	People have access to health promoting information, services and/or support which meets their individual needs and circumstances
8	**Environment**
	Individuals, groups, communities and agencies influence and create environments which promote people's health and well being
9	**Outcomes of Promoting Health**
	Health promoting activity has a sustainable effect that improves the public's health

---

Activity

Go to the Department of Health website and review the impact these two documents have on your own clinical care. Identify how leadership is dealing with the monitoring and audit that is suggested.

Monitoring quality is often confused with the terms audit or evaluation. The following definitions may help differentiate the terms:

- **Monitoring:** The continuous or regularly repeated observations or measurements of important parts of the service related to structure process output or outcome.
- **Audit:** A discrete activity composing of a detailed periodic review of part or whole of a service or a procedure. In audit, there is an explicit search for improvement. This means that the importance of an audit extends beyond monitoring into developing the service.
- **Evaluation:** Refers to the judgments concerning information arising from a monitoring system.

On the clinical side, there has been a move towards multidisciplinary team audits (clinical audit). These audits focus more on the patient experiences or 'journey' rather than on the various individual services provided.

Clinical Effectiveness

This is about whether patient outcomes are achieved by the right health care interventions. Research is needed to identify what the relationship between outcomes and interventions may be. However, some health care professionals do not always see themselves as scientists or researchers but as 'action orientated doers' (Parkin and Bullock, 2005). However, those that use the health service are looking to see the effectiveness of health care, more so than ever and so research is important. Hunt (2001) notes that the main key advances in the last century have depended on professionals working with the public to advance practice through research. Nurse / Midwifery Consultancy is seen as a key driver for some professional research-mindedness in nursing and midwifery.

There are many questions about certain health care interventions where even the research is ambiguous. However, Muir Gray (1997) points to key questions about the use of research as evidence for health care. These are related to the relevance of the research, the range of outcomes and effects, generalisability, and whether any intervention does more harm than good. This must be taken in the context of a traditional science background, and generalisability may not always fit with the nature of qualitative research. Effective therapeutic care on an individual basis is often difficult to measure. This, therefore, has to be balanced against the context of the centralising management of the health service. Hamer and Collinson (2005: 92) highlight the present day sophistication in quality management with the developing NHS Performance Management Framework, 'Star Rating', and embedded clinical effectiveness in every field of practice.

The NHS Performance Assessment Framework

The Department of Health, through its Executive, proposed the NHS Performance Assessment Framework in 1999, which provided a range of performance measures for the benefit of all health service stakeholders. Performance Indicators (PIs) in the Health Service have been valued for the following reasons:

- To ensure that NHS goals are achieved
- To be accountable to a growing range of stakeholders
- To survive through competition.

Below is a table of the six proposed quality dimensions.

Quality dimension NHS Executive (1999)	Patients as stakeholders	GPs as stakeholders	Health ministers as stakeholders
Health Improvement			
Fair Access			
Effective delivery of appropriate health care			
Efficiency			
Patient/carer experience			
Health outcomes of NHS care			

Activity

Rank the Quality dimensions from 1 to 6 under each of the three perspectives.

Patients will probably prioritise their own individual experiences in terms of effectiveness and efficiency of services. GPs will probably be more concerned with treatment effectiveness, outcomes and efficiency dimensions. Health ministers will probably view the criteria of health improvement, access, efficiency and outcomes as priorities on which to base their communications with the electorate. This shows that not all stakeholders have the same quality perspectives and there are tensions about priorities. One of the core values for the government is the issue of health equity and fairness within the health service.

Health Equity and Health Equality

Equity concerns fairness, impartiality and treating like cases alike. It could be seen as a separate entity or as a sub criterion of effectiveness. It is concerned with treating it's patients and clients equally when they are in similar situations. Health equality is seen as the condition of being equal and concerns the removal of disadvantage.

In terms of the NHS Performance Framework, there is a need to measure health inequality and health inequity. Health inequality relates to differences in health experience and outcomes between different population groups; health inequity relates to differences in opportunities for different population groups, which result in unequal

- life chances
- access to health services
- nutritious food
- adequate housing, etc.

Sir Donald Acheson (1998) set up the notion of auditing health equity. Health Equity Audit was set as a performance indicator requirement in 2002 for PCTs in order to inform the implementation of local delivery plans, community and local neighbourhood renewal strategies in light of addressing health inequalities. It was meant to provide a systematic framework for PCTs to recognise common understanding of key local health inequalities. This was to ensure action for enabling resources to be allocated to address these inequalities. The overall aim of the audit was not to distribute resources equally but rather in relation to need. Not all PCTs have been able to respond to this activity in the same way and the data required for the audit activity has been difficult to acquire, so it is unclear whether this has been overshadowed by other performance indicators such as waiting times or cost containment.

Clinical Risk Management

In order to minimise errors and complaints in the health service, risk management is a very important aspect to prevent litigation. Lilley and Lambden (1999) identify three aims to risk management that can broadly be seen as:

- Reducing or eliminating the harm to the patient
- Dealing with affected patient and supporting clinical staff
- Safeguarding the organisational assets.

In terms of a risk assessment for moving and handling, you will see the importance of these aims for patients who are not able to move themselves easily. If every bed in hospital had a slip sheet, maybe more nurses would use them and avoid discomfort/injury to the patient, risk of back injury and reduce high absenteeism and even litigation for the Trusts.

Lilley and Lambden also identified the four principles of risk management

- Risk identification
- Risk analysis
- Risk control
- Risk cost.

Risk management does involve the ability of all staff to report adverse problems and events without fear of being made a personal scapegoat. This will require courage and more positive support for 'whistle-blowing', which is not always easy for new staff, who do not always understand the organisational culture and the impact of them acknowledging any problems.

Quality Assurance

The ability of the health service to assure quality is an important means of building public confidence but must be taken in the light of what staff feel are important standards. The use of care pathways is one example of what patients/clients will expect and what commissioners will expect to build into their contracts. While this is only an example of how quality might be assured, it is also a method of establishing an evaluative process, which is what quality assurance, clinical audit and clinical governance is really all about.

Staff Development

Ultimately, quality relies on well trained and critical practitioners who are well motivated and enthusiastic to improve care continuously. Clinical governance, therefore, relies on professional regulation and lifelong learning. The importance of staff development is essential but does depend on health organisations having the finances to deal with this. In NHS Trusts with high financial deficits, training budgets are the first to go. The question of who funds staff development is, then, an important issue, as ultimately this aspect of quality underpins the health service clinical governance theme.

Professional Development and
Clinical Supervision

Health care professionals are expected to engage in professional development activities within their sphere of work. Leadership is key to this engagement in learning; through encouragement and direction staff can be motivated to recognise and utilise alternative learning activities in order to keep up to date and fulfil professional body requirements. Learning can cover a spectrum of activities that relate to direct involvement with client/patient, relatives as well as colleagues and other members of their health care team. Clinical supervision as an aspect of quality, that allows professional and team growth, is generally influenced by two main issues:

- The nature and scope of the post and the intrinsic demands for giving information and helping others to understand, apply and use information
- Supporting and facilitating the learning and development of junior colleagues and students.

There are many definitions of clinical supervision. One 'clinical supervision' website by Steve Cottrell and Georgina Smith highlights a definition given by the NHS Executive in 1993:

> A term used to describe a formal process of professional support and learning which enables individual practitioners to develop knowledge and competence, assume responsibility for their own practice and enhance consumer protection and safety of care in complex clinical situations. It is central to the process of learning and to the expansion of the scope of practice and should be seen as a means of encouraging self assessment and analytical and reflective skills. http://www.clinical-supervision.com/default.htm

The clinical supervisor has an important role in helping the clinical supervisee achieve developmental growth through

- Creating a context of curiosity for the supervisee
- Generating multiple perspectives on a situation
- Inviting supervisees to arrive at their own solutions
- Giving positive feedback
- Confirming a supervised person's ability
- Creating new perspectives on professional–patient relationships.

A contract for clinical supervision can clarify the expectations of this activity for both parties. Table 10.6 is an example of such a contract.

Table 10.6 Example of clinical supervision contract

Joint responsibilities	Supervisee responsibility	Supervisor responsibility
To work together to facilitate in-depth reflection on issues affecting practice, so developing both personally and professionally to develop a high level of clinical expertise. To meet on average once per calendar month for one hour or as necessary To protect the time and space for clinical supervision, by keeping to agreed appointments and time boundaries. Privacy will be respected and interruptions avoided. To provide a record for our employer, showing the times and the dates of the clinical supervision sessions. Any other notes made about the sessions during or after the sessions will be kept by the supervisee. Although these are personal to the supervisee, they may be subpoenaed by a court of law or viewed by the employer if clinical supervision is part of the employment contract. We will work to the supervisee's agenda, within the framework and focus negotiated at the beginning of each session. However, the supervisor reserves the right to highlight items apparently neglected or unnoticed by the supervisee. We will work respectfully, both of us being open to feedback about how we handle the clinical supervision sessions. We both agree to challenge aspects of this agreement that may be in dispute.	Prepare for the sessions, for example, by having an agenda or preparing notes or transcripts. Making effective use of the time, including punctuality, the outcomes and any actions perhaps taken as a result of clinical supervision. Be willing to learn, to develop clinical skills and be open to receiving support and challenge.	Keep all information confidential that is revealed in the clinical supervision sessions except for these exceptions: when any unsafe, unethical or illegal practice is evident; repeatedly failed attendance at sessions. In the event of an exception arising, an attempt to persuade and support to deal appropriately with the issue directly yourself. If I remain concerned I will reveal the information only after informing you that I am going to do so. At all times work to protect confidentiality. Not allow any management supervision to be part of the clinical supervision session. Offer advice, support, and supportive challenge to enable reflection in depth on issues affecting practice. Be committed to continually developing as a practising professional. Use own clinical supervision to support and develop own abilities as a clinical supervisor and clinician, without breaking confidentiality.

Accountability and Quality

Accountability for practice involves 'moving with the times' and not just rely-ing on what was taught during initial training. Knowledge and skills from the past will not be adequate to meet the demands of today and the future. Therefore, professional responsibility involves being accountable for updat-ing these areas and being research minded. The various professional bodies expect everyone to maintain a portfolio of evidence in order to demonstrate exactly this. Professional leaders should be able to assess whether individuals in the team are keeping up to date with current developments in order to maintain credibility and accountability. Accountability is about a personal and team philosophy of continuous improvement in order to improve patient care so that patient centredness is embedded in professional day-to-day work. Martin (2001a, 2001b) identifies that quality care standards are linked with top decision making and highlights the role of health and social service bodies, which are accountable for strategically shaping the quality of our services for patients at present.

Conclusion

The main emphasis of this chapter has been to examine the concepts of qual-ity and attempt to relate them to professional practice. An overview of some of the historical developments and policy in quality has been highlighted and then taken into the context of the contemporary health service towards the concepts of clinical governance, clinical audit, clinical effectiveness and clinical risk management. A number of quality models have been briefly explored. Finally, the importance of staff development and clinical supervision have been examined to reflect the relevance for leaders to develop and motivate their teams towards self mastery for the benefit of patients and clients and improvements in care.

Summary of Key Points

This chapter has identified the importance of leadership and quality in the health service in order to meet the identified learning outcomes:

▸ **Identify the importance of quality in the health service for better patient outcomes**
   This was discussed in the context of present quality agendas through a variety of policy drivers.
▸ **Discuss the historical developments that led to the present quality agenda**
   The historical developments towards the present quality NHS agenda related to

a number of quality gurus and their influence on the health service and health care delivery.

▶ **Discuss the importance of clinical governance, audit, effectiveness and risk management** These aspects of contemporary policy were explored and debated within the finite resources of health services.

▶ **Compare a variety of quality models to inform effective leadership for continuous improvement of health care delivery** A number of models of quality including TQM, EFQM and clinical governance were examined within the context of current patient care delivery.

▶ **Relate the importance of leadership in clinical supervision as a method of developing professional learning** The notion of leadership and clinical supervision, as elements of clinical governance, highlighted the requirement for identifying learning needs and planning for professional development.

Further Reading

Parsley K and Corrigan P (1999) *Quality Improvement in Healthcare: Putting Evidence into Practice* (2nd edition). Gloucester: Stanley Thornes (Publishers) Ltd.

Peters T and Waterman R (1988) *In Search of Excellence*. London: Harper Collins.

Salvage J (1995) *NDUs: A Force for Change*. London: Scutari.

Wright S (1993) 'The Standard guide to ... achieving change quietly', *Nursing Standard* 7 (26): 52–4.

11　Leadership for Change

Learning Outcomes

By the end of this chapter you will have had the opportunity to:
▶ Explore change theory
▶ Discuss the need for effective leadership throughout the change process
▶ Recognise effective change environments
▶ Debate the effects of change on individuals, groups and organisations
▶ Explore the value of Action Learning Sets in supporting change.

Introduction

This chapter attempts to draw together the various notions of leadership and examine their effects on leading for change. Leadership during periods of change can be extremely difficult so it is important to know just how the information in the preceding chapters and the theories of effective change management can be used together in order to work in an effective and harmonious environment. Well-handled change is seen to be for the benefit of all rather than something that is imposed upon the workforce. Organisational change is a complex and well-researched area. This chapter will explain the process of change management and discuss the behaviours that might be seen in the organisation during change. Experience dictates that in many situations the process of change is not given enough attention to ensure that change is successful and as painless as possible. It may seem difficult, at times of change, to think about the future – particularly when there appears to be government induced change-after-change legislation. Few periods of history can be thought of as *transforming* but currently we appear to be living through one of those periods, particularly in health care. Today we are facing two major conflicting challenges: control of health care costs and provision of quality care to all patients and clients. These two factors are fundamentally altering the health care delivery system and so impact on the ability to lead effectively during change.

Defining Change

Although change appears constant and indeed a frequent event in health and health care, it is not always clear what it means. There are a number of definitions of change. Clarke and Copcutt (1997: 2) noted that

> Change is not a single process or group of processes: It ... does not exist at all. It is an ideal, a story made by everyone who is experiencing discontinuity. Viewed as a cause of events, by others as a consequence, it can be the disease, diagnosis and the cure.

Activity

What does the above definition mean to you? How does it relate to any recent personal change you have encountered?

It could infer that change is what you want it to be. A recent personal change involved buying a new DVD recorder (cause of events) on the basis of a little savings put by (consequence). There was a concern and indeed stress about learning how to use it and to its full potential (disease). My daughter, who had received one at Christmas, thought it was a wonderful present and said we should get our own for 'one stop' viewing and persuaded us that we needed one to prevent the usual conflicts over TV viewing (diagnosis). The benefit gained which helped with the decision to buy was that several remote controls would go and there would be a more simplistic approach to TV viewing (cure).

A more simplistic definition of change by Sullivan and Decker (2001: 6) is

> Making something different from what it was.

Figure 11.1 Linear continuum

From simple to complex definitions it appears that there will be some form of movement along a continuum which could be either linear (as above) or cyclic.

Theories of Change Management

From the plethora of published material on issues of change management, many models might seem relevant in the area of health and social care. Ackerman (1997) identified three types of change:

- **Developmental change**: Planned or emergent incremental change focusing on the improvement of skills and processes
- **Transitional change**: Planned and more radical organisational change (based on work of Lewin, 1951; Kanter, 1983)
- **Transformational change**: Radical organisational changes of structure, processes, culture and strategy based on learning and adaptation.

One widely recognised model of change, which is perhaps simplistic but well understood, is described by Lewin (1951), who suggests that there are three key stages to any change. These changes are:

1 **Unfreeze** or unlock from the existing level of behaviour
2 **Change** the behaviour or move to a new level
3 **Refreeze** the behaviour at the new level.

Lewin's three stage model can be applied to almost all change situations in order to analyse the success and failure of the whole process. In 1958, Lippet et al. suggested a three phase model that can be utilised alongside Lewin's model:

1 The **clarification** or diagnosis of the problem
2 The **examination** of alternatives and establishing a plan of action for the change
3 The **transformation** of intentions into actions to bring about change.

These two models jointly (Figure 11.2) create a useful cyclic process model that is applicable to the situation undergoing or requiring change. However, it should be noted that change in any health service is not always seen as being this simple.

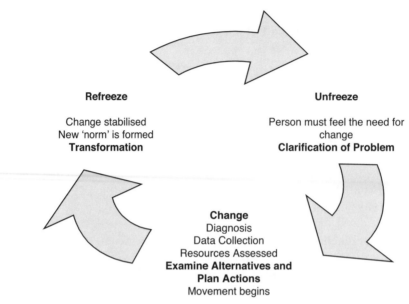

Refreeze
Change stabilised
New 'norm' is formed
Transformation

Unfreeze
Person must feel the need for change
Clarification of Problem

Change
Diagnosis
Data Collection
Resources Assessed
Examine Alternatives and Plan Actions
Movement begins

Figure 11.2 Cyclical process model. A combination of Lewin (1951) and Lippet et al. (1958)

Swansburg and Swansburg (1998) note other theorists, such as Havelock (1973) and Rogers (1983), who suggest more comprehensive staged models for change and innovation (see Table 11.1).

Table 11.1 Roger (1983) vs Havelock (1973) models of change

Rogers' (1983) Five Stage Diffusion of Innovation Model	Havelock's (1973) Six Stage Model
1 Awareness	1 Build Relationship
2 Interest	2 Diagnose Problem
3 Evaluation	3 Acquire Resources
4 Trial	4 Choose Solution
5 Adoption	5 Gain Acceptance
	6 Stabilisation and Self Renewal

Activity

Do you have any preference for Rogers' or Havelock's models?

It appears that Havelock, despite being an earlier model, has integrated the importance of relationships and people into the model. This reflects a focus on whether people in the team will actually identify with a need for change.

Upton and Brooks (1995) note various perspectives related to change management which help in trying to see the need for change. These perspectives can be viewed as the:

1 Very broad trends at a national and international level
2 Regional and localised changes that affect patterns of service delivery
3 The leader as an instrument of change.

The first two perspectives are very important in understanding why change may be necessary but the third is vital if you are to lead a change effectively. Without this understanding it would be very difficult for you as a leader or manager to ensure that what you are doing fits with prevailing trends in society and health care delivery.

Broad Trends

Undertaking a PEST analysis (Political, Economic, Social and Technological) to identify current trends will reveal where there may be problems. By discussing these briefly, we can see what impact each might have on health care delivery.

Political Context

Recent policy changes, starting with Labour's Health Act (DOH, 1999b), culminating in the NHS Plan (2000); this focused on the emergent and powerful role of Primary Care Trusts in a market health economy, a focus on quality, performance standards and patient power. Together with this are changes in taxation policy, particularly granting tax relief for the elderly with private medical insurance, strengthening audit requirements and public accountability while still allowing for local decision making. European Union health insurance membership reflecting a health care provision that addresses mobility and travel trends of populations and the amalgamation of regional ambulance services (DOH, 2005) are some of the more recent changes that have to be considered. All these changes are purported to squeeze more out of the NHS while devolving accountability and responsibility away from central government to a level closer to the patient.

Economic Context

Most of the developed world's governments are looking at ways in which they can contain the health care expenditure by rationalising or prioritising treatments, set ceilings on procedure costs and achieve cost improvements.

There are attempts to integrate cost, quality and outcome in order to aid decision making by policy makers and planners.

Social Context

As the population lives longer, the cost of care is increasing for the vulnerable and chronically ill. This, alongside global mobility from countries with poorer health care provision, is out of line with other demographic factors. There are also higher consumer expectations about the breadth and quality of services that are received. Also, there is greater sophistication in terms of understanding and choosing what is needed or wanted, which all add to the overall cost of health and social care.

Technological Context

Discoveries in fields of health care interventions, medicine and total health systems continue to reshape the NHS and look likely to accelerate. Of course, this aspect is harder to predict but potentially may have the greatest impact on health care delivery. Overall, it requires a high degree of flexibility and ability to respond quickly and effectively to change within the service.

Local Influences

If one conducts a Force Field Analysis that includes both hard (quantitative) and soft (qualitative) factors it is possible to depict how important the proposed change might be and to predict its success. An example of a part analysis might be seen when a new 12-hour working shift pattern is suggested (Figure 11.3).

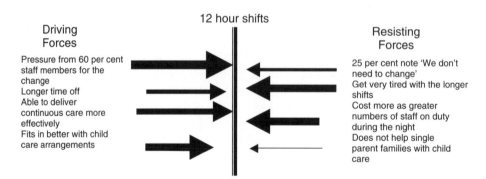

Figure 11.3 Force Field Analysis for change related to implementing 12 hour shift pattern

You can see from the strength of the arrows, that some of the forces are much stronger than others, so that the overall need for change appears to be the stronger argument and it would therefore be useful to continue to plan for change. This change must be planned effectively and initially should be considered as a pilot project with an evaluation date to see whether the change should continue.

Activity

Think of a situation, within your clinical area, where a change may be necessary and draw up a force field analysis of the need for that change.

You might have found this relatively easy. Did it give the results you expected? Did it highlight the need for the proposed change? Often the results of such an exercise demonstrate that the proposed change is not quite as strongly required as first thought. It also helps to identify the restraining factors, so that appropriate strategies might be considered, but it is important to gather a project team if you can so that you get a good picture of the current situation. This will help the team develop an ownership of the proposed change. You could ask some of the following questions to indicate how ready for change the workplace team is:

1 How ingrained are the various forces?
2 Which ones are the most open to reduction?
3 What influence can we use to help overcome difficulties or constraints?
4 Are there things we need to find out in order to get a clearer picture of the local influences?

The Leader as an Instrument of Change

In previous chapters, we discussed the benefits of knowing about your leadership/followership style (Chapter 1) and also your problem solving style (Chapter 2). Now we can take the perspective of the leader being an instrument of change. You, as the leader, need to play to your strengths rather than your weaknesses or blind spots and use a reflective approach within your team when driving through change. It is important to remember that you will be seen as a role model and others will look to you for direction, motivation and commitment. The way in which you handle the process of change, the stress involved and the way in which you interact with others will determine the success or failure of the change project.

The Process of Change

In order to ensure a successful change then the present situation must be considered and information gathered in order to set the direction for improvement. Galbraith's star model (2001) highlights the complexity of change within organisations and how change should 'fit' within a number of elements in the organisation (Figure 11.4). For instance, changing the way tasks are carried out has implications for the organisational objectives, people, information, structures and rewards.

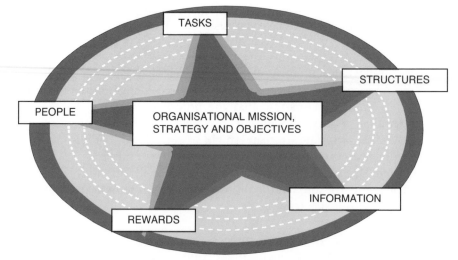

Figure 11.4 Galbraith's star model (2001)
Source: Galbraith, 2001
Reproduced with permission

Within the change process the initial stage of unfreezing, problem diagnosis or awareness should highlight issues related to elements of Galbraith's model. The next phase of planning and preparation will be where a change method from a number of alternative solutions is developed. It is not enough to say this, that or the other must stop or must change; there must be negotiation of a plan that can be communicated to the team and wider audience. Following the change there must be a review to ensure that the change has occurred (refreezing), evaluate the impact on health care delivery and that the motivation to operate in the 'new' way is maintained.

Response to Change

Kramer (1974) identified a phenomenon described as the 'Reality Shock' that was seen to occur when a student nurse becomes a registered nurse. A conflict between the student nurse's expectations of the role and its reality in the work setting emerged. The four phases of role transition from student to professional identified in Chapter 9 are:

1 Honeymoon phase
2 Shock phase
3 Recovery phase
4 Resolution phase.

While Kramer's work related to a nursing scenario, these findings are well known stages expected of any project change. It is natural that when a change is proposed there will be some reaction to the event. The point where the *need* for change becomes a *desire* to change is accepted as being a pivotal point and therefore the start of the movement process. If we take as an example the changes to moving and handling procedures, it was during the 1990s that the great risks of poor moving and handling practices in clinical care were identified. The RCN initiated change for professional groups amid little or no debate with external organisations. Due to the lack of involvement of care organisations, acceptance of change was not easy; there was no clear starting point and it is difficult to identify when the 'need for change' became a 'desire for change'.

Reactions to change are often surprising to change leaders because of the wide spectrum of emotions involved. The table below offers ten potential reactions to bereavement identified by Kubler-Ross (1970). While her work examined the reactions to death and dying, the emotional features can be applied to all change – as those who experience the change are being drawn away from their comfort zone into an unknown area. The ten phases are highlighted in Table 11.2.

Table 11.2 Phases of emotional change (adapted from Kubler-Ross, 1970)

Equilibrium	The current situation where everyone knows what is expected of him or her and feels comfortable. It is recognised by high energy and emotional/ intellectual balance. Personal and professional goals are synchronised.
Denial	Here the practitioner denies the reality of the need for change. Negative changes occur in physical, cognitive and emotional functioning.
Anger	Here the practitioner may demonstrate apathy, rage, envy, resentment or indeed any negative trait to demonstrate their feelings.
Bargaining	In an attempt to eliminate the change, energy is used in bargaining.
Chaos	Noted by diffused energy, feelings of powerlessness, insecurity and loss of identity, which can be diminished by effective leadership throughout the change process.
Depression	Here the practitioner may demonstrate self-pity as their defence mechanisms are no longer operable.
Resignation	The proposed change is accepted passively but without enthusiasm.

(Continued)

Table 11.2 Phases of emotional change (adapted from Kubler-Ross, 1970) (continued)

Openness	There is some willingness to accept new roles or assignments that have resulted from the change.
Readiness	Here we see the beginnings of acceptance and practitioners may demonstrate a wilful expenditure of energy to explore new events, with physical, cognitive and emotional elements involved.
Re-emergence	Practitioner again feels empowered and begins initiating projects and ideas.

There are many reasons why resistance to change occurs and leaders need to try and anticipate these and understand them as natural phenomena. Kotter and Scheslinger (1979) identified four key reasons:

Self Interest People resist change if they perceive that they may lose out in some way. This could be as simple as loss of power or input in decision making. There are many individuals that simply resent being told what to do. Similarly, staff tend to think that their own approach is the best with sayings such as 'this is how it has always been done so why change' and 'if it ain't broke don't fix it'.

Misunderstanding and lack of trust Strangely, efforts to create safer working systems can be negatively received and not trusted. It is vital that the leader engenders enthusiasm for the proposed change, letting all the team know what is happening at each stage in order to combat this element and take on board their individual issues into the change plan.

Different assessments or expectations There are often different perceptions of the change process from the people involved. Indeed, the cost of the proposed change must be considered in influencing the outcome. The force field analysis plays a large part in determining where change is

needed and cost of that change will lead to success. Conflict is seen when the benefits of a proposed change are biased towards one group's needs at the expense of another group. So if the change is seen to benefit only the organisational management structure but add further work for the workforce there is likely to be little cooperation with the process.

Leading the Team Through Change

Leaders need to assess the willingness of each individual to take on board change. There will be some people in the team who do not inherently like any sort of change and will demonstrate a low tolerance to any new initiatives. Within some areas of the health service there has been constant change over recent years and team members may exhibit signs of change fatigue in these rapidly developing areas due to constant patterns of change. However, there may be many gradients of change makers and change resisters. Within any team, there will be individuals who react to change in many different ways (Table 11.3).

Table 11.3 Types of individuals (adapted from Rogers and Shoemaker, 1971)

Change (progressivism)	
Innovator (Change Maker)	Proactive during the process of change, e.g., implements new policy or procedure
Early Adopter	Readily accepts the change, e.g., another professional adapts to the change
Early Majority	First group to follow early adopter, e.g., local team becomes involved in the change
Later Majority	Other groups follow suit, e.g., other teams introduce the policy
Laggards	A reticent group who tend to remain sceptical, although not openly hostile to change, e.g., colleagues who compare but do not take part
Rejecters (Change Resister)	Openly oppose change, e.g., individuals resist becoming involved in the implementation of the policy
Status Quo (traditionalism)	

This might seem quite a simplistic view and tends to categorise individual team members in relation to how they may react to change at one point in time rather than seeing individuals as changing as the process progresses.

Activity

Think back to Chapter 2 (Leadership/Followership and MBTI® exercises) to see if you can spot any trends. Then ask yourself the following questions:

- Which behavioural pattern (above) do you most often adopt in response to change?
- Does your behaviour always fit this pattern or does it change depending on the situation or your maturity?

You will not be surprised to know that your attitude towards change depends on a number of factors; the situation you find yourself in has a great part to play together with whether you see the change as having a positive influence on your employment position. You might think of other factors that have influenced you in the past and made you behave like a laggard rather than an early adopter. It is now prudent to explore the effects of successful and unsuccessful change and the ways in which a leader can affect outcomes.

Successful vs Unsuccessful Change

In health care provision, the need for change has never been greater both in practice and management systems. The effective leader will recognise that change brings with it a number of feelings, including a sense of achievement, loss, pride and stress. As a leader, it is important that you understand the change development because leaders must be able to give a rationale for it and communicate an understandable plan to those who must manage the change and incorporate it into their lives (Malloch and Porter-O'Grady, 2005). Effective leaders will embrace change and lead health-care delivery forward; they will exhibit exceptional planning skills and be flexible in adapting to the change they have directly initiated.

As previously discussed, the feelings generated when change is imminent are similar to those experienced during bereavement or loss. Unplanned change may be accidental or change by drift (Marquis and Huston, 2006: 171) – this is particularly noticeable when the *change is imposed* and a selection of obstructive behaviours may be seen. By contrast, during a change that is expected, rehearsed and informed, the behaviours exhibited are more complimentary and positive in their manner. Planned change occurs because of an intended effort by the change agent. As a leader, you will need to be that change agent and make efforts in planning change carefully.

It is clear that initiating and coordinating change requires well-developed leadership and management skills. Dye (2000) goes as far as to say that one of the most fundamental values that differentiates effective leaders from average ones is the desire to 'make a difference'.

Unplanned Change

Activity

Try to remember a time in your life that involved unnecessary or unplanned change.
Why did you think it was unnecessary?
Did it follow Lewin's or Lippet et al.'s model?
What could have been done to make the change more acceptable?

A colleague told me about her shift patterns at work, in a local GP practice, being changed overnight and with no consultation. When she spoke to her manager, she was told that her contract allowed this to happen and that there was no need for consultation. My colleague was not happy and felt that she had to find new employment as there was no way the employers were going to change their minds. Following her resignation, channels of negotiation were opened and an agreement was reached. Clearly when this situation is related to Lewin's model one can see that there was no opportunity for 'unfreezing', whereby the situation is recognised as requiring change, but the managers went straight to the 'change' element with very little success. Had the situation been handled differently with discussion and information being offered throughout there may not have been as much resistance to the change thereby leading to greater success.

All too often leaders of change have a plan but do not share it and encourage input from others. They might not see the importance of effective communication. For instance, if the plan/change is seen as short term the leader can become short-sighted, or if it is someone else's idea and is not 'owned' by the leader communication can be weak. Whatever the situation we must all recognise that change occurs and so we must be able to plan in order to manage that change. One example of this could be government deliberations related to the recent amalgamation of the small regional ambulance services into larger organisations in order to deliver better care to the patient (DOH, 2005). The thinking supporting this change was of increasing efficiency and cutting costs, due to fewer people being paid at the higher end of the salary scale. This white paper noted the opportunity to build on the significant improvements of the past few years and a statement was made to radically improve the services provided. It set out how ambulance services can be transformed from a service focusing primarily on resuscitation, trauma and acute care towards becoming the mobile health resource for the whole NHS. The object was to improve leadership, both clinical and managerial, so that the organisational structure, culture and style matched new models of care. Unfortunately, in terms of communication to the people involved 'at the rock face', it was not sufficiently detailed. Ambulance personnel perceived the real change issue being an effect on job security during and after the change. As such, the change took place in an atmosphere of distrust and uncertainty, which lasted for many months. Figure 11.5 depicts the effects on people when the change is not handled well and very few people know what is happening, why it is happening or how long the change will take.

All change cannot be contained, directed or managed. Unplanned change will continue to happen in a haphazard way but planned change will be targeted and purposeful. When managers make decisions that appear to be unrelated to current work practices it can be unsettling for the workforce. The uncertainty of the whole process means that decisions may be based on unspoken, sometimes unconscious assumptions about the organisation, its environment and future (Mintzberg, 1989), so resistance may be high. The common mistakes made when change is difficult or unsuccessful are as followed:

- Inappropriate time scales
- Unclear aims
- Inadequate resources

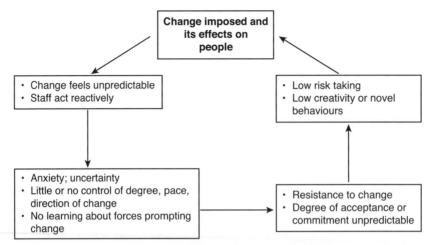

Figure 11.5 Effects of imposed change

- Ignoring knock-on effects
- Contamination in trying to change too many things at once
- Hijacking–where someone who may wish to settle an old score tries to sabotage the new project
- Incorrect diagnosis–limited Force Field Analysis or knee jerk reaction to solving the problem
- Lack of ownership.

Planned Change

Planned change is well thought out, timely and necessary. The rhetoric of planned change features all the positive aspects of informing the workforce what is happening and why. It is a reasoned and well thought out activity that will have a positive benefit for care delivery. In reality, the change may be thought to be well planned but there may be pockets of the workforce who have a less rosy view of the change. Figure 11.6 depicts the effects on people when the change is handled well and everyone knows what is happening, why it is happening and how long the change will take.

Kotter and Schlesinger (1979) described a broader range of strategies the leader of change might consider in order to facilitate a more successful process. They are:

- Education and persuasion
- Participation and involvement
- Facilitation and support
- Negotiation and agreement
- Manipulation and co-option
- Implicit or explicit coercion
- Review and monitoring.

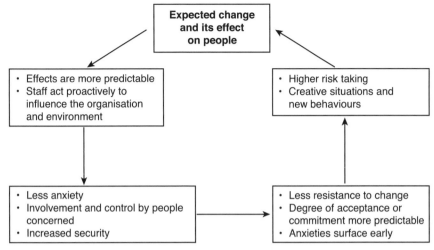

Figure 11.6 Effects of planned change

Activity

Can you think of a well planned change in your practice area?
Jot down which elements within Figure 11.6 were successful.

You might have thought of many instances where change was discussed and started well but hit difficulties and the whole process became confused due to slippage or various interpretations of people's expectations. In hindsight you may have thought that those leading the change could have managed the change approach better. Bennis et al. (1969) identified three simple strategies to promote organisational or group change (Table 11.4).

Table 11.4 Strategies for group change (Bennis et al., 1969)

Strategy	Use
• Power–coercive approach	This can be used when resistance is expected but when acceptance is not important to power source. The importance of power, control, authority and threat of job loss to gain compliance with change – 'do it or leave!'
• Normative–re-educative approach	This is based on the need for good working relationships as a method of inducing support for change. It focuses on these relationship needs and stresses the importance of 'going with the majority.'
• Rational–empirical approach	Uses knowledge to encourage change. Once individuals understand the need for individual change and organisational change, they will cooperate. It focuses on training and communication. It is used when little resistance is anticipated.

Education and persuasion One of the most used ways of minimising resistance to change is through educating people about the need for change. Education is vital during the 'unfreezing' stage of the change process. However, persuasion is required within the approach. There are a variety of approaches to education and persuasion that might be of help:

- The legal argument
- The ethical argument
- The financial argument
- The evidence argument
- Meeting professional standards.

Participation and involvement It is important that staff, carers and those receiving care are involved with the decision-making process.

Facilitation and support If negative feelings towards the change are exhibited then it is important to consider the empathetic and sympathetic approaches of facilitation. Training is usually seen as a good start to the support process, moving on to co-working and effective supervision during the change. Skilled facilitators should spend time preparing as well as understanding the factual content of the change.

Negotiation and agreement As part of acceptance of the new methods and behaviours there may be issues for group agreement. In order to reach a consensus and agreement, it may be necessary to negotiate the way forward in small steps to allow the 'later majority, laggards and rejecters' to reach an acceptable outcome. However you reach the desired outcome you, as leader, must ensure that undue pressure is not placed on any one individual.

Manipulation and co-option If the change process is not working, it may be necessary to resort to a more subversive method in order to manipulate people to agree. Co-opting a hesitant member of staff to assist in the process may give them ownership and can be very effective in getting them 'on side'. Once this has been achieved they may bring others with them, so assisting in the smooth running of the process. Should you have a group member who is strongly opposed to the change they may try to hijack the outcome and affect the dynamics of the group. The infiltration of a key supportive individual might assist in changing the views of that person.

Implicit or explicit coercion When all else fails, creating a power base where the change leader could offer some sort of reward for adhering to the change or punishment for resisting it can be resorted to. Some care organisations resort to considering disciplinary actions if the change is not implemented. This can only be considered as a last resort. It must be remembered that if punishment is the driving force behind the change then there is a very real possibility that once these threats are removed the resisting group will go back to their old ways.

Review and monitoring As with all changes there must be an evaluative period to conclude. The change should be measured and related to how well the new change has been accepted and adopted. The review needs to be ongoing in order to ensure that the old practices are not reverted to.

Experiences for Successful Change

> ### Activity
>
> Have you been involved in a change situation where there was resistance to a particular change?
> Consider the way this resistance was overcome and make notes on the effect the change had on the group.

I can remember a time where we wanted to introduce 'pre-operative visiting' for all our patients so that they would know what to expect in the anaesthetic room. We did not want to tell the patients about the details of surgery in case of raising anxieties. At the time, it was felt that all patients would want to know what was going to happen to them in the anaesthetic; they were shown photographs of the anaesthetic environment, briefly told about the monitoring equipment to be used and any questions they wanted to ask were answered. Clearly, for one anxious patient this was too much information and he declined the operation. Following this episode the surgeon forbade the anaesthetic staff from going near his patients. We had to write a script so that the surgeon could see what his patients were being told but for a while we only went to see the patients if requested. The change had been implemented without full communication with all involved but fortunately, a compromise was reached which served the needs of all concerned. It is therefore prudent to consider the following when driving through a change in the workplace (Table 11.5).

Table 11.5 Considerations for driving through change

Direction	Everyone clearly understands what is happening. There is a sense of purpose.
Timescales	Clear and relevant – may be by using a GANTT chart.
Communication	If ineffectual then there are clear grounds for rumour, innuendo and gossip. Gets rid of hidden agendas.
Consultation	Staff need to be informed and involved at every stage of the change.
Resources	Time, money, people, materials – where will they come from and how will they be paid for? Increasingly, employers rely on goodwill that may lead to employee resentment.
Making change real	Involve yourself and behave in ways consistent with the change you are trying to bring about.
Job security	During organisational mergers and reconfigurations, people need to know their place in the new structure. They will not commit to change if their personal place is not secured.

Action Learning Sets

More and more, the use of action learning sets are utilised to facilitate change in the health service, although they can be seen as taking valuable resources in a time-strapped health service environment (Malloch and Porter-O'Grady, 2005: 153). Action learning sets help individuals see the need for change and bring their own personal relationship into the change process. Action learning is seen in the context of learning and reflection, supported by colleagues, with the purpose of change. It is based on the following principles of team working

- Meeting regularly
- Consistent membership
- Addressing member's problem tasks
- Sharing, support, questioning
- Group success
- Review
- Facilitation.

In order for action learning to succeed, there is a need to agree the following ground rules

- Confidentiality
- Commitment and continuity of attendance
- Clarity of objectives
- Constructive challenge
- Work as a group of peers
- Recognise individual strengths/limitations
- The role of the facilitator is clearly defined.

Scenarios for change are set up and the facilitator assumes a questioning stance. The whole group engage with helping individuals face their particular change difficulty. The elements in Figure 11.7 could be questionable frameworks in order to ensure all involved recognise the change issues and have ownership of that process.

Rayner et al. (2002) identify that action learning offers a unique opportunity to develop leadership skills in a safe, non-threatening situation. The ability of leaders or facilitators to analyse problems, gain personal confidence and identify solutions for change for the benefit of clinical effectiveness are paramount. Douglas and Machin (2004) emphasised the value of action learning sets for interdisciplinary collaboration in their grounded theory research in mental health.

The skills, knowledge and experience of the individuals whose responsibility it is to bring about change are varied and complex. It is vital that they consider the intricacies of people's response to change and how that might make the path to change difficult, full of barriers and pitfalls. Good preparation

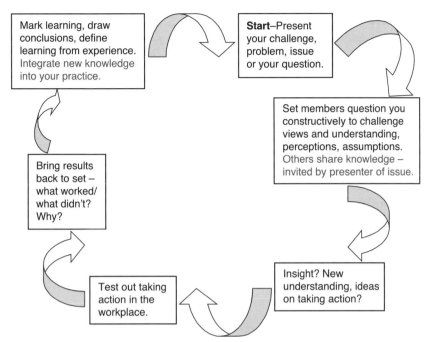

**Figure 11.7 Action learning model (www.natpact.nhs.uk/uploads/Action%
20Learning%20Models.doc, accessed 10.04.07)**

and planning of the process and involvement of interested parties at all stages
helps to ensure appropriate support, encouragement and action so increasing
the potential for successful change.

Summary of Key Points

This chapter has explored a variety of strategies that can lead to successful change.
These are:

▶ **Explore change theory** A number of definitions, theories, models and perspectives
  have been utilised to reflect a breadth of theory underpinning the concept of change.
▶ **Discuss the need for effective leadership throughout the change process** The
  importance of leadership to shape change and lead people through the process
  of change was explored and there were a number of strategies proposed for
  effective leadership in this area.
▶ **Recognise effective change environments** Planned and unplanned change outcomes
  were discussed and the implications for success and difficulties were explored.
▶ **Debate the effects of change on individuals, groups and organisations** The variety of
  effects of change on health care teams and individuals were debated and the
  impact on improving and changing care for patients and clients was highlighted.
▶ **Explore the value of Action Learning Sets in supporting change** This model of
  change was linked to the notion of team learning, problem solving and reflection
  using a facilitative approach.

Further Reading

Baulcomb J S (2003) 'Management of change through force-field analysis', *Journal of Nursing Management* 11: 275–280.

Davies C, Finlay L and Bullman A (2000) *Changing Practice in Health and Social Care.* London: Sage/The Open University.

Gerrish K (2000) 'Still fumbling along? A comparative study of newly qualified nurse's perception of the transition from student to qualified nurse', *Journal of Advanced Nursing* 32 (2): 473–480.

Gough P (2001) 'Changing culture and deprofessionalisation', *Nursing Management* 7 (9): 8–9.

Paton R and McCalman J (2000) *Change Management: A Guide to Effective Implementation* (2nd edition). London: Sage.

12 Conclusion

Learning Outcomes

By the end of this chapter you will have had the opportunity to:
► Recap on the scope and focus of the totality of this leadership text.
► Discuss the notion of studying 'Futures' in the context of health care.
► Consider the need for change to address the future and the importance of the leadership role in driving through change for the benefit of patient and clients.

Introduction

Malloch and Porter-O'Grady (2005: 180) state that

> Like any other pursuit, leadership is a journey. The only difference with regard to leadership is that leadership is a journey with no permanent destination.

This book has demonstrated how we might embark on that journey, support actions with theory and successfully arrive at our individual and collective destinations. The leadership role reflects the journey of life and as such is not only confined to our professional role but also to how we conduct ourselves in the community as a whole. This chapter, therefore, attempts to highlight the discussions from all chapters and draw together elements of the leadership process through a variety of activities. By doing this you will be able to practise an integrative approach to leadership for yourself and perhaps change the behaviour of others around you.

Leadership is often seen as a cure for all difficulties in any organisation experiencing challenges and the health care industry is no different. Antrobus and

Edmonds (1997) tell us that when change is imposed on the health service it reacts, and because health care professions are seen to traditionally lack leaders it is transformed by a drive to bring in enhanced leadership. In recognising this phenomenon it is prudent to consider ways in which each of us can develop as potential leaders in the world of today and for tomorrow. Changes are occurring on a scale as important as those of the industrial revolution and the health service needs to anticipate and respond to these changes.

Résumé of Chapters

The first four chapters concentrated on the leader as an individual and their ability to recognise these leadership qualities in themselves. Chapter 1 discussed the concepts of leadership and followership; it highlighted that, despite our nominated or employment position we will oscillate between these two concepts. As the text went on to define leadership and establish the importance of the changing environment related to health care, we argued that leadership training per se would not produce the quality of leaders required to push through change. A more sustainable solution lay with the development of what was termed 'growth cultures', in order to develop leaders with a number of characteristics, including emotional intelligence. However, when comparing leadership and management it was also noted that while management roles are appointed, leadership is often seen as coming from anywhere within a team.

Following this Chapter 2 debated the importance of clinical leaders in health care practice today. Through the work of Maxwell (1999) we examined some of the 21 indispensable characteristics of a leader. Whether you feel you are more coercive than affiliative, or more authoritative than democratic there will be times when you fluctuate between all the styles mentioned by the National Professional Qualification for Headship (NPQH, 2005). By reflecting on personal experiences of leadership in clinical practice it is possible to develop self-awareness and thus become able to interact in a more efficient and effective way. The use of evidence-based practice allows us to develop practice mastery. Identifying yourself as a master of your own specific professional practice may come after many years in the clinical area. Sometimes much time can be lost when you put yourself in the hands of others to direct your professional development but, when you look back, you realise that you could have reached a career fulfilment much earlier, if you had relied on your own determination. 'Self-Mastery' is about empowering *yourself* to reach your own goals and dreams.

Chapter 3 went on to discuss the breadth of the concept of culture and the relevance of cultural diversity influencing health and health care, which led on to a review of leadership in the context of cultural diversity and to explore theoretical models of transcultural care. Clearly, in order to lead a culturally diverse team, one must understand the needs of people from other diverse groups. When leading, one must be sure to:

- Examine the diversity of the workgroup so that you can get breadth of perspectives for the solutions
- Understand how team members respond to conflict and their expectations
- Work towards understanding the benefits of diversity and appreciate all contributions
- Avoid assumptions that cultural groups act and respond in the same way
- Avoid labelling
- Value everyone's differences and recognise similarities
- Play close attention to both verbal and non-verbal communication for cultural cues
- Assist those in minority groups to be successful
- Include them in informal networking within the team culture.

From here, Chapter 4 began to map the evolution of leadership theories in relation to how they affected health work practices. The ability to identify, compare and contrast the various leadership theories means that you should be able to reflect why you have acted in a certain way, but also how you might act or lead in the future. These theories will help you understand the effects of your preferred style upon a given situation. This is not to say that you will always consciously confront a situation and stop to think, 'Which approach will I use here?' but if asked to justify your actions these theories may help to support a rationale for your actions, hence utilising an evidence base for your leadership practice.

Moving on from 'you' as a leader, the next four chapters examined the notion of effective leadership in the team. Chapter 5 defined 'group' and 'team' and examined the values of team membership and their formation, the classification of work groups, the application of team leadership and the notion of effective leadership teams and their impact on the learning environment in health care.

Chapter 6 progressed the team perspective to describe various forms of communication and discuss the importance of effective communication. Poor communication is often cited as the fundamental reason for failure within the team or by the leadership. The chapter highlighted the communication process, discussed the interrelated ideas of leadership, motivation and communication. It then considered the benefits of 'Active Listening' and Neuro-Linguistic Programming. The legal and ethical issues related to effective communication were also discussed in order to make sure that all concerned understand the aims and objectives of effective communication whether this be upward or top-down in nature.

Chapter 7 discussed the concept of problem solving, examined some of the models and discussed some of the ways in which effective decision making can encroach on care delivery. Arguments related to task allocation vs holistic care vs care pathways were raised. Rational and creative problem solving approaches and techniques were examined in order to deal with the complexity of health care dilemmas. Also, the importance of the patient participating in the problem solving process was outlined to fit with the ethos of a *Patient Led NHS* (DoH, 2006b).

The final chapter (Chapter 8) in the team section was devoted to managing conflict. The concept of conflict and a range of conflict management models were examined. This then led on to explore the importance of conflict management within the context of problem solving. It is useful to understand the three levels of conflict when leading teams in health care. These conflict levels are the intrapersonal, interpersonal and intergroup. A good leader should anticipate and recognise these as different but also recognise the variety of strategies that attempt to manage these types of conflict competently.

Following on from the team focus, the next three chapters examined the perspective of leadership within the whole organisation. Chapter 9 attempted to relate the importance of organisational life by discussing the features of strategy, structures and systems. It also explored the notion of organisational culture, reflecting the nature of organisational roles and examining professional responsibility and accountability. This highlighted the importance of authority and delegation for leaders. Leadership requires a close relationship with the Human Resource function in an organisation in order to promote equity, equality and development leading to a well motivated workforce. Leaders need to be able to identify the importance of having the right staff to provide the right health care service. Formal management communication networks and liaisons are required in order to work effectively within employment contracts to support the leadership role.

Chapter 10 went on to identify the importance of quality management in the health service for better patient outcomes and outlined the historical developments that lead to the present quality agenda. TQM©, EFQM, clinical governance, audit, effectiveness and risk management were scrutinised in order to compare a variety of quality models. Effective leadership for continuous improvement of health care delivery was related to the notion of clinical supervision as a method of developing professional competence for quality patient care.

Chapter 11 then discussed change theory and the impact this has on the team. Effective leadership throughout the change process is vital in order to move forward with purpose. The effects of change on individuals, groups and organisations were explored. The effective leader needs to recognise that change brings with it a number of team emotions, including a sense of achievement, loss, pride and stress; it is the leader's role to ensure all participants in the change are able to cope with the situation and see the benefits for practice.

Leading Health Care in the Future

The speed of economic, political, social and technological change in the world today has implications for changing health services that are 'fit for purpose'. It is easy to look back at some glorious era, say, when the NHS was 'born' and believe that with a few adjustments we can go back to this health service where people were only too glad to be able to get their glasses provided by the NHS. The health services of the future will need to be very different and this requires leaders to push these developments through. Leaders need to have an 'eye' for the future and some literature evidence has tried to capture the notion of 'future building' exercises. This is seen as more than just crystal ball gazing but is now a management discipline in its own right. Rogers (1997: 1) signals that 'the future is a part of the consciousness of every human being', but highlights the assumption that 'Futures' studies are not predictable and is not an exact science. Warner et al. (1998: 8) identify a number of reasons why it is important to look to the future. These are to:

- predict developments in the future
- provide early warning of potential opportunities as well as threatening developments
- stimulate a learning environment for creative ideas
- enable people to determine their own preferred future
- explore options
- support policy formation.

It is also important to note some of the following global trends:

- Information industry replacing manufacturing
- Increasing urbanisation
- More migration of peoples
- More fragmented family lives
- Persistence of economic inequalities
- Increasing elderly and also carer population
- Declining birth rate and deferred child rearing
- A growing interest in environmental issues
- Increasing expectations – gerontocracy (power of older people) and better informed people requiring more health choices
- Various forms of health care privatisation

- Changing health care professional structures: more flexibility and more team working towards a generic workforce providing better transparent accountability.

A PSI Report (Northcott, 1991), using multiple methodology research for forecasting, found that important medical developments from biotechnology were expected that would affect the food we ate, the ability for genetic profiling (p. 217) and expected environmental issues in Britain. The PSI report also highlighted the specific information technology revolution that would influence health services, through:

- Storage of patient records
- Diagnostic aids including kits for self diagnosis, based on computed tomography (CT scanning) and monoclonal antibodies and biosensors
- Epidemiological analysis
- Drug monitoring
- Surgical and medical interventions: use of fibre optics, lasers and lithotripters
- Aids for handicapping conditions
- Health care education, especially in distance learning applications.

However, it was noted that these developments would be constrained by budgets, information technology security, technical skills of staff and the culture in health and social care. Warner et al. (1998) also forecast that the following health challenges will present themselves:

- Increasing non-communicable diseases, e.g., circulatory, cancer, gastrointestinal and metabolic disorders
- Increasing communicable diseases
- Nutritional
- Increase in mental ill health
- Increase in reproductive technologies.

The PSI report (p. 303) also noted that accidents and violence were now seen as the main causes of morbidity in the under-30 age group. From these trends there are going to be tensions in how health care services will cope with these demands on it. Will there be greater emphasis on primary care or acute care? Will cure and palliation override preventative services? How will those with a little voice get their health care services when those with a louder voice shout for their demands? What will be the impact of caring on families, especially as family life is more diverse and fragmented? How will the health care professional roles evolve?

Future scenarios for health care provision will be influenced by the wider global economy and also the national policies of the time. The following direction could be dependent on:

- Policies that move to the left: economic strength and greater consumer choice, which will be supported by greater governmental spending on health and social care
- Policies that move to the right: the free market and individual choice towards greater privatisation in health care services
- Environmentalist policies that focus on rights of the population to have a healthier and safer environment
- Policies that focus on the middle ground of all of the above.

Leaders need to consider these drivers for change and monitor directions of the health service they provide.

Activity

A leader has a role in ensuring the success of any change in the workplace by supporting participants of that change and challenging them to extend their practice. Consider how you would support your colleagues while developing your leadership role.

- List the attributes you feel are necessary to ensure you complete this role effectively.
- Consider which attributes you feel are strong in your leadership style.
- List and suggest how you can address the weaknesses you identified.

You may have considered a number of requisites highlighted when you completed the Leadership/Followership Styles questionnaire (Chapter 2). Essentially you need to demonstrate awareness with regards to enhancing and developing leadership roles within your team and develop the professional respect of colleagues together with the necessary expertise and experience to carry out the role. There are many other examples you might have identified. It is important to remember that when leading, effective goal setting must be applied and communicated so that everyone involved knows what is expected of them and can fulfil their potential. You may think of your role in terms of a flow chart like the one depicted in Figure 12.1, either cyclic or linear, so ensuring that all participants are 'kept in the loop'.

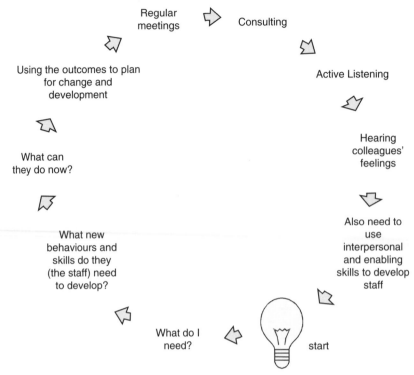

Figure 12.1 Forward planning and developing a leadership role

---

Activity

Drawing on all the concepts discussed within this book we can attempt to look at the future.

Consider the changing role of the health care leader.

- How would you design the basic competencies of the leader to reflect the needs of the twenty-third century in a technology healing context?
- What knowledge would be essential for the processes of rework?
- What protective skills would be necessary for the leader?
- What would you leave behind that would not compromise the future value of health care provision?

Letting go of the past is a difficult exercise and requires careful analysis of what should be retained and what might be given up. If we consider the basic competencies of the health care leader we recognise that there is a need for better communication skills, so that everyone in the organisation knows what is happening and why. Similarly, there may be a case for changing work priorities; in the past evidence suggested that 'holism' was the way forward rather than task orientation. It would be interesting to debate whether the constant demands put on health care services means this notion of holistic care is something of a luxury?

Activity

Ask the following questions in order to evaluate how you perform as a leader personally and as a leader within your clinical environment:

For me

- How well am I doing?
- How do I compare with highly effective leaders – how should I be doing?
- What more should I aim to achieve to make it happen next year?
- What must I do to make it happen?
- What is my timetable for action and how shall I monitor progress?

For my clinical area

- How well *are* we doing?
- How do we compare with similar clinical areas – how well should we be doing?
- What more should the clinical area do to make it happen?
- What must the clinical area do to make it happen?
- What should the clinical area's timetable for action be and how should progress be monitored?

The models of excellence enable you to set the results of your own diagnostic data against the evidence from highly effective leaders in other clinical areas. By asking these questions and then answering them, you should see more clearly the links between personal and clinical target-setting and achieve a more coherent approach to your role in clinical improvement and leadership.

Conclusion

It is vital that effective health care leaders in the future take cognisance of the theories related to leadership. This book has attempted to demonstrate how this can be done in a variety of situations; it offers some solutions and ways in which you can apply theory to practice in a variety of health care settings. In the words of Nelson Mandela:

> It is better to lead from behind and to put others in front, especially when you celebrate victory when nice things occur. You take the front line when there is danger. Then people will appreciate your leadership.

Summary of Key Points

This chapter has briefly looked at various aspects of leadership in order to meet the identified learning outcomes. These were:

▶ **Recap on the scope and focus of the totality of this leadership text** We took an opportunity to briefly note the focus of each chapter for revision.

▶ **Discuss the notion of studying 'Futures' in the context of health care**. This highlighted the novelty of studying how the future could be seen in some years hence and how this would affect leadership in health care.

▶ **Consider the need for change to address the future and the importance of the leadership role in driving through change for the benefit of patient and clients** Ultimately the focus of this text concerns leadership, which hopefully you considered as synonymous with the notion of change and, therefore, also with the future which is an unknown feature we have to grapple with for delivering quality services for our patients and clients.

References

Acheson D (1998) *The Independent Inquiry into Inequalities in Health*. London: HMSO.

Ackerman L (1997) 'Change in development, transition or transformation: the question of change in organisations'. In D Van Eynde, J Hoy and D Van Eynde (eds) *Organisation Development Classics*. San Francisco: Jossey Bass.

Ackoff R L (1981) 'The art and science of mess management'. In C Maby and B Mayonwhite (eds) (1993) *Managing Change* (2nd edition). London: Paul Chapman, Open University. pp. 47–54.

Adair J (1979) *Action Centred Leadership*. Aldershot: Gower Press.

Adair J (1990) *Great Leaders*. Brookwood Talbot: Adair Press.

Adair J (1993) *Effective Leadership. How to Develop Leadership Skills*. London: Pan.

Adair J (1997) *Decision Making and Problem Solving*. London: Institute of Personnel and Development.

Adair J (2003) *The Inspirational Leader. How to Motivate, Encourage and Achieve Success*. London: Kogan Page.

Almost J (2006) 'Conflict within nursing work environments: concept analysis', *Journal of Advanced Nursing* 53 (4): 444–453.

Antrobus S and Edmonds J (1997) *Nursing Leadership: Study Guide*. MSc Nursing Module NUM63U. London: RCN Institute.

Armstrong M (1990) *How to be a Better Manager* (3rd edition). London: Kogan Page.

Bales R F and Strodtbeck F L (1951) 'Phases in group problem solving', *Journal of Abnormal and Social Psychology* 46: 485–495.

Bandler R and Grindler J (1990) *Frogs into Princes: Introduction to Neurolinguistic Programming*. London: Eden Grove Editions.

Barge J K (1996) 'Leadership skills and dialectics of leadership in group decision making', cited in P G Northouse (2001) *Leadership: Theory and Practice* (2nd edition). London: Sage.

Barnard C (1938) *The Functions of the Executive*. Oxford: Oxford University Press.

Barzey S (2005) 'Dealing with difficult people and situations', *Nursing Times* 101 (16): 62–63.

Bass B (1985) *Leadership and Performance Beyond Expectations*. New York: Free Press.

Bass B and Avolio B J (1990) 'Developing transformational leadership: 1992 and beyond', *Journal of European Industrial Training* 14: 21–27.

Bassett C (ed.) (1999) *Clinical Supervision – A Guide for Implementation*. London: Nursing Time Books.

Belbin R M (2000) *Beyond the Team*. London: Butterworth-Heinemann.

Benner P (1984) *From Novice to Expert – Excellence and Power in Clinical Nursing Practice*. California: Addison Wesley.

Benner P and Tanner C (1987) 'Clinical decision making: how expert nurses use intuition', *American Journal of Nursing* 87 (1): 23–31.

Bennett M (1986) 'A development approach to training for intercultural sensitivity', *International Journal of Relations* 10: 179–196.

Bennis W G (1999) 'The leadership advantage', *Leader to Leader* 12, Spring.

Bennis W G and Shepherd H A (1956) 'A theory of group development', *Human Relations* 9: 415–437 in Hartley P (1997) *Group Communication*. London: Routledge.

Bennis W G and Nanus B (1985) *Leadership: Strategies for Taking Charge*. New York: Harper & Row.

Bennis W G, Benne K and Chin R (eds) (1969) *The Planning of Change* (2nd edition). New York: Holt, Reinhart, Winston.

Bennis W G, Parikh J and Leesom R (1994) *Beyond Leadership: Balancing Economics, Ethics and Ecology*. London: Blackwell.

Bernhard L A and Walsh M (1995) *Leadership: Key to Professionalization of Nursing* (3rd Edition). Missouri: Mosby.

Berry L, Zeithami V and Parasuraman A (1988) 'The service quality puzzle', *Business Horizon* Sept–Oct: 35–43 in Moullin M (2002) *Delivering Excellence in Health and Social Care*. Buckingham: Open University Press.

Blake R R and Mouton J S (1985) *The Managerial Grid 111*. Houston: Gulf Publishing Company.

Buchanan D and Huczynski A (2004) *Organisational Behaviour* (5th edition). London: Prentice Hall.

Buchanan D and Badham R (1999) *Power, Politics and Organizational Change*. London: Sage.

Buckenham M A (1988) 'Student nurse perception of the staff nurse role', *Journal of Advanced Nursing* 13: 662–670.

Buckingham C and Adams A (2000) 'Clarifying clinical decision making: interpreting nursing intuition, heurists and medical diagnosis', *Journal of Advanced Nursing* 32(4): 990–998.

Bucknall T (2000) 'Critical care nurses decision-making activities in the natural setting', *Journal of Clinical Nursing* 9 (1): 25–36.

Burns J M (1978) *Leadership*. New York: Harper and Row.

Burnside R (1991) 'Visioning: building pictures of the future', in J Henry and D Walker *Managing Innovation*. London: Sage.

Cable D M and Parsons C K (2001) 'Socialisation tactics and person–organisation fit', *Personnel Psychology* 54 (1): 1–24.

Cardwell M, Clark L and Meldrum C (1996) *Psychology for A-Level*. London: Collins Educational.

Carlyle T (1841 [1907]) *Heroes and Hero Worship*. Boston: Adams.

Castledine G (1998) *Writing, Documentation and Communication Skills for Nurses*. London: Quay Books.

Chartered Institute of Management Accountants (CIMA) (1998) *Organisational Management and Development* (3rd edition). London: BPP.

Clarke J E and Copcutt L (1997) *Management for Nurses and Healthcare Professionals*. London: Churchill Livingstone.

Collins (1986) *Paperback Thesaurus in A to Z form*. London: Collins.

Collins J (2001) 'Level 5 leadership: the triumph of humility and fierce resolve', *Harvard Business Review* (January): 67–76.

Collins J (2001a) *Good to be Great*. New York: Random House Business Books.

Cortis J (2003) 'Managing society's differences and diversity', *Nursing Standard* 18 (14, 15, 16): 33–39.

Covey S (1990) *The Seven Habits of Highly Effective People: Powerful Lessons in Personal Change*. New York: Fireside.

Crinson I (1999) 'Clinical governance: the new NHS, new responsibilities', *British Journal of Nursing* 8 (7): 449–453.

Crosby P B (1984) *Quality Without Tears*. New York: McGraw–Hill.

Cunningham I (1986) *Leadership Development – Mapping the Field*. (Unpublished paper) Ashbridge Management College, Berkhamstead.

Cyert R M and March J G (1963) *A Behavioural Theory of the Firm*. London: Prentice Hall.

Daft R L (2005) *The Leadership Experience* (3rd edition). Canada: Thomson South-Western.

Daft R L (2006) *The New Era of Management* (international edition). Canada: Thomson South Western.

De Bono E (1990) *Lateral Thinking: Creativity Step By Step*. New York: HarperCollins.

Deming W Edwards (1986) *Out of the Crisis*. Cambridge: Cambridge University Press.

Department of Health (1992) *Minding the Quality*. Consultation Document, Audit Commission.

Department of Health (1997a) *Report on the Review of Patient Identifiable Information. (The Caldicott Report)*. London: Department of Health.

Department of Health (1997b) *The New NHS: Modern and Dependable*. London: Department of Health.

Department of Health (1998) *A First Class Service: Quality in the New NHS Health Services*. London: The Stationery Office.

Department of Health (1999a) *Making a Difference. Strengthening the Nursing, Midwifery and Health Visiting Contribution to Health and Health Care*. London: Her Majesty's Stationery Office.

Department of Health (1999b) *Working Together with Health Information*. London: Department of Health.

Department of Health (1999c) *The Health Act*. London: Department of Health.

Department of Health (2000a) *The NHS Plan*. London: The Stationery Office.

Department of Health (2000b) *Research and Development for a First Class Service: R & D Funding in the NHS*. London: Department of Health.

Department of Health (2001a) *Agenda for Change*. London: Department of Health.

Department of Health (2001b) *Essence of Care*. London: The Stationery Office.

Department of Health (2002) *National Service Framework*. London: Department of Health.

Department of Health (2003) *Essence of Care: Patient-Focused Benchmarks for Clinical Governance*. London: The Stationery Office.

Department of Health (2004) *The NHS Knowledge and Skills Framework (NHS KSF) and the Development Review Process*. London: The Stationery Office.

Department of Health (2005) *Taking Health Care to the Patient: Transforming NHS Ambulance Services*. London: Department of Health.

Department of Health (2006a) *Our Health, Our Care, Our Say: A New Direction for Community Services*. London: The Stationery Office.

Department of Health (2006b) *A Patient Led NHS*. London: Department of Health.

Department of Health (2006c) *Essence of Care Benchmarks for Promoting Health.* London: The Stationery Office.

Dimond B (1999) *Legal Aspects of Physiotherapy.* London: Blackwell Science.

Dimond B (2002) *Legal Aspects of Radiology and Radiography.* London: Blackwell Science.

Dimond B (2004a) *Legal Aspects of Occupational Therapy* (2nd edition). London: Blackwell Publishing.

Dimond B (2004b) *Legal Aspects of Nursing* (4th edition). London: Blackwell Publishing.

Dimond B (2006) *The Legal Aspects of Midwifery* (3rd edition). Edinburgh: Books for Midwives.

Doherty C and Doherty W (2005) 'Patients preferences for involvement in clinical decision-making in secondary care and the factors that influence their preferences', *Journal of Nursing Management* 13 (2): 119–127.

Donahue M P (1985) *Nursing – The Finest Art Missouri.* Missouri: Mosby.

Donebedian A (1966) *Evaluating the Quality of Medical Care.* Millbank Memorial Fund Quarterly, 44: 166–206.

Donebedian A (1986) 'Criteria and standards for quality assessment and monitoring', *Quality Rev Bulletin* 2 (3): 99–100.

Douglas S and Machin T (2004) 'A model for setting up interdisciplinary collaborative working in groups: lessons from an experience of action learning', *Journal of Psychiatric and Mental Health Nursing* 11 (2): 189–193.

Dowding L and Barr J (2002) *Managing in Health Care: A Guide for Nurses, Midwives and Health Visitors.* London: Pearson Education.

Drucker P (1967) The Effective Executive. In H Flanagan and P Spurgeon (1996) *Public Sector Managerial Effectiveness.* Milton Keynes: Open University Press.

Drucker P F (1989) *The Practice of Management.* London: Heinemann.

Drummond H (1992) *The Quality Movement.* London: Kogan Page.

Duchscher J E B (2001) 'Out of the real world: newly graduated nurses in acute care speak out', *Journal of Nursing Administration* 31 (9): 426–439.

Dunitz M (1995) *Clinical Audit.* London: Martin Dunitz Ltd.

Dye C F (2000) 'Leadership in healthcare. Values at the top'. In B L Marquis and C J Huston (2006) *Leadership Roles and Management Functions in Nursing: Theory and Application.* Lippincott: Williams & Wilkins.

European Foundation for Quality Management (EQFM) (1999) *The EFQM Excellence Model: Public and Voluntary Sectors.* Brussels: EFQM.

Farrell G (2001) 'From tall poppies to squashed weeds: why don't nurses pull together more?', *Journal of Advanced Nursing* 35 (1): 26–33.

Fayol H (1925) *General and Industrial Management.* London: Pitman and Sons.

Fiedler F E (1967) *A Theory of Leadership Effectiveness.* New York: McGraw-Hill.

Fletcher L and Buka P (1999) *A Legal Framework for Caring.* London: Macmillan.

Foot M and Hook C (1996) *Introducing Human Resource Management.* London: Longman.

French W L and Bell C H (1990) *Organization Development: Behavioural Science Interventions for Organization Improvement* (4th edition). London: Prentice Hall.

Freud S (1911) *Interpretation of Dreams* (3rd edition) (Translated by A A Bill). USA: Plain Label Books.

Frew D R (1977) 'Leadership and followership', *Personnel Journal* 54 (2): 90–97.

Galbraith J R (2001) *Designing Organisations: An Executive Guide to Strategy, Structure and Process* (2nd rev edition). San Francisco: Jossey Bass.

Garbett R (1998) 'Clinical governance?', *Nursing Times Learning Curve* 2 (7):15.

Gardner H (1990) *Leading Minds*. London: Harper Collins.

Gibbs G (1988) *Learning by Doing: A Guide to Teaching and Learning Methods*. Further Education Unit: Oxford Polytechnic.

Giger J N and Davidhizar RE (1999) *Transcultural Nursing*. Baltimore: Mosby.

Giuliani R W (2002) *Leadership*. New York: Hyperion.

Gorlay R (1998) *Dealing with Difficult Staff in the NHS*. Buckingham: Open University Press.

Gould T and Merrett H (1992) *Introducing Quality Assurance into the NHS*. London: Macmillan.

Greenbaum H W (1974) 'The audit of organisational communications'. In J Weightman (1999) *Introduducing Organisational Behaviour*. Harlow: Addison Wesley Longman.

Greenleaf R K (1977) *Servant Leadership: A Journey in the Nature of Legitimate Power and Greatness*. New York: Paulist.

Greenleaf R K (1998) *Power of Servant Leadership*. San Francisco, CA: Berrett-Koehler Publishing Inc.

Grohar-Murray M E and DiCroce H R (2002) *Leadership and Management in Nursing* (3rd edition). London: Prentice Hall.

Grossman S and Valiga T M (2000) *The New Leadership Challenge: Creating the Future of Nursing*. Philadelphia: FA Davis.

Gulick L (1937) 'Notes on the theory of the organisation'. In L Gulick and L Urwick (eds) *Papers on the Science of Administration*. New York: Institute of Public Administration.

Haddad A M (1992) 'Ethical problems in home health care', *Journal of Nursing Administration* 22 (3): 46–51.

Hamer S and Collinson G (2005) *Achieving Evidence-based Practice* (2nd edition). London: Ballière Tindall Elsevier.

Handy C B (1985) *Understanding Organisations* (3rd edition). London: Penguin Business.

Harrison S (2004) 'Racism and the NHS', *Nursing Standard* 19 (6): 12–14.

Hartley P (1997) *Group Communication*. London: Routledge.

Havelock R G (1973) *The Change Agent's Guide to Innovation in Education*. Englewood Cliffs, NJ: Educational Technology.

Hayes J (2002) *The Theory and Practice of Change Management*. Basingstoke: Palgrave.

Health Professions Council (HPC) (2004) *Standards of Conduct, Performance and Ethics*. London: HPC.

Health Professions Council. www. hpc-uk. org accessed on 21.08.07.

Hersey P and Blanchard K (1977) *Management of Organisational Behaviour: Utilising Human Resources* (3rd edition). New Jersey: Prentice Hall.

Herzberg F (1966) *Work and the Nature of Man*. London: Staples Press.

Hewison A and Stanton A (2003) 'From conflict to collaboration? Contrasts and convergence in the development of nursing and management theory (2)', *Journal of Nursing Management* 11 (1): 15–24.

Hewitt P (2005) www.dh.gov.uk, accessed on 20.03.07.

Hibbs T (2005) NHS Head of News Press Release, March 22.

Hill K S (2004) 'Defy the decades with multigenerational teams', *Nursing Management* (USA) 35 (1): 32–35.

Hofsted G (1980) *Culture's Consequences*. Beverley Hills: Sage Publications, in Open University (1985) International Perspectives Unit 16, Block V Wider perspectives, *Managing in Organisations*. Milton Keynes: Open University Press.

Holdaway K and Kogan H (eds) (1997) *The Healthcare Management Handbook* (2nd edition). London: Institute of Health Services Management/ Kogan Page.

Honey P (1997) *Improve your People Skills* (2nd edition). London: The Chartered Institute of Personnel and Development.

Howatson-Jones I L (2004) 'The servant leader', *Nursing Management* 11 (3): 20–24.

Huczynski A and Buchanan D (1991) *Organisational Behaviour: An Introductory Text* (2nd edition). London: Prentice Hall.

Humphries J (1998) *Managing Successful Teams*. Oxford: How To Books.

Hunt J (2001) 'Research into practice: the foundation for evidence based care', *Cancer Nursing* 24: 78–87.

Iles V and Sutherland K (2001) *Organisational Change: Managing Change in the NHS*. London: The National Co-ordinating Centre for NHS Service Delivery, Organization, Research and Development.

Ishikawa K (1985) *What is Total Quality Control?* Englewood Cliffs: Prentice-Hall Inc.

Janis I L (1982) *Groupthink* (2nd edition). Boston: Houghton Miflin.

Johnson G and Scholes K (1989) *Exploring Corporate Strategy*. London: Prentice Hall.

Juran J M (1986) 'The quality trilogy' *Quality Progress* 19 (8): 9–24.

Kagawa-Singer M and Chung R (1994) 'A paradigm of culturally based care in ethnic minority populations', *Journal of Community Psychology* 22 (3): 192–208.

Kanter R M (1983) *The Change Masters*. London: George Allen.

Kanter R M (1991) 'Change Master skills: what it takes to be creative'. In J Henry and D Walker (eds) *Managing Innovation*. London: Sage/Open University.

Keighley T (1989) 'Developments in Quality Assurance', *Senior Nurse* 9: 7–10.

Kelly-Heidenthal P (2004) *Essentials of Nursing Leadership and Management*. New York: Thomson Delmar Learning.

Kemp N Richardson (1990) *Quality Assurance in Nursing Practice*. London: Butterworth Heinemann.

Kilner T (2004) 'Desirable attributes of the ambulance technician, paramedic, and clinical supervisor: findings from a Delphi study', *Emergency Medicine Journal* 21: 374–378.

Kitson A (1988) in WMHA (1990) *Quality and Standard Setting Workshop*. Directorate of Nursing and Quality. Birmingham: WMHA.

Koch T (1992) 'A review of nursing quality assurance', *Journal of Advanced Nursing* 17: 785–794.

Kotter J P and Schlesinger L A (1979) 'Choosing strategies for change', *Harvard Business Review*, March/April in J Hayes (2002) *The Theory and Practice of Change Management*. Hampshire: Palgrave.

Kramer M (1974) *Reality Shock–Why Nurses Leave Nursing*. Missouri: Mosby.

Kubler-Ross E (1970) *On Death and Dying*. London: Tavistock Publications.

Lancaster J (1999) *Nursing Issues in Leading and Managing Change*. Charlottesville, VA: Mosby.

Lansdale B M (2002) *Cultivating Inspired Leaders*. West Hartford, CT: Kumarian Press.

Lasswell H D (1948) 'The structure and function of communication in society'. In L L Bryson (ed.) *The Communication of Ideas*. New York: Harper and Brothers.

Leavitt H J (1951) 'Some effects of certain communication patterns on group performance' *Journal of Abnormal and Social Psychology* 46: 38–40.

Leavitt H (1965) 'Applied organisational change in industry: structural, technological and humanistic approaches'. In J G March (ed.) *Handbook of Organisations*. Chicago: Rand McNally.

Leavitt H (1978) *Managerial Psychology* (4th edition). Chicago: University of Chicago Press.

Leavitt H J (2005) *Top Down: Why Hierarchies are Here to Stay and How to Manage them More Effectively*. Boston, MA: Harvard Business School Press.

Lee D and Newby H (1983) *The Problem of Sociology*. London: Hutchinson University Library.

Leininger M (1997) 'Transcultural nursing research to transform nursing education and practice: 40 years image', *Journal of Nursing Scholarship* 29: 341–347.

Levitt T (1972) 'Production-line approach to service', *Harvard Business Review* 50 (5): 41–52.

Lewin K (1951) *Field Theory in Social Sciences*. New York: Harper & Row.

Lewin K, Lippitt R and White R K (1939) 'Patterns of aggressive behaviour in experimentally created social climates', *Journal of Social Psychology* 10: 271–299.

Lilley R (1999) *Making Sense of Clinical Governance*. Oxon: Radcliffe Medical Press.

Lilley R and Lambden P (1999) *Making Sense of Risk Management: A Workbook for Primary Care*. Oxon: Radcliffe Medical Press.

Lindbloom C (1959) 'The science of muddling through', *Administrative Science Review* 19: 79–99.

Linstead S, Fulop L and Lilley S (2004) *Management and Organization: A Critical Reader*. Hampshire: Palgrave Macmillan.

Lippet R, Watson J and Wesley B (1958) *The Theory of Planned Change*. New York: Harcourt, Brace, Jovanovich.

Lucas S (1999) *The Passionate Organisation*. New York: American Management Association.

Lumby J (1991) 'Threads of an emerging discipline'. In G Gray and R Pratt (eds) *Towards a Discipline in Nursing*. London: Churchill Livingstone.

Lyons M F (2002) 'Leadership and followership', *The Physician Executive* Jan/Feb: 91–93.

MacDonald A and Ling J (2002) 'Growing leaders: preparing the workforce for the future', *Nursing Management* 8 (10): 10–14.

Malby R (1994) *The Challenges for Nursing and Midwifery in the 21st Century: A Briefing Document*. Leeds: University of Leeds.

Malloch K and Porter-O'Grady T (2005) *The Quantum Leader Applications for the New World of Work*. London: Jones and Bartlett Publishers.

Manthey M and Millar D (1994) 'Empowerment through levels of authority', *Journal of Nursing Administration* 24 (7/8): 23.

Markham G (2005) 'Gender in leadership', *Nursing Management* 3 (1): 18–19.

Marquis B L and Huston C L (2006) *Leadership Roles and Management Functions in Nursing: Theory and Application* (5th edition). Philadelphia: Lippincott.

Marriner Tomey A (2004) *Guide to Nursing Management and Leadership* (7ᵗʰ edition). Missouri: Mosby.

Martin C A (2003) 'Transitional timelines', *Nursing Management* (USA) 34 (4): 25–26, 28.

Martin V (2001a) 'Mapping the service', *Nursing Management* 7 (9): 32–36.

Martin V (2001b) 'Service planning and governance', *Nursing Management* 8 (3): 33–37.

Maslow A (1987) *Motivation and Personality* (3rd edition). Harlow: Addison Wesley.

Maxwell J C (1999) *The 21 Indispensable Qualities of a Leader*. Nashville: Thomas Nelson.

Maxwell R J (1984) 'Quality assurance in health', *British Medical Journal* 288: 1470–1472.

McAlpine A (2000) *The New Machiavelli: The Art of Politics in Business*. New York: John Wiley Inc.

McClelland D C (1984) *Human Motivation*. New Jersey: Longman Higher Education.

McElhaney R (1996) 'Conflict management in nursing administration', *Nursing Management* 24: 65–66. In P E B Valentine (2001) 'A gender perspective on conflict management strategies of nurses', *Journal of Nursing Scholarship* 33 (1): 69–74.

McGregor D (1987) *The Human Side of Enterprise*. London: Penguin.

McNeese-Smith D K and Crook M (2003) 'Nursing values and a changing nurse workforce: values, age, and job stages', *Journal of Nursing Administration* 33 (5): 260–270.

McSweeney P (1997) 'Quality in primary care: management challenges for new Health Authorities', *Total Quality Management* 8 (5): 243–253.

Mears P and Voehl F (1994) *Team Building: A Structured Learning Approach*. Delray Beach: St Lucie Press.

Miner J B (1980) *Theories of Organisational Behaviour*. New York: Dryden Press.

Mintzberg H J (1989) *Mintzberg on Managament: Inside Our Strange World of Organisations*. New York: Free Press.

Mintzberg H, Quinn J B and Ghoshal S (1998) *The Strategy Process*. Hemel Hempstead: Prentice Hall.

Morgan J and Everitt T (1990) *Introducing Quality Management: A Training Manual*. SE Staffordshire HA/Birmingham University, Kall Kwick Printing St Helens.

Moullin M (2002) *Delivering Excellence in Health and Social Care*. Buckingham: Open University Press.

Muir Gray J A (1997) *Evidence–Based Healthcare: How to make Health Policy and Management Decisions*. London: Churchill Livingstone.

Muir N (2004) 'Clinical decision-making: theory and practice', *Nursing Standard* 18 (36): 47–52.

Mulholland J (1995) 'Nursing, humanism and trans-cultural theory: the bracketing out of reality', *Journal of Advanced Nursing* 22 (5): 442–449.

Mullaly S (2001) 'Leadership and politics', *Nursing Management* 8 (4): 21–27.

Mullins L J (1999) *Management and Organisational Behaviour* (5th edition). New York: Prentice Hall/Financial Times.

Mullins L J (2005) *Management and Organisational Behaviour* (7th edition). New York: Prentice Hall/ Financial Times.

Myers-Briggs I (1995) *Gifts Differing: Understanding Personality Type.* Palo Alto, CA: Davies-Black Publishing.

National Audit Office (2007) *Improving Quality and Safety – Progress in Implementing Clinical Governance: Lessons for the New Primary Care Trusts.* London: NAO.

National Professional Qualification for Headship (NPQH) (2005) Securing the commitment of others to the vision *(D1.2)* in *National College for School Leadership.* London: NPQH.

NHS Careers (2007) www.nhscareers.nhs.uk

NHS Executive (1998) *Clinical Effectiveness.* NT/NHSE.

NHS Executive (1999) *The NHS Performance Assessment Framework.* Weatherby: Department of Health.

NHS Management Executive (1993) *The Quality Journey.* Health Publications Unit.

Nightingale F (1859) 'Notes on nursing'. In R van der Peet (1995) *The Nightingale Model of Nursing.* Edinburgh: Campion Press.

Northcott J (1991) *Britain in 2010: The PSI Report.* London: Policy Studies Institute.

Nursing and Midwifery Council (NMC) (2002) *Code of Professional Conduct* London: NMC.

Open University (1996) *P679 Planning and Managing Change.* Buckingham: Open University Press.

Ouchi W (1981) *Theory Z: How Americans Business Can Meet the Japanese Challenge.* Harlow: Addison Wesley.

Ovretveit J (1992) *Health Service Quality.* London: Blackwell Scientific Publications.

Owen J (2005) *How to Lead.* Harlow: Pearson Education Limited.

Palfrey C (2000) *Key Concepts in Health Care Policy and Planning.* London: Macmillan.

Parkin C and Bullock I (2005) 'Evidence-based healthcare: development and audit in clinical standard for research and its impact on an NHS Trust', *Journal of Clinical Nursing* 14 (4): 418–425.

Pearson A, Borbasi S, Fitzgerald M, Kowanko I and Walsh K (1997) 'Evidence based nursing: an examination of nursing within the international evidence based health care practice movement', *RCNA Discussion Document No. 1 Nursing Review.* Sydney.

Pedlar M (1997) *The Learning Company: A Strategy for Sustainable Development.* (2nd edition). London: Mcgraw-Hill.

Perren L and Tavakoli I (1997) 'Mission impossible without commitment', *Professional Manager* July: 14–15.

Pondy L R (1967) 'Organisational conflict: concepts and models', *Administrative Science Quarterly* 12: 296–320.

Porter M (1980) *Competitive Strategy: Techniques for Analyzing Industries and Competitors.* New York: The Free Press.

Porter-O'Grady T (2003) 'A different age for leadership, part 2: new rules, new roles', *Journal of Nursing Administration* 33 (3): 173–178.

Rafferty A (1993) *Leading questions: a discussion paper on the issues of nurse leadership.* King's Fund Centre.

Rahim M A (1983) 'A measure of styles of handling interpersonal conflict', *Academy of Management Journal* 26: 368–375.

Rahim M A (1985) 'A strategy for managing conflict in complex organisations', *Human Relations* 38: 81–89.

Rayner D, Chisholm H and Appleby H (2002) 'Developing leadership through action learning', *Nursing Standard* 16 (29): 37–39.

Redfern S J and Norman I J (1990) 'Measuring the quality of nursing care: a consideration of different approaches', *Journal of Advanced Nursing* 15: 1260–1271.

Rippon S (2001) 'How does your garden grow?', *Nursing Management* 8 (7): 11–15.

Robertson C (1997) *The Wordsworth Dictionary of Quotations*. London: Wordsworth Editions Ltd.

Robotham A and Frost M (2000) *Health Visiting Specialist Community Public Health Nursing* (2nd edition). London: Elsevier.

Rogers E and Shoemaker F (1971) *Communication of Innovations: A Cross-cultural Report*. New York: The Free Press.

Rogers E M (1983) *Diffusion of Innovations* (3rd edition). New York: Free Press.

Rogers M (1997) *Canadian Nursing in the Year 2020: Five Futures Scenarios*. New York: Canadian Nurses Association.

Rosener J (1990) 'Ways women lead Harvard Business Review'. In G Markham (1996) 'Gender in leadership', *Nursing Management* 3 (1): 18–19.

Rost J C and Barker R A (2000) 'Leadership education in colleges: toward a 21st century paradigm', *Journal of Leadership Studies* 7 (1): 3–12.

Royal College of Nursing (RCN) (2005) *Working with Care: Improving Working Relationships in Healthcare*. London: RCN.

Royal College of Nursing (RCN) (1988) *The Dynamic Standard Setting System, Standards of Care Project*. London: RCN.

Royal College of Nursing (RCN) (1998) *Guidance for Nurses on Clinical Governance*. London: RCN.

Sadler P (2003) *Leadership* (2nd edition). London: Kogan Page.

Sale D (1990) *Quality Assurance*. London: Macmillan.

Sardar Z and Van Loon B (1997) *Cultural Studies for Beginners*. Cambridge: Icon Books Ltd.

Scally G and Donaldson L (1998) 'Clinical governance and the drive for quality improvement in the new NHS in England', *British Medical Journal* 317: 61–65.

Schein E H (1985) *Organizational Culture and Leadership*. California: Jossey–Bass.

Schein E H (1992) 'Coming to a new awareness of organizational culture'. In G Salaman (ed.) *Human Resource Strategies*. London: Sage.

Schmalenburg C and Kramer M (1979) *Coping with Reality Shock*. Wakefield, MA: Nursing Resources.

Schön D (1987) *Educating the Reflective Practitioner: Towards a New Design for Teaching and Learning in the Professions*. San Francisco: Jossey Bass.

Scott I (1998) 'Challenging the future', *Nursing Management* 4 (9): 18–21.

Senge P (1990) *The Fifth Discipline: The Art and Practice of the Learning Organisation*. New York: Doubleday.

Shannon CE and Weaver W (1954) *The Mathematical Theory of Communication*. Illinois: University of Illinois Press.

Shirley S (1991) 'Corporate strategy and entrepreneurial vision'. In J Henry and D Walker *Managing Innovation*. London: Sage.

Shorten A and Wallace M (1997) 'Evidence based practice: the future is clear', *Australian Nursing Journal* 4 (6): 22–4 in B J Taylor (2000) *Reflective Practice: A Guide for Nurses and Midwives*. Buckingham: Open University Press.

Silva M C (1977) 'Philosophy, science and theory: interrelationships and implications for nursing research', *Image* 9 (3): 59–63.

Simon H A (1960a) *Administrative Behaviour*. New York: Macmillan.

Simon H A (1960b) 'The corporation: will it be managed by machines?' In H Leavitt and L R Pondy *Readings in Managerial Psychology*. Chicago: University of Chicago Press.

Simon H A (1977) *The New Science of Management Decision* (revised edition). London: Prentice Hall.

Simon H A (1990) 'Cognitive science: the newest science of the artificial', *Cognitive Science* 4: 33–46.

Smith G (1995) *Managing to Succeed*. Hertfordshire: Prentice Hall.

Snow J (2001) 'Looking beyond nursing for clues to effective leadership', *Journal of Nursing Administration* 31 (9): 440–443.

Sofarelli D and Brown D (1998) 'The need for nursing leadership in uncertain times', *Journal of Nursing Management* 6: 201–207.

Spector R (2000) *Cultural Diversity in Health and Illness*. Norwalk, CT: Appleton and Lange.

Starns P (2000) *Nurses at War: Women in the Frontline 1939-45*. Stroud: Sutton Publishing Ltd.

Stewart I M (1918) 'Popular fallacies about nursing education', *The Modern Hospital* 18 (1). In Donahue M P (1985) *Nursing – The Finest Art*. Missouri: Mosby.

Stewart R (1996) *Leading in the NHS: A Practical Guide* (2nd edition). London: Macmillan Business.

Stott K (1992) *Making Management Work*. London: Prentice Hall.

Stott K and Walker A (1995) *Making Management Work A Practical Approach*. London: Prentice Hall.

Sullivan E J and Decker P J (1997) *Effective Leadership and Management in Nursing*. Menlo Park, CA: Addison Wesley.

Sullivan E J and Decker P J (2001) *Effective Leadership and Management in Nursing* (5th edition). Menlo Park, CA: Addison Wesley.

Sullivan E J and Decker P J (2000) *Effective Leadership and Management in Nursing*. (5th edition). London: Benjamin Cummings.

Swansburg R C and Swansburg R J (1998) *Introductory Management and Leadership for Nurses* (2nd edition). Boston: Jones and Bartlett Publishers.

Tannenbaum R and Schmidt W H (1958) 'How to choose a leadership pattern', *Harvard Business Review* 36: 95–101.

Tappen R, Weiss S and Whitehead D (2004a) 'Tools for leadership and management problem solving'. In R Tappen, S Weiss and D Whitehead *Essentials of Nursing Leadership and Management* (3rd edition). Philadelphia: FA Davis.

Tappen R, Weiss S and Whitehead D (2004b) *Essentials of Nursing Leadership and Management* (3rd edition). Philadelphia: FA Davis Company.

Taylor B J (2000) *Reflective Practice: A Guide for Nurses and Midwives*. Buckingham: Open University Press.

Taylor F W (1947) *Scientific Management*. New York: Harper & Row.

Thomas K W (1976) 'Conflict and conflict management'. In M D Dunnette (ed.) *Handbook of Industrial and Organisational Psychology*. Chicago: Rand McNally.

Thomas K W (1977) 'Towards multidimensional values in teaching: the example of conflict behaviours', *Academy of Management Review* July: 487.

Thomas S P (2003) 'Horizontal hostility', *American Journal of Nursing* 103 (10): 87.

Toon P (1994) *What is Good General Practice?* London: RCGP.

Tuckman B W (1965) 'Developmental sequence in small groups', *Psychological Bulletin* 63: 384–99.

Tuckman B C and Jensen M A (1977) 'Stages of small group development revisited', *Group and Organization Studies* 2 (4): 419–427.

Tylor E B (1871) 'Primitive cultures'. In Z Sardar and B Van Loon (1997) *Cultural Studies for Beginners*. Cambridge: Icon Books Ltd.

Upton T and Brooks B (NAHAT) (1995) *Managing Change in the NHS*. London: Kogan Page.

Valentine P E B (1995) 'Management of conflict: Do nurses/women handle it differently?', *Journal of Advanced Nursing* 22: 142–149.

Valentine P E B (2001) 'A gender perspective on conflict management strategies of nurses', *Journal of Nursing Scholarship* 33 (1): 69–74.

VanGundy A B (1988) *Techniques of Structured Problem Solving* (2nd edition). London: Van Nostrand Reinhold.

Vroom V H and Yetton P W (1973) *Leadership and Decision Making*. Pittsburg: University of Pittsburg Press.

Vroom V and Jago A G (1988) *The New Leadership*. New Jersey: Prentice Hall.

Walker L O and Avant K C (1994) *Strategies for Theory Construction in Nursing* (3rd edition). Norwalk, CT: Appleton and Lange.

Wanless D (2002) *Securing Good Health: Taking a Long Term View*. London: Department of Health.

Wanless D (2004) *Securing Good Health for the Whole Population*. London: Department of Health.

Warner M, Longley M, Gould E and Picek A (1998) *Healthcare Futures 2010*. Pontypridd: University of Glamorgan/Welsh Institute for Health and Social Care.

Weightman J (1999) *Introducing Organisational Behaviour*. Harlow: Addison Wesley Longman.

Weisbord M (1976) 'Organisational diagnosis: six places to look with or without a theory', *Group and Organisational Studies* 1: 430–447. In V Iles and K Sutherland (2001) *Organisational Change: Managing Change in the NHS*. London: The National Co-ordinating Centre for NHS Service Delivery, Organization, Research and Development.

Wheelan S (1994) 'Group process: a developmental perspective'. In P Hartley (1997) *Group Communication*. London: Routledge.

White R K and Lippitt R (1960) 'Autocracy and democracy: an experimental inquiry'. In B L Marquis and C J Huston (2006) *Leadership Roles and Management Functions in Nursing: Theory and Application* (5th edition). Philadelphia: Lippincott.

Whitehead D (2006) 'Workplace health promotion: the role and responsibilities of health care managers', *Journal of Nursing Management* 14 (1): 59–68.

Wood J (1997) *Communication, Gender and Culture* (2nd edition). Cincinnati, OH: Wadsworth Publishing Co.

World Health Organisation (1977) *Health For All*. Geneva: WHO.

World Health Organisation (1983) *The Principles of Quality Assurance*. Copenhagen: WHO (Report on a WHO meeting).

World Health Organisation (1986) *The Ottawa Charter*. Geneva: WHO.

Wright T (2000) 'The phantom menace', *Nursing Management* 6 (5): 5. www.nlp3.co.uk/personal.html accessed on 21.08.07.

Young A P (1989) *Legal Problems in Nursing Practice*. New York: Harper and Row.

Young A P (1994a) *Law and Professional Conduct in Nursing*. London: Scutari Press.

Young K (1994b) 'An evaluative study of a community health service development', *Journal of Advanced Nursing* 19: 58–65.

Young A P (1995) 'The legal dimension'. In J Tingle and A Cribb (eds) *Nursing Law and Ethics*. Oxford: Blackwell Scientific.

Yuki G, Goron A and Taber T (2002) 'A hierarchical taxonomy of leadership behaviour. Integrating a half century of behaviour research', *Journal of Leadership and Organizational Studies* 9 (1): 15–32.

Index